Professor Kirkham holds degrees from Lehigh University and the University of North Carolina at Chapel Hill. He has published extensively on Mrs. Stowe and is presently preparing a complete collection of her letters. He is also the compiler of *Indices to American Literary Annuals and Gift Books, 1825–1865*.

THE BUILDING OF
Uncle Tom's Cabin

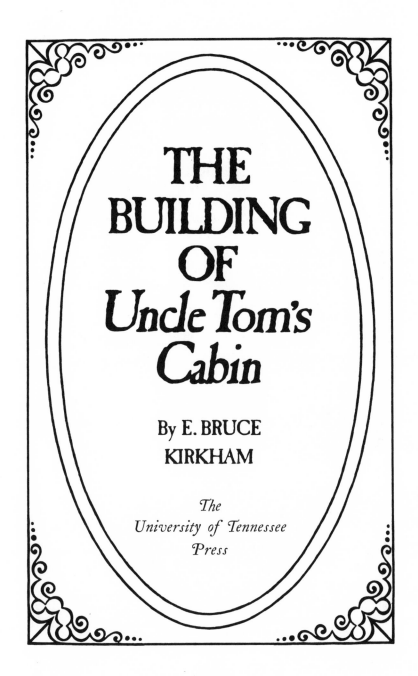

THE BUILDING OF
Uncle Tom's Cabin

By E. BRUCE
KIRKHAM

*The
University of Tennessee
Press*

FRONTISPIECE

Harriet Beecher Stowe is shown at her writing table, probably in her first Hartford house, in this 1866 engraving. *Courtesy of Stowe-Day Memorial Library and Historical Foundation, Hartford, Conn.*

Library of Congress Cataloging in Publication Data

Kirkham, Edwin Bruce, 1938–
  The building of Uncle Tom's cabin
  Bibliography: p.
  Includes index.
  1. Stowe, Harriet Elizabeth Beecher, 1811–1896.
Uncle Tom's cabin. I. Title.
PS2954.U6K5   813'.3   76–49637
ISBN 0–87049–205–5

For Kathy

PREFACE

Aside from her fame as the writer of the world's best-selling novel, Harriet Beecher Stowe is mentioned in most literary histories only as a shaper of the local-color genre and as the woman who broke the Byron incest scandal. The author of *Uncle Tom's Cabin* is labeled a careless craftsman who wrote without revision, without knowledge of her subject, and without artistic sensibility; she wrote for money; she was one of Hawthorne's "damn scribbling women." This study has been undertaken to modify those judgments.

Mrs. Stowe's apprenticeship as a writer was long and extensive: *Uncle Tom's Cabin* came seventeen years after she had published her first sketch. At various times she wrote to supplement or provide the family income, but she was not a hack writer. When she had time to work carefully, she often wrote rather well. But occasionally she was too busy or the muse was silent and she could not compose, no matter how great the financial need. She did have both a fairly standard method of composition and a few sets of favorite rhetorical devices—she was particularly fond of the debate, the moral lecture, and the allegorical representation of characters in terms of pure good versus pure evil. Yet when she was deeply stirred or had at hand personal experiences to use as warp or woof in her literary fabric, she could create scenes and characters capable of standing with those of her contemporaries who have received greater critical acclaim. If composition was often rushed, her revision was extensive when she had the time. Even the earliest pieces give evidence of textual tinkering. The productions of her pen were not masterpieces. No one would claim that *Uncle Tom's Cabin* ranks as a literary work equal to *Moby Dick* or *The Scarlet Letter,* although its social and historical impact has been far greater. Some writers have claimed that Mrs. Stowe's novel changed the course of history. On the other hand, few of her works should be classed with those of Mrs. Sigourney, Mrs. Hale, Mrs. Warner, or Fanny Fern.

The problems facing the scholar interested in investigating *Uncle Tom's Cabin,* or any other work by Harriet Beecher Stowe, are manifold. Copies of the *National Era,* the newspaper in which the novel was serialized, are available only on microfilm or in a few research libraries. The collected edition (1896) is textually unreliable, and first editions beginning in 1833 are often difficult, sometimes impossible, to obtain. Holograph manuscripts have not survived for most of the novels and are extant for only a few of the sketches. There is no edition of her letters, and the few printed in the early biographies have been excerpted, punctuated, and silently emended by the friends or relatives who wrote the studies filled with undocumented legends and misstatements of fact. The most "definitive" biography is now thirty-six years old.

As is the case with many other works in American literature, there are no critical articles of worth on *Uncle Tom's Cabin* prior to 1930. Much of what was published in the nineteenth and early twentieth centuries was either biographical in nature or sentimental in approach. The worst pieces are both. Most of the articles published between 1930 and 1950 were sloppily done by uncritical writers for popular magazines; little appeared in scholarly journals. The centennial year (1952) brought forth a number of reappraisals, mostly from critics who were rereading the book for the first time and found it to be better than they had remembered it. In the past ten years the number of scholarly articles has increased slightly, but the foundations of the valuable critical structure have barely been laid. The blame for Mrs. Stowe's neglect, however, cannot be laid entirely at the doors of unsympathetic scholars. Until the 1950's, most of the primary material was in private hands. Happily, the situation today is improved. Libraries have increased their holdings and generously extend permission to quote passages from their collections of Mrs. Stowe's letters and manuscripts.

Without the aid of the staffs of libraries and historical societies, this study would not have been possible. My debts are greatest to the major repositories: the Arthur and Elizabeth Schlesinger Library on the History of Women in America at Radcliffe College, the Henry Huntington Library and Art Gallery, the Rutherford B. Hayes Library, the Manuscript Division of the New York Public Library, the Henry W. and Albert A. Berg Collection at the New York Public Library, the Clifton Waller Barrett Collection in the Alderman Library at the University of Virginia, and the Stowe-Day Foundation Library. Many people answered letters, checked holdings, and made copies (sometimes typed whole letters) at these and the other libraries listed in the notes, giving freely of their time; their gift is here inadequately acknowledged.

For their helpful comments I wish to thank Raymond Adams, John C. Broderick, C. Carroll Hollis, C. Hugh Holman, Louis D. Rubin, Joseph Van Why, and Nathalia Wright. Their positive contributions will please the reader of this study; all the shortcomings and infelicities are mine. Without the gracious permission of David Stowe, executor of the papers of Harriet Beecher Stowe, none of his great-grandmother's letters or manuscripts could have been included here. I thank him especially for his encouragement and help.

For financial assistance I thank the Smith Research Fund of the University of North Carolina, the English Department of the University of North Carolina, the Trustees of Ball State University, the English Department of Ball State University, the Ball State Foundation, and the Trustees of the Stowe-Day Foundation.

Barbara Gnaideck, Karen Radigan, Bonnie Wade, and Cynthia Harter helped to prepare the manuscript, typed correspondence, and kept all running smoothly without complaint. Their help was indispensable.

And for continuous help and encouragement, and allowing another woman in my life, I thank my wife.

CONTENTS

ILLUSTRATIONS

Part I – BACKGROUND

Chapter 1.

LITCHFIELD AND HARTFORD: 1811-1832

At times it must have appeared to the average American of the nineteenth century that, in the words of Dr. Leonard Bacon, "this country is inhabited by saints, sinners and Beechers"[1] and that the first two were controlled if not outnumbered by the last. Beechers, at one time or another, lived in forty-eight towns in seventeen states ranging geographically from Maine to Florida, Massachusetts to Louisiana, South Carolina to Iowa. Few Americans could have escaped them. Those who did not read Harriet's books read about Henry Ward's trial for adultery. If they praised James's leadership of the First North Carolina

---

[1] The five semistandard biographies of Mrs. Stowe are Annie Fields's *Life and Letters*, Charles Stowe's *Harriet Beecher Stowe*, Charles and Lyman Stowe's *Harriet Beecher Stowe*, Lyman Stowe's *Saints Sinners and Beechers*, and Forrest Wilson's *Crusader in Crinoline*. In order to keep the footnotes to a workable minimum, all biographical information cited in this study will be left undocumented if it appears in two or more of these works. When the material quoted can be found in only one work, or when there is some disagreement among the authors, the footnote will either indicate the single source or the most trustworthy. The passage to which this first footnote refers may be found in Lyman Stowe, 7. For biographies of Lyman Beecher see Stuart C. Henry, *Unvanquished Puritan*; for Catharine see Kathryn Kish Sklar, *Catharine Beecher*; for Henry Ward see William C. Beecher and Samuel Scoville, *Henry Ward Beecher*, and Jane Shaffer Elsmere, *Henry Ward Beecher*, the best of the more than half dozen about him; and for Edward see Robert Meredith, *Edward Beecher*. The other family members await their biographers.

3

Colored Volunteers, they also wondered about George's accidental death. So ubiquitous were the members of the family that it was no surprise to find Charles superintending public education in Florida and Thomas K. marrying Samuel L. Clemens to Olivia Langdon and, in Forrest Wilson's words, "drinking beer, playing cards, and holding Sunday evening services in the Opera House"[2] in Elmira, New York. Sightseers who once came to hear Henry Ward preach and found Thomas K. instead learned what many Americans knew: Beechers were not to be taken lightly. As the gawkers were leaving, Thomas K. announced that "all those who came here this morning to worship Henry Ward Beecher may now withdraw from the church—all who came to worship God may remain."[3]

As well known and influential as her brothers and sisters were, however, all of them together did not surpass the fame of their quiet sister Harriet. *Uncle Tom's Cabin* was not born, as she often maintained, in a vision she had in one of the straight-backed pews of a great frame church one Sunday morning in Brunswick, Maine. The seeds which gave slow birth to the weekly installments through the hot summer, brilliant fall, and freezing winter of 1851 and continued to germinate in the always welcome New England spring of 1852 had been sown in many towns in many states: Litchfield, Nutplains, and Hartford, Connecticut; Boston, Massachusetts; Cincinnati and Chillicothe, Ohio; Newark, New Jersey; New Orleans, Louisiana; Jacksonville and Alton, Illinois; Huntsville, Alabama; small towns in Kentucky, Ohio, Kansas, and Indiana; and other places without names in states both north and south. But in order to chronicle the sowing we must begin as Harriet began—in Litchfield, Connecticut.

Born June 14, 1811, Harriet Elizabeth was the seventh child and fourth daughter (the second to be named Harriet) of the Reverend Lyman and Roxanna Foote Beecher. The first Harriet,

---

[2]Forrest Wilson, 557.   [3]Lyman Stowe, 380.

Birthplace at Litchfield, Conn.

The rambling Beecher house, birthplace and childhood home of the author of *Uncle Tom's Cabin,* once stood on the west side of North Street in Litchfield. *Courtesy of Stowe-Day Memorial Library and Historical Foundation, Hartford, Conn.*

5

born in 1808, lived less than a year. There were five other children in the house north of the square in Litchfield, and six more would arrive. Together they would be called "Beecher's dozen," and Harriet would survive all but four of them; the other eight had all died before 1896.

Harriet lived in the big, rambling house until she went to Hartford in 1824. Here in Litchfield she lost her mother and met the first of her stepmothers. Here she wrote her first composition and acted in her first play, her sister Catharine's[4] adaptation of Maria Edgeworth's "The Unknown Friend," a burlesque of the sensitive, romantic young girl. Here she shared Catharine's grief over the drowning of her fiancé and watched Catharine lose her faith and her father try, without success, to restore it. In Litchfield she heard her father preach and found the sermon as unintelligible as Choctaw. And here she first met Negroes.

Her mother died when Harriet was four. In all her later reminiscences she said she remembered her mother vividly. The fact was, however, that most of what she remembered was based on family stories rather than on her unaided memory. The pleasant aura of maternal goodness which surrounded Harriet was real enough, but the tale of the prize tulip bulbs being eaten for onions is based on fireside reminiscences. Harriet was to "remember" thus again and again. In other instances, such as her Aunt Mary Foote's tales of life in Jamaica, we know she deceived herself because the aunt died when Harriet was only two. But what is important here is not so much the validity of the source or the accuracy of Harriet's chronology as the fact that she vividly recalled incidents about her mother, aunts, and cousins.

Of her father, there are stronger impressions and memories. Born in 1775, Lyman Beecher lived during the two greatest

---

[4] Although she sometimes spelled her sister's name with an *e*, she seems to have preferred the *a* spelling.

wars his country was to know. Too young to remember the early years of the Revolution, he was to die in 1863 ignorant of the results of the Civil War—a man, some said, of his age; others saw him as the last Puritan, the stubborn defender of a dying faith.

Regarded by many as the best preacher in America, a reputation which would, in time, descend to his son Henry Ward, Lyman was a defender rather than an innovator; he preached the theology of Jonathan Edwards long after it had passed its prime. Discussion and debate exhilarated him, but controversy which he felt could serve no useful purpose except to excite people and upset the status quo he avoided. He attacked slavery in the form of the slave trade when it was safe to do so, but he backed down when William Lloyd Garrison asked him to become a militant abolitionist, tried to conciliate Theodore Weld, the firebrand of Lane Seminary, and urged moral suasion and the Christian example as the most effective means of freeing the slave. He was a man fixed in his habits as proved by his advocacy of colonization to his death in 1863, whereas the movement had been effectively destroyed thirty years before.

Yet there were contradictions in the man. A descendant has noted that he was Old-School Presbyterian in that he embraced the doctrine of foreordination, yet he believed in the New-School doctrine of man's free agency in his acts. He pursued, as he put it, "the measures best calculated . . . to get the slaves out of bondage in the shortest time, and best manner,"[5] a course which led him to abolitionist acts and colonizationist rationalizations. To say that he was a heretic or a timeserver or an opportunist is to misread the man. He was aware of the problems facing himself and his age in the areas of religion and slavery and acted as he saw best in each individual case. If one act was contradictory to the other in terms of party loyalty, so be it; the end was what was important.

[5] Lyman Stowe, 66.

Lyman Beecher was a gentle father. He enjoyed hunting and fishing with the boys and nut-gathering with all the children, turning the chores of woodcutting and cider making into games almost as much fun as arguing points of theology at the dinner table. He had an apparently unlimited confidence in himself as a debater and savior of souls. When he heard of the death of Lord Byron, he is reported to have said that, if the poet "could only have talked with [Nathaniel W.] Taylor and me, it might have got him out of his troubles."[6] His daughter Harriet some years later said that her early life was spent in "a great household inspired by a spirit of cheerfulness and hilarity."[7] There were many pleasant memories and many standard family jokes which were told over and over, but a more balanced picture of the influences that were at work will be found only by one's moving outside the family group.

Although Negro servants were present in the Beecher household, Harriet's first knowledge of the evils of slavery came from her mother's sister, Mary. In 1803 Mary Foote had married John James Hubbard, a Jamaica merchant. John hired Mary's brother, Samuel, as a clerk in his business house, and all went off to the island. Mary was appalled by what she found. Her husband was the father of many of his slaves. As one of the family later wrote: "What she saw and heard of slavery filled her with constant horror and loathing. She has said that she has often sat by the windows on a tropical night, when all was still, and wished that the island might sink in the ocean, with all its sin and misery, and that she might sink with it."[8] After a year, she left her husband, returned home with Samuel, and lived in Nutplains until her death at the age of twenty-eight.

Young Harriet's horizons were expanded by her travels back and forth from Litchfield to Hartford, Guildford, and Nutplains, as well as by her relatives, some of whom were like Uncle

[6] Fields, 40.

[7] *Ibid.*, 42.

[8] Lyman Beecher, *Autobiography*, ed. Barbara M. Cross, I, 94.

Samuel Foote, who had been all over the world and read and spoke both French and Spanish. But there were other sources of knowledge closer to home, and Harriet was exposed to these earlier and more often than to the others.

Harriet's stepmother had read Miss Edgeworth's "Frank" to her, an interminable collection of moral sketches designed to edify young minds. Harriet apparently also read Richardson's *Sir Charles Grandison,* for she later referred to the title character as an "old bore." The days in Nutplains she spent listening to her mother's family read Scott's ballads and Rees's *Cyclopedia* aloud.

Although Lyman bought only those books recommended in the *Christian Spectator* and disapproved of novel reading generally, copies of Byron's poems were somehow gotten into the house[9] to supplement the diet of Mather's *Magnalia,* Bunyan's *Pilgrim's Progress,* Bell's *Sermons,* Bonnett's *Inquiries,* Bogue's *Essays,* Toplady on predestination, Law's *Serious Call,* Cruden's *Concordance,* and, of course, the Bible.

From the *Magnalia,* Harriet gleaned example after example of the wondrous workings of God's Providence. In Maria Edgeworth's "Frank," she saw applied the ethics and morals she had found in her Bible. Bunyan's *Pilgrim's Progress* further reenforced the religious influence on her life. The plethora of moral literature, combined with family conversations that often sounded more like sermons than small talk, produced a tone and style of writing which she was never able to shake off. Time and again in the early sketches, and later in *Uncle Tom's Cabin,* in *Dred,* and elsewhere, Harriet paused and pointed out the moral of the previous scene, lest the reader miss the point. When she did not preach to the reader, she had one character preach to another or set up pseudo-Socratic debates in order to lead the "dear reader" to truth as she saw it.

Her symbolism, such as it is, is as obvious as Bunyan's

[9] Uncle Sam Foote was probably the smuggler. Lyman Beecher, *Autobiography,* 161.

allegory. Good, white Little Eva is to be contrasted with mischievous, black little Topsy; good, fun-loving Shelby slaves are to be compared with idle, evil Legree slaves; Ophelia St. Clare with Marie St. Clare; Shelby's cook Chloe with St. Clare's Dinah; and so on throughout the novel. The reader meets Bunyanesque black and white allegorical figures but never a gray.

In 1817, when Harriet was six, two years after her mother had died, Lyman Beecher was asked to deliver an ordination sermon at the Park Street Church in Boston. During his protracted stay, battling Unitarianism in the center of New England culture, he met Miss Harriet Porter of Portland, Maine, and married her the following fall. The children liked her immediately, and the next six years were pleasant for the young Harriet. Her father discovered Scott and permitted the children to read him. Lyman himself often read to the family from *Paradise Lost;* Milton was impeccable. Aunt Esther Beecher, looking one afternoon for something to give Harriet to read to keep her quiet, handed her a copy of Byron's *Corsair.* Harriet was delighted to pursue her magnificent author and, caught up in the Byron craze along with the rest of the young ladies at Miss Pierce's Academy, was soon reading *Manfred* and *Childe Harold.*

But there was also sadness in these years. Little brother Charles had trouble with a broken leg; the Beechers had to take in boarders to make ends meet; and Alexander Metcalf Fisher, Catharine's twenty-eight-year-old fiancé, was drowned at sea.

Seeking solace, Catharine, then twenty-two, took a job teaching school in New London, but the work could not shut out the religious doubts that plagued her. Harriet, aged eleven, was also worried, but about her own salvation. Byron had died; death was all around her. Eventually both girls made their peace with their father—whose theology troubled them—and with themselves, but the faiths that emerged from these crises were not of Lyman Beecher's making.

Deciding upon teaching as a career, Catharine set about to

start a school. In the spring of 1824, she traveled the twenty-three miles from Litchfield to Hartford and, with her sister Mary, opened the Hartford Female Academy with less than a dozen pupils. In the fall of 1824, the enrollment had risen to a little over two dozen, and one of the new girls was sister Harriet.

Lyman Beecher had arranged for Harriet to board at the home of Isaac Bull. Hartford was a new setting, a strange metropolis of five to six thousand people, but she knew the principal of the school, of course, and soon made a few friends—Catherine Cogswell and Georgiana May—although she was rather shy and retiring and preferred her books to conversation or new faces.

Her prodigious memory was already filled with countless hymns and Bible chapters, and now she studied arithmetic, composition, Latin, French, and Italian. But when she was caught by her sister "wasting her time" writing "Cleon," an iambic pentameter drama about a Christian in Nero's Rome, she was set to work doing something more useful: abstracting Joseph Butler's *The Analogy of Religion, Natural and Revealed, to the Constitution and Course of Nature.* The following autumn, Catharine had her sister teach Butler to students of Harriet's own age. This was not to be the last time Catharine was to halt or redirect Harriet's writing efforts.

That summer, as the result of a visit to Litchfield, where she heard her father preach, Harriet was converted, and Lyman was delighted. With one more soul accounted for, Lyman accepted a call from the Hanover Street Church in Boston and, the following spring, gathering up what was left of the family in Litchfield, moved there. His son Edward, recently graduated from Andover, had been in charge of the Hartford Latin School; he joined the family in Boston as pastor of the Park Street Church.[10] For the next six years Harriet was to spend much of her time commuting back and forth from Hartford to Boston. In the spring of 1827, Uncle Samuel Foote, recently returned from

---

[10] Harriet Beecher Stowe, "Catharine E. Beecher," *Our Famous Women*, ed. Harriet Beecher Stowe et al., 86.

his last sea voyage, married Elizabeth Elliot of Guilford and, having explored foreign strands, turned his face west and moved with his new wife to Cincinnati, where he joined his brother, John F., who had settled there some time before. Within the span of five years, most of the Beecher clan would follow.

Lyman Beecher, defender of evangelical Boston, was also a busy man. Recognizing that he was fighting a religious battle with political overtones, he organized the Hanover Association of Young Men, which exerted some political influence through its temperance and Blue Law activities.[11] Ever an enemy of strong drink, Lyman had preached many sermons on the subject and in 1827 had published a collection called *Six Sermons on the Nature, Occasion, Signs, Evils, and Remedy of Intemperance.* The abhorrence of strong drink was pervasive in the family. Some years later, Catharine wrote a temperance song that was published in a Cincinnati paper[12]; all seven sons preached temperance sermons at one time or another (except, possibly, Thomas K.), and it should be noted that many of the characters in *Uncle Tom's Cabin* reveal their moral and spiritual weaknesses through their use of or dependence on liquor.

One man who came often to hear Lyman Beecher in the first few years of his tenancy of the Hanover Street pulpit was a young newspaper editor, William Lloyd Garrison. According to one of his biographers, he "became a warm admirer of Dr. Beecher, partly on account of his attitude on the Temperance question, but still more because of his great powers as a preacher."[13] When, on October 15, 1830, Garrison himself lectured on abolition at Julian Hall in Boston, he was honored to find Beecher in the audience.[14] Later, he appealed to Beecher to join him in the fight for the immediate abolition of slavery. The

---

[11] John L. Thomas, *The Liberator*, 56–58.

[12] Catharine E. Beecher, "Song for the Youth's Temperance Society of Cincinnati," *Western Monthly Magazine* 3 (1835), 182–83.

[13] Oliver Johnson, *William Lloyd Garrison and His Times*, 44.

[14] Wendell P. and Francis J. Garrison, *William Lloyd Garrison,* I, 212.

preacher demurred; he had too many irons in the fire. Garrison replied that it was better for him to let the irons burn than "to neglect [his] duty to the slave." Beecher, secure in his position as spiritual leader and no doubt feeling superior by virtue of his age, said he found Garrison's idea of immediate emancipation "repulsive." "'Your zeal,' he said, 'is commendable, but you are misguided. If you will give up your fanatical notions and be guided by us [the clergy] we will make you the Wilberforce of America.'"[15] Beecher had, unconsciously, spoken for the Boston clergy as a whole; Garrison got no support and never forgave Lyman Beecher.[16]

Thereafter, Garrison's *Liberator* followed Beecher's career carefully, reporting sermons, noting his membership in various organizations, chronicling his travels, and always attacking. When Beecher took up a Fourth of July collection for the Colonization Society, whose opponents, he called "a few foolish whites," the paper noted that he advocated colonization "on the curious ground that 'the Blacks are justly entitled to the whole Southern territory'; and how shall we liquidate their claim? By sending them to Africa."[17]

It reported Beecher's Thanksgiving sermon in Cincinnati and his speech before the Colonization Society in Pittsburgh, and commented at another time that "Dr. Beecher . . . stands very far below him [William Ellery Channing] in moral dignity, in relation to the great question of slavery." Garrison attacked again when Beecher said, in denouncing the public desecration of the Sabbath, "the Sabbath is the *great sun of the moral world*." The *Liberator* answered that the Gospel says the Lord God is the sun, and that Beecher refused to see that slavery violates all Ten Commandments and excludes two and one half million countrymen from any Sabbath. "Dr. Beecher," it continued, "advocated leaving the system alone, as being sure to come to an end

---

[15] Johnson, 44; Garrison and Garrison, 215; Forrest Wilson, 149.
[16] Johnson, 45.
[17] Garrison and Garrison, I, 261.

in the course of a couple of centuries." Beecher denounced atheism, the paper pointed out, but not the slave system based on it; rejected fatalism, yet supported the Colonization Society, "which held that the blacks were fated to remain degraded in this country."[18]

As time went on, many Beechers were to reject colonization as a solution to the problem of the peculiar institution. Some were to do it publicly; others would maintain a façade of belief while helping escaped slaves to freedom. The fact that every member of the family, including the Doctor himself, modified his stand is overlooked by such partisan biographers of Garrison as Oliver Johnson, who says that, "if Lyman Beecher had been true to Christ and to liberty in that trying hour, the whole course of American history in regard to slavery would have been changed, and the slaves might have been emancipated without the shedding of blood." But Lyman missed his chance and "linked his name forever with those of the trimmers and compromisers of that day."[19] In fact, of course, neither Lyman nor his daughter caused or could have prevented the war single-handedly, despite Johnson's statement to the contrary.

Among the many who heard Beecher in Boston when he was at the height of his powers was a young Alabamian and slaveholder, James G. Birney. Birney had not come north, however, to attend Lyman's church. In fact, by the time he arrived in Boston, he had already accomplished the purpose of his long trip. He had come seeking teachers and had found them at the Hartford Female Seminary. He visited Catharine Beecher at her home on Monday, September 13, 1830. They talked for some time, and she gave him her book on education, which he read that night. He visited again the next day, and again they talked about the proposed Huntsville Female Academy back in Alabama. Catharine suggested three names to him: Miss Brown, Miss Southmayd, and Miss Baldwin. The Academy was

[18] *Ibid.*, I, 106–9.   [19] Johnson, 177.

started,[20] but Birney and the Beechers were not to part forever. In the near future in Cincinnati, Harriet, Catharine, and Birney would have, as mutual friends, Salmon P. Chase, the lawyer who defended fugitive slaves; Gamaliel Bailey, the abolitionist editor; and the uncles Foote. In a very few years Birney would shift from colonization to abolition, becoming an active abolitionist publisher, and in ten years he would run for President of the United States on an Abolition-Liberty party ticket. One of the threads of the fabric of *Uncle Tom's Cabin* had its first fibers twisted in Hartford in September 1830 when Harriet met this future leading citizen of Cincinnati.

That same year was a momentous one for Lyman Beecher and his son Edward. Lyman was offered the presidency of Lane Theological Seminary, a new Presbyterian school in Cincinnati. Excited as he was by the prospect of winning the West from the infidels and Catholics, however, he was to delay for more than a year before accepting the proffered appointment.

While Lyman deliberated, his son Edward left Boston to accept the presidency of the newly founded Illinois College in Jacksonville, Illinois. He had joined with Leonard Bacon and four others at Yale when they organized the Anti-Slavery Association on July 6, 1825,[21] and he took these same political views with him to Illinois in September 1830. He would later chronicle the famous Alton Riots, in which he was almost shot, and would, in the words of Lawrence Lader, become an abolitionist "strongly counter to . . . his father."[22] It was Edward whom Harriet visited in Boston two decades later on her way to a new house in Brunswick, and it was Edward's wife who, still later, sent the famous letter to Harriet urging her to write something about slavery.

Of Harriet's few letters that have survived this period, one in

[20] Betty Fladeland, *James Gillespie Birney*, 46; William Birney, *James G. Birney*, 92.

[21] Leonard Woolsey Bacon, *Anti-Slavery before Garrison*, 26.

[22] Lawrence Lader, *The Bold Brahmins*, 78.

particular indicates that she was even then preparing herself for some sort of literary activity. In an 1830 letter to her best friend and former roommate, Mary Dutton, then teaching in New Haven, Harriet wrote:

> I am quite busy preparing for my composition class—Have been reading Raselas & writing a little in imitation of Dr. Johnson's style—think it is improving me by giving a command of language—The man writes as if some Fairy had spell bound him & given him the task of putting every word in his great dictionary in his book as a means of release—I have been spouting at Catharine respecting *"general & transcendental truths"* & "errors of exageratory declamation" every since. For half an afternoon I was quite *"ore rotundo"* & could not even shut a closet door except in a double antithesis—My plan this summer is to have the young ladies imitate the style of various authors & read the English Classics—Respecting composition I think that never yet have time & attention enough been given to it to have it well taught—I mean it shall be this summer. —

She also asked Mary, "If you see A. Baldwin tell him that I shall write him a series of 'Sketches of female characters' as soon as I can get a letter from him to make it excusable for me to write to him."[23] Where and when the promised sketches were published, if, indeed, they were ever written, is not known. Although others in her family were publishing, Harriet's first known piece in print did not appear until after she had moved to Cincinnati.

In May of 1832, after a good bit of procrastination, Lyman Beecher accepted the appointment at Lane and started to lay plans for the trip west. Harriet spent at least part of the summer in Nutplains with Uncle Sam Foote, who was back east on a visit. She certainly asked him about Cincinnati, and, tale spin-

---

[23] Beinecke Collection, Yale Univ. Library. Unpublished with the exception of a single line printed in Edward Wagenknecht, *Harriet Beecher Stowe*, 237, n. 7. Here and throughout the study original spellings have been retained.

Nine children gather to honor Lyman Beecher on his eightieth birth-
day in 1855. Matthew Brady was the photographer. From left to
right, seated, are Isabella, Catharine, Lyman, Mary, and Harriet;
standing, Thomas, William, Edward, Charles, and Henry Ward.
Superimposed on the Brady photograph are insets of sons James (left)
and George (right). *Courtesy of Stowe-Day Memorial Library and Historical Foundation.*

17

ner that he was, he certainly told her more than she needed to know.

Early in October the caravan set out. Not all of the family made the trip. Harriet's two older brothers had earlier left the family circle: brother Edward was already west at Jacksonville; brother William was at Newport, Rhode Island. Two of her younger brothers were at school: Henry Ward was at Amherst, and Charles, born in 1815, was at Bowdoin. But it was still a very impressive group, Lyman, his wife, Aunt Esther Beecher, and the children (Catharine, Mary, Harriet, Isabella, Thomas K., and James, the baby, only four years old) made up the first contingent. George, then at Yale, was to follow soon to take up his studies at Lane under his father's direction. And, at Dartmouth College, an admirer of Dr. Beecher who had been doing editorial work in Boston for the *Recorder* when the Doctor was there had accepted the Chair of Languages at Dartmouth and was courting Eliza Tyler, daughter of the president. His name was Calvin Ellis Stowe, and he would soon follow the Beecher clan to Cincinnati and become one of the first faculty members at Lane Seminary.

Chapter 2.

CINCINNATI: 1832-1849

"The Queen City," "The Athens of the West" its promoters called Cincinnati, the cultural center of the trans-Allegheny frontier, an oasis of refinement and the arts on the banks of the beautiful blue Ohio. It was "Porkopolis," a roaring, meatpacking riverport to its detractors—a new city, a strange city; yet Harriet's letters reveal that coming to Cincinnati was like coming home. Every place the twenty-one-year-old school teacher went she met friends and relatives from Litchfield, Hartford, and Boston. The tap roots of heritage in Cincinnati ran north and east. But the city was planted on the banks of the Ohio, the Jordan between slavery and freedom, and its feeder roots—its economic roots—extended south across the river and down the river to the Mississippi, to Memphis and Natchez and Vicksburg, and, finally, New Orleans. Cincinnati, whether it liked it or not, was a Southern city on Northern soil. Many men, both black and white, were to mistake geographic location for political persuasion. From the 1830s to the 1850s Cincinnati and Ohio were a battleground for the proslavery and antislavery forces, and Harriet lived in the thick of the undeclared war.

The American Colonization Society had been founded in 1817 to solve the Negro question. Slavery was to be ended and the troublesome freedmen disposed of by the very simple and logical means of sending all the blacks back to what Gilbert Barnes identifies as their "'native home,' an unhealthful strip of jungle on the coast of Liberia in Africa."[1] In fact, it was race, not slavery, that primarily concerned the colonizationists. In P. J. Staudenraus's words, the Negro represented a second race,

> a socially inferior and repressed nation dragged to the Western Hemisphere in chains and abused with impunity. Negro slavery was but a symbol of a previous transgression against God's rulership over the universe . . . . Removal of the alien race would atone for the African slave trade, root out slavery, restore the "Africans" to their divinely ordained home, civilize the dark continent, and hasten the coming of the American milennium when one happy, united, homogeneous race of freedmen would tread the land.[2]

Colonization was the ideal solution; the evangelical aspects particularly appealed to the missionary zeal of the American people. With so much to recommend it, how could anyone argue the merits of the Society's program? In the beginning, few did.

By the early 1820s, when Harriet was a schoolgirl in Hartford, colonization groups were spread wide over the land. *The African Repository and Colonization Journal* issued its first number in March 1825 under the editorship of Ralph Randolph Purley. Leonard Bacon, Edward Beecher's professor at Yale, spoke on colonization in Boston in 1824 and, according to Staudenraus, Lydia Huntley Sigourney, "the Sweet Singer of Hartford" and the century's most prolific American poetess, became "New England's most famous lady colonizationist" and a leading figure in Hartford's Female African Society.[3] Lyman Beecher was a staunch colonizationist, as were many other prominent men of the time. Leaders from all walks of life supported a

[1] Gilbert Hobbs Barnes, *The Antislavery Impulse*, 27.
[2] P. J. Staudenraus, *African Colonization*, vii–viii.
[3] *Ibid.*, 100, 119, 127.

movement which helped to assuage whatever guilt they felt about the plight of the Negro by giving them the impression that they were doing some positive good.

Whatever small good the colonizationists were doing, however, was brought to an abrupt end in 1831 by two men, one white and one black. On the first day of January 1831, shortly after Lyman Beecher had denied him the support of the Boston clergy, William Lloyd Garrison published the first issue of his *Liberator;* the following August, Nat Turner led a slave revolt in Southampton County, Virginia. Of the two events, Turner's was to have the greater immediate effect. Louis Filler's *Crusade against Slavery* records that members of the Virginia House of Delegates, who had been on the verge of abolishing slavery, suddenly felt they were "legislating for their lives." The results of extended debate confirmed the necessity of slavery to the Virginia way of life, led to stringent laws governing the life of the Negro, and "spelled the total collapse of reform in that state."[4] Antislavery forces, both colonizationist and abolitionist, would never again represent a sizable portion of the population in the South.

William Lloyd Garrison's paper and the philosophy it voiced aroused stronger hatreds in both North and South than any single man or periodical had done in the history of the country, for Garrison was an immediatist; his solution to the problem of slavery was immediate and total freedom for the Negro without compensation to the slaveholder. The Southerner, fearing for his life should the slaves band together and rise under the incitement of such a policy as the *Liberator* advocated, saw nothing but economic ruin for his cotton-based economy should he be forced to hire his labor. The Northerner also feared the cheap labor of freed Negroes, and despite the solemn pronouncements about equality in God's sight, was no more ready to accept the Negro

[4] Louis Filler, *Crusade against Slavery*, 53–54.

as a social equal than was the Virginia gentleman he hypocriti-
cally accused of prejudice.[5]

The editor of the *Liberator* called a meeting on November
13,1831, to form the New England Anti-Slavery Society; fifteen men came. Many others had been frightened away by
Garrison's call for immediate abolition. With the zeal of an
angry prophet, Garrison attacked all who disagreed with him.
He later renounced allegiance to his country, nominated Jesus
Christ for President, called the Sabbath an outworn supersti-
tion, and eventually denounced religious denominations in the
country one by one as they either ignored or opposed him.[6] He
urged separation from the union, which was held together, he
said, by a Constitution which protected slaveholders. In short,
he offended many and converted few. People who knew nothing
about abolition and cared little about slavery knew the name
"Garrison" as that of a madman.

Early in the course of his attacks on various groups he singled
out the Colonization Society in his pamphlet *Thoughts on African
Colonization,* published in 1832. Colonization, he said, rested
on four principles: persecution (conditions were made so unpleasant for the Negro that he wanted to go to Africa), falsehood
(the Negroes were no more natives of Africa than the whites
were of Great Britain), cowardice (blacks were said to be a
menace), and infidelity (the black and white races had to be
enemies as long as the blacks were here). Garrison strode on for
over 130 pages, attacking at every step.[7] The colonization
apologists were unable to answer him to the satisfaction of many
people. The population, if not pro-Garrison at this point, was
certainly not pro-colonization. But Lyman Beecher, the first

---

[5] Two good studies of Northern prejudice and anti-Negro feeling are Leon F.
Litwack, *North of Slavery*, and Lorman Ratner, *Powder Keg*. For a striking but
representative incident see Alfred T. Child, Jr., "Prudence Crandall and the Canterbury Experiment," *Bulletin of the Friends Historical Association* 22 (1933), 35–55;
Filler, 64–65; and Samuel J. May, *Recollections*, 39–72.

[6] Barnes, 44, 93, 94.

[7] William Lloyd Garrison, *African Colonization*, 57–61.

president of Lane Seminary, and many of the faculty stood fast against the tide.

At the annual meeting of the Colonization Society in Cincinnati, January 14, 1833, Beecher called the efforts of the Colonization Society "wise and successful" and "approved of Heaven, to facilitate the education and emancipation of slaves, and the abolition of slavery, at home." He hoped that the "introduction of christianity, and civilization, and civil liberty, and the extinction of the slave trade [would] in some measure repay injured Africa for her protracted and unutterable sufferings and wrongs."[8] The following year, again in Cincinnati, he repeated that slavery was wrong and should be ended, "not however, by force, nor by national legislation, nor by fomenting insurrection, nor by the violation of the constitution and the dissolution of the union; but by information, and argument, and moral suasion—and by the spontaneous action of the slave-holding states."[9] It was his desire to avoid debilitating battle that prompted Beecher, in that same year, to help found the American Union for the Relief and Improvement of the Colored Race. He hoped that a common ground might be found for the abolitionists and the colonizationists, but he was wrong. One by one his own children left the colonization fold to become abolitionists until only Harriet and Catharine remained with their father, but the abolition which attracted George and Edward and Charles and William and Henry Ward and the new Lane faculty member, Calvin Stowe, was not New England's abolition, Garrison's abolition. It was born in New York state, and its leader was an old acquaintance of Lyman.

Charles Grandison Finney had begun his great religious revival in Oneida, New York, in 1824. More reasoned than emotional, Finney's appeal to the people lay in his disregard for

[8] *Proceedings of the Cincinnati Colonization Society*, 2.

[9] The speech is quoted from the Connecticut *Observer*, July 28, 1834, p. 118, where Theodore Weld read it; *Letters of Theodore Weld, Angelina Grimké Weld, and Sarah Grimké*, ed. Dwight L. Dumond and Gilbert H. Barnes, 165.

the traditional Calvinist emphasis on original sin, the elect, and the ineffectiveness of good works. He preached that "all sin consists in selfishness; and all holiness or virtue in disinterested benevolence." Salvation thus marked for the individual not the end of a painful life, but the beginning of a fruitful life, the aim of which was benevolent activity here on earth. The natural consequence of such a philosophy was social reform.[10] Temperance, communistic communities, abolition, and a host of other activities rose in the 1830s and '40s as a direct result of his emphasis on disinterested benevolence.

Although Lyman Beecher too, believed in the efficacy of revivals, he was unable to accept Finney's denial of the truth of basic Calvinist tenets. They met in New Lebanon, New York, in 1827—the Western prophet and the Eastern patriarch—and they fought. As they disagreed on religious principles, they also held opposing views on slavery. Consistent with his theological position, Beecher wanted to wait for God to work out the problem in His time and according to His plan; Finney urged personal involvement now. It was not to be Finney who would give Beecher his most unhappy moments, however, but rather one of Finney's converts, Theodore Dwight Weld.

In October of 1833, Weld joined the newly formed New York City Anti-Slavery Society. The members were immediate abolitionists, but with a difference: the New York doctrine was immediate abolition gradually accomplished; i.e., "at the earliest possible period consistent with the best good of the slaves, they should be fully emancipated." Compared with Garrison, Weld was a gradualist; but compared with Beecher and other colonizationists, he was an immediatist. People who feared Garrison but hated slavery welcomed the opportunity to fight the evil in principle without the threat of being overrun by an ignorant mass of blacks. Antislavery forces grew under Weld's leadership as they had never done or could have done under

---

[10] Barnes, 10–11, who cites "Sermon I: Sinners Bound to Change Their Own Hearts" of Finney's *Sermons on Important Subjects* (New York, 1836), 3–42.

Garrison's more radical doctrines. It was the abolition of Weld, not that of Garrison, which changed the West and the nation. It was Weld who converted a staunch Alabamian colonizationist, James G. Birney, into an abolitionist. Birney, friend of Catharine and Harriet Beecher from that day in Hartford when he had come to the seminary looking for teachers, was soon to move to Ohio, to Cincinnati, and start an abolitionist newspaper. And it was Weld's abolition which destroyed Lane Seminary in a microcosm of the national battle between colonizationists and abolitionists.

Lane Seminary had been started in 1829 when Elnathan Kemper of Walnut Hill outside Cincinnati gave the land for it with the condition that, should the school fail, the property was to be equally divided among four philanthropic groups, one of which was the American Colonization Society. More than $80,000 was pledged form various sources for professorships and buildings, on the condition that Lyman Beecher come west and become both president and professor of theology. He was elected president on October 22, 1830, and visited Cincinnati for the first time in April 1832 with his daughter Catharine. He accepted the appointment in July, went west with his family in November, and was installed the day after Christmas the same year. On August 9, 1832, Calvin Ellis Stowe was elected to the Lane faculty. He left his position as professor of languages at Dartmouth and assumed his duties as professor of Biblical literature, lecturer on church history, and librarian in July of 1833. Along with his titles, Stowe had a new wife: Eliza Tyler, the daughter of Dartmouth's president. [11] Eliza Tyler Stowe and Harriet Beecher quickly became close friends.

As the student body was from both the North and the South, slavery was often a topic for discussion. A colonization society had been established at the school with Beecher's blessing

---

[11]*Lane Theological Seminary*, 9, 11, 16, 19. See also John Vant Stephens, *Lane Seminary*. Most of the manuscript records of this period of Lane are in the McGraw Memorial Library, McCormick Theological Seminary, Chicago.

shortly after the opening session, but some of the students pressed argument upon argument in favor of abolition. Finally, in February of 1834, with the permission of the president, the student body debated the question: "Ought the people of the slaveholding states to abolish slavery immediately?"[12] In a spurt of enthusiasm, Beecher had offered to participate; on second thought, he declined. But almost the entire faculty attended at least some of the meetings, and, as one historian has found, Beecher "had a written statement of his views, drafted by Catharine, read to the students."[13] The letter urged the combination of abolition and colonization forces, the familiar Beecher position.

The meetings were held on eighteen successive nights for two and one-half hours a night. Students Theodore Weld and William Allan spoke on conditions in Alabama; Asa Stone told of the life of the slave in Mississippi; James Bradley, the only Negro student, recounted his experiences as a slave; James A. Thome of Kentucky said that slavery demoralized the sons of planters and degraded society generally; Huntington Lyman described slave life in Louisiana. In all, there were speeches by seventeen eyewitnesses, one of them a former slave. About half of the speakers were sons of slaveholders, another was a former slaveholder, and the remainder had resided in or had traveled through slave states. After nine nights the question was voted upon, and immediate abolition was endorsed overwhelmingly. The meetings were more revivals than debates.

The remaining nine meetings were devoted to an examination of the position of the colonizationists. When colonization as a solution to the problem of slavery was voted upon, all but one vote were against it. An antislavery society was founded

[12] Barnes, 66.

[13] Robert Samuel Fletcher, *Oberlin College*, 152. Fletcher cites Huntington Lyman's letter of March 4, 1834, printed in the *Emancipator* on Mar. 25, 1834, and H. B. Stanton's letter of Mar. 10, 1834, printed in the New York *Evangelist* on Mar. 22, 1834, reprinted in the *Emancipator* on Mar. 25, 1834. Barnes, 66–67, appears to be wrong in saying that Catharine read the statement.

with the purpose, not of instructing the slaves to rebel, not of urging the free states to intervene, not of pressing congressional interference, but of encouraging the slaveholders to live by the spirit of the gospel. The members were to go forth as teachers and lecturers to start schools and lyceums.[14]

The seminary students immediately set about preaching abolition in both Cincinnati and the surrounding area. They established schools for Negro children and, to a degree that upset the townspeople, mixed with the black population socially.[15] To Beecher, the social mixing was both unwise and harmful to the school, and he also believed that the students were neglecting their studies.[16] To the seminary's twenty-five trustees, twenty-one of whom were colonizationists, the abolitionist activity was frightening.[17] Therefore, on August 16, 1834, while Beecher was away in the East raising funds, the board met, prohibited societies not related to the curriculum, and abolished the antislavery society. When Beecher returned, he addressed a letter to the student body in an attempt to defend the trustees' action, but it apparently had little effect. Two days later, twenty-eight students requested dismissal from school; the next day eleven more followed suit. On the seventeenth, Theodore Weld, student and leader of the revolt, submitted a letter requesting the same action.[18]

Weld took a shrewd position in attacking the board of trustees; he did not mention the merits of abolition but instead argued for free speech. His principle was that *"free discussion, with a correspondent effort, is a DUTY, and of course a RIGHT"* and at Lane *"free discussion and correspondent action have been prohibited by law."*[19] The trustees realized their mistake and

---

[14] Fletcher, 152–54.
[15] Benjamin P. Thomas, *Theodore Weld*, 72.
[16] Fletcher, 156.
[17] [Theodore Dwight Weld], *Statement*, 21.
[18] Fletcher, 158, 161–66.
[19] [Weld], *Statement*, 3, 4.

repealed the rules in November, but it was too late.[20] Lane, despite Beecher's reputation, was never to recover.

The abolition agitation had its effect on Harriet during this period, but her activities are easier to chronicle than her thoughts because, as one of her biographers, Forrest Wilson, has pointed out, "She was never one to ally herself uncompromisingly even in private communications with causes that were unpopular or dubious, however much she might secretly believe in them. . . . Abolition was unpopular with the kind of people Harriet knew, and therefore she could not espouse it," even in personal letters. Thus when she went with Mary Dutton on a trip to Kentucky in 1833 to visit the home of one of their students, whose parents owned slaves, she wrote no one at the time about her impressions of this, her only firsthand experience with slavery. Almost twenty years later, however, Mary commented: "Harriet did not seem to notice anything that happened, but sat much of the time as though abstracted in thought. When the negroes did funny things and cut up capers, she did not seem to pay the slightest attention to them. Afterwards, however, in reading 'Uncle Tom' I recognized scene after scene of that visit portrayed with the most minute fidelity, and knew at once where the material for that portion of the story had been gathered."[21] To appear to be woolgathering only to reproduce an incident or conversation verbatim at some future date was a trait she was never to lose.

In October 1834, Harriet accompanied her father to the meeting of the Cincinnati Synod in Ripley, Ohio. While there, they stayed with Reverend John Rankin, an important station master on the underground railroad. Rankin told the Beechers and Professor Stowe, who was also staying with him, about an interesting incident which had occurred a few years back. A young Negro girl had escaped from slavery by crossing the Ohio

[20] Calvin Ellis Stowe, Letter to the New York *Evangelist*, Nov. 10, 1834, quoted in the *Emancipator*, Dec. 2, 1834.

[21] Forrest Wilson, 196, 120.

Seventeen months after the death of his first wife, Calvin Stowe married her best friend Harriet Beecher. *Courtesy of Stowe-Day Memorial Library and Historical Foundation.*

River on the ice floes. Harriet said nothing; she just listened. Years later, when asked where she got the story of Eliza's miraculous crossing, Harriet said it was from an antislavery periodical she had recently read.[22] As will be seen, the article she referred to does exist, and it is altogether possible that she did see it while writing her novel, but it surely must have served as catalyst to resurrect a weak memory, not as initial input.

During the same fall, Harriet had returned from a trip to Amherst for Henry Ward's graduation to discover that Eliza Tyler Stowe had died of cholera on August 6. All the Beechers tried to comfort Calvin Stowe in his loss, but Harriet seemed to be most helpful. She had been Eliza's closest friend, and Calvin turned to her now in his hour of grief. Gratitude on his part and Harriet's helpfulness eventually developed into a stronger attachment, resulting in marriage on January 6, 1836. Nine months and twenty-three days later Harriet gave birth to twin girls. One was named Eliza Tyler Stowe, for Calvin's first wife, and the other, Harriet Beecher Stowe, for his second wife.

Calvin sailed from New York for Europe on June 8, 1836, to study the Prussian educational system and to buy books for the Lane Seminary Library; he did not return until early the following year. A steady stream of letters from his wife helped to keep him informed of events in Cincinnati, however, during an exciting summer indeed, for this was the time of the Birney riots. Harriet described them in her long letters to Calvin.

> The excitement about Birney continues to increase. . . . A meeting has been convoked by means of a handbill, in which some of the most respectable men of the city are invited by name to come together and consider the question whether they will allow Mr. Birney to continue his paper in the city. . . . The mob madness is certainly upon this city when men of sense and standing will pass resolutions approving in so many words of things done contrary to law, as one of the resolutions of this meeting did. . . . For my part, I can easily see how such

[22]*Ibid.*, 144–46.

This portrait of Harriet Beecher Stowe, painted in oil by Alanson
Fisher in 1853 when she was forty-two years old, hangs in Professor
Stowe's bedroom in the Stowe House. *Courtesy of Stowe-Day Memorial
Library and Historical Foundation.*

proceedings may make converts to abolitionism for already my sympathies are strongly enlisted for Mr. Birney, and I hope that he will stand his ground and assert his rights. The office is fire-proof, and enclosed by high walls. I wish he would man it with armed men and see what can be done. If I were a man I would go, for one, and take good care of at least one window.[23]

James G. Birney had just started what was to be one of the longest-running abolition papers in the state; it did not cease publication until 1847. He had come over to the abolition cause shortly after the Lane disputes. He had been reading antislavery works by Wilberforce, Clarkeson, George Thompson, and Charles Stuart, and had subscribed to the *Emancipator* and the New York *Evangelist.* Theodore Weld went to see him late in 1834, and before Weld left, Birney told him he was through with colonization. He then published his *Letter to the Churches, to the Ministers and Elders of the Presbyterian Churches in Kentucky,* in which he indicted slavery on religious grounds. The pamphlet was printed in the Cincinnati *Journal* the same year.[24] In October 1835 Birney moved to Cincinnati.

His experiences with the paper were typical of the problems which many abolitionist editors encountered. Feeling ran high everywhere in the North, but it was particularly strong in Cincinnati, situated, as the city was, on the border between the slave and free states. Cincinnati was no stranger to violence; steamboat explosions, river gang fights, sailor brawls were common in all river towns. But newspapers tend to stir up a different class of people, the middle class, the reading public, and the Cincinnati *Weekly Herald and Philanthropist*—commonly known as the *Philanthropist*—stirred up Cincinnati. Riots broke out, property was damaged, lives were threatened —all of which became grist for Birney's weekly paper.

Birney had trouble with his *Philanthropist* almost from the start. Seeking a more liberal atmosphere than Cincinnati offered, he published the first number in New Richmond, Ohio,

---

[23] Charles Stowe, 82–84.   [24] Fladeland, 80, 96–97.

January 1, 1836. He soon discovered that he had chosen the wrong town, and number twelve came out in Cincinnati. Number thirteen appeared in New Richmond; Birney's life had been threatened in Cincinnati. Then New Richmond proved even more inhospitable, and he moved back to Cincinnati for good, under the wing of the state antislavery society. There was some trouble getting the paper out for July 15: eight men had gone into the print shop the night of the twelfth, destroyed paper and type, and disassembled the press. On the twenty-third, over a thousand people attended an antiabolition rally. They wanted Birney and his kind out of the city. On July 28, at another meeting, many strongly defended Birney's right of free speech. But the antiabolitionists were in no mood to listen to legal arguments about constitutional rights. Two days later the mob struck again, tore the printing office apart, and threw the press into the river. The riots lasted for three days, but, to everyone's surprise and Harriet's delight, the *Philanthropist* came out on schedule on August 5, 1836.[25] Nevertheless the anger of the anti-Birney faction did not dissipate quickly. Seven months later, on March 31, 1837, Birney reported that he had received misspelled notes threatening his life, but by the end of the year subscriptions were up enough for him to announce a bigger page and new, larger type. He finally tired of fighting, sold the paper, and went into politics, but the paper and the fight went on.

In the issue of July 31, 1838, the new editor, Gamaliel Bailey, reported that he had received the names of 308 antislavery societies in the state; 196 had reported their membership which totaled about 16,000. Figuring on this basis an average of 78.5 members per society, Bailey estimated that an additional 8,000 members belonged to the 102 societies that had not reported, bringing the grand total to about 25,000 abolitionists in a state population that totaled 1.5 million in 1840.

In addition to extracts and reprints from other papers, poetry

[25]*Ibid.*, 139–41; James G. Birney, *Late Riotous Proceedings*, *passim*.

33

and reviews, the *Philanthropist* maintained a good coverage of abolition and other newsworthy events within the city and state. Although the abolitionist position is impossible to ignore, the paper was more than simply propaganda. In it can be traced, for example, the movements and involvements of the Beecher clan in Cincinnati and abolition affairs.

In 1836 Angelina Grimké, later the wife of Theodore Weld, wrote an *Appeal to the Christian Women of the Southern States,* in which she argued for female participation in the abolitionist cause: abolitionists were pacific and moral; emancipation would not breed rapine and murder; Southern slavery was not the same as Biblical slavery and could not equate to it; therefore, the women of the South should pray over the matter, free their slaves, and protect them.[26] The following year Catharine Beecher supplied a rebuttal in her *Essay on Slavery and Abolitionism, with Reference to the Duty of American Females.*

It was both "unwise and inexpedient for ladies of the non-slave-holding States to unite themselves in Abolition Societies," Catharine argued. Abolitionists and their measures were un-Christian and divisive. Garrison professed Christianity but was an "avowed opponent of most of its institutions" and attacked the Colonization Society, a worthy group of individuals. Abolitionism was the course "calculated to awaken illegal acts of violence," and when such acts had occurred, the abolitionists rejoiced. "Christianity is a system of persuasion . . . abolitionism . . . is a system of coercion by public opinion." Therefore "*calm,* rational Christian discussion" was the "only proper method of securing the end of slavery." The women of the world were "to win every thing by peace and love."[27]

Angelina Grimké struck back with a series of letters to Catharine published in the *Liberator* the same year.[28] The

---

[26] Angelina Grimké, *Appeal.*

[27] C[atharine Elizabeth] Beecher, *Essay,* 6, 13–14, 21, 23, 46, 137, 100.

[28] The series ran in the *Liberator* from June 23 to Nov. 3, 1837. They were later

Philanthropist reprinted them beginning September 29 with Letter VII and concluding with Letter XIII on November 28. Point by point Catharine's arguments were answered; piece by piece the colonization argument was taken apart. Catharine was the earliest of the children to publish antislavery material and the last to leave the colonization fold.

When the reports of the family activity cited in the *Philanthropist* are supplemented by Birney's correspondence, a fairly clear picture emerges of the way the various members were involved in the antislavery movements in the thirties. In a letter to Lewis Tappan, written April 29, 1836, Birney stated that the Presbyterian Church in Cincinnati was beginning to be troubled by the subject of slavery.

> Dr. Beecher, when a few weeks ago the Resolutions of the Chillicothe Pres'ty were introduced into the Cin'i Presby., and an attempt was made to give them the go-by, said it must not be done, the subject would have to be discussed and it was useless to attempt to elude it. . . . There is, if I do not mistake, a great change with reference to this matter among those who are under Dr. B's influence. His son William at Putnam is no longer an 'abolitionist—but'—He has dropped the 'but.' His son, George, is nearly full blown.[29]

The letter was printed in the *Emancipator,* a New York antislavery paper, reprinted in the *Philanthropist* of June 3, 1836.

Birney wrote to Tappan again in September and told him that Reverend George Beecher had joined the Anti-Slavery Society at Batavia, Ohio, and was to be appointed "lecturer for Claremont County." In October, Elizur Wright told Birney that the Anti-Slavery Office in New York had just sent a commission to George Beecher at the recommendation of Weld, who had converted him to abolition at Lane during the debates, and that

---

collected and issued as a pamphlet: *Letters to Catherine [sic] E. Beecher, in Reply to an Essay on Slavery and Abolitionism.*

[29] James G. Birney, *Letters*, ed. Dwight L. Dumond, 321.

"if he accepts and can be spared from the West, we want him to take by the horns the ecclesiastical *bull* that was lately calved in Connecticut, . . . a Slave-holding State" in their opinion.[30] A letter of appeal to the people of Claremont County on behalf of the Anti-Slavery Society published in the *Philanthropist* for May 12,1837, was signed by George Beecher. Apparently he declined the offer to go back to the East. Another letter from Birney to Tappan, written in July 1837, mentioned that Horace Bushnell, a man who had the distinction of being both antislavery and anti-Negro,[31] had spoken at Lyman Beecher's church, "where before he would not have been permitted to speak at all."[32]

In the summer of 1837, Harriet, pregnant again, went to visit her brother William in Putnam, Ohio. In one of the letters she wrote to Calvin, who stayed at home in Cincinnati, is another of her early references to abolition.

> The good people here, you know, are about half abolitionists. A lady who takes a leading part in the female society in the place, yesterday called and brought Catharine the proceedings of the Female Anti-Slavery Convention.
>
> I should think them about as ultra as to measures as anything that had been attempted, though I am glad to see a better spirit than marks such proceedings generally.
>
> Today I read in Mr. Birney's *Philantropist.* Abolitionism being the fashion here, it is natural to look at its papers.
>
> It does seem to me that there needs to be an intermediate society. If not, as light increases, all the excesses of the abolition party will not prevent humane and conscientious men from joining it.
>
> Pray, what is there in Cincinnati to satisfy one whose mind is awakened on this subject? No one can have the system of slavery

[30] *Ibid.*, 360, 365.
[31] Charles C. Cole, Jr., "Horace Bushnell and the Slavery Question," *New England Quarterly* 23 (1950), 19–30.
[32] James G. Birney, *Letters*, 399.

brought before him without an irrepressible desire to *do* something, and what is there to be done?[33]

In early 1837, the Stowes reopened their Walnut Hills house after Calvin's return from Prussia and hired a Negro girl to work for them. She said she was free, but they learned that she was a fugitive slave and that her master was in Cincinnati looking for her. Calvin and Henry Ward spirited the girl off through the night to the home of John Van Zandt.[34]

In October, Reverend Edward Beecher attended the Illinois Anti-Slavery Convention as a member from Jacksonville.[35] Later in the same month Edward preached on slavery twice at the formation of the state Anti-Slavery Society in Alton, Illinois. On November 7, Edward's friend Elijah Lovejoy was shot to death by a mob in Alton which had come to destroy his printing press; in the words of Robert Meredith, "No other personal incident of the anti-slavery struggle, except the hanging of John Brown . . . so overwhelmed the North."[36] Early in 1838, Edward published his *Narrative of the Riots at Alton* and became the second child of Lyman Beecher, after Catharine, to write an antislavery work.[37]

In December 1837, the *Philanthropist's* editor Bailey wrote from Cincinnati that Lyman Beecher was still uncertain as to what course he wished to pursue in regard to slavery, that Reverend George Beecher was firmly in their camp, and that he had far more hope that Calvin Stowe would come over than he did that Lyman would. Even though Stowe would not lecture for them, he did preach a sermon on Lovejoy's death.[38] Five

---

[33] Forrest Wilson, 196.

[34] Lyman Stowe, 175.

[35] *Philanthropist*, Oct. 13, 1837.

[36] Robert Meredith, "Introduction," *Riots at Alton by Edward Beecher*, v.

[37] The only modern edition is that cited in the previous note. The only record of the famous trial that followed the riot is William S. Lincoln, *Alton Trials*.

[38] James G. Birney, *Letters*, 434.

months later, the *Philanthropist* ran a letter from Edward Beecher at Illinois College in which he said that he would "find great pleasure in attending the meeting of the American Anti-Slavery Society, and doing all in [his] power to promote its interest, and to promote the holy cause in which it is engaged."[39] The following month, the Reverend William Beecher, who had a church in Putnam, Ohio, opened a meeting marking the Third Anniversary of the Ohio Anti-Slavery Society with a prayer and a few remarks, and was appointed to the Committee on Resolutions and the Committee on Free Labor Products. In his prayer he expressed sentiments remarkably parallel to those of his brother Edward: the antislavery cause "is truly a religious one; and . . . its unparalleled success in opposition to the most powerful and inveterate hostility, is unquestionably the work of God, and is to be regarded as a signal answer to the prayers of his people."[40]

By 1838, all of Harriet's older brothers—William, Edward, and George—had left colonization and become abolitionists. Henry Ward, two years Harriet's junior, who had gone to the West in 1834 after graduating from Amherst, had not yet capitulated. During the summer of 1836 he had filled in for editor Thomas Brainerd of the Cincinnati *Journal* when he went to the East with Lyman. Two years later, on the Fourth of July, speaking in the town of his first parish, Lawrenceburgh, Indiana, Henry Ward contended that freedom for the blacks, in the words of one biographer, "could never be accomplished by the methods followed by the Abolitionists."[41] Though he was continually trying to break free of Lyman's spell, it would be almost twelve years—1850—before he would desert his father by attacking Louis A. Godey's *Lady's Book,* which, he main-

[39]*Philanthropist*, May 29, 1838.
[40]*Ibid.*, June 12, 1838.
[41]Paxton Hibben, *Henry Ward Beecher*, 92.

tained, had defended Southern institutions by not attacking them.[42]

But both his father and others seem to have been softening. With the influences of abolition pervasive, indications of a change of attitude toward abolition on the part of those left in Cincinnati were noted by Bailey in a letter to Birney in October 1838.

> Our doctors etc. have at length mustered courage enough to venture into our office. Professor Stowe has been in several times—by the way he is a good abolitionist, and has promised to aid us in the attempt we are about making to establish a large depository here. Even Dr. Beecher happened in the other afternoon—I showed him a Liberator which contained a "broadside from Dr. Beecher." I do believe that, though a little skittish himself, he is quite willing that others should turn his artillery against slavery.[43]

Events went on in Cincinnati as they had in the earlier years. There were periodic riots, kidnappings, murders, and cholera epidemics. A number of debates were staged on the question of abolition versus colonization, or slavery versus antislavery.[44] Steamboats blew up with frightening frequency, often taking hundreds of lives, but for Harriet it seems to have been a time of little development in her progress toward *Uncle Tom's Cabin*.

In fact, with the birth of Henry Ellis Stowe on January 14, 1838, and the departure of Henry Ward for a new church in Indianapolis in 1839, there began a decade of Harriet's life which might well be called a period of pain and suffering. She gave birth to three more children—Frederick William in 1840, Georgiana May in 1843, and Samuel Charles in 1848—and lost the last in a cholera epidemic. Her brother George died after

---

[42] *Independent*, Jan. 14, 1850, cited in Hibben, 139.

[43] James G. Birney, *Letters*, 474.

[44] As one of many examples see Rev. J. Blanchard and N. L. Rice, *Debate on Slavery*.

accidentally shooting himself in the mouth while cleaning a shotgun in the garden of his home in Rochester, New York. She was bedridden again and again, if not by the aftereffects of childbirth, then by an acute neuralgic condition which repeatedly deprived her of her sight. Forrest Wilson calls 1841 a "blank year," a year in which she hardly wrote a letter. She took the water cure at Brattleboro, Vermont, from March 1846 to May 1847. Calvin replaced her at the spa for some fifteen months commencing in June 1848, leaving her in Cincinnati with the children. He was not in Cincinnati when the baby, Samuel Charles, died July 24, 1849.

Consideration of these various events lends some support to Forrest Wilson's remark that, of the years 1842–1851, "no other period of her earlier life had so little effect upon Harriet's writing."[45] This statement is strengthened by the scarcity, through those years, of references in the family correspondence that bear upon Harriet's development as either a novelist or an antislavery advocate. On the other hand, an examination of both her published writings and those of her family present this decade as one of considerable practice in technique through contributions to periodicals, and of progress in her thinking about abolition.

[45] Forrest Wilson, 209, 215.

Chapter 3.

CONTRIBUTIONS TO PERIODICALS

The Beechers were a reading and a writing family. In 1832, the year Harriet arrived in Cincinnati, Lyman, Cousin Samuel Foote, his brother John P., Reverend and Mrs. E. B. Hall, Judge Timothy Walker, and others founded one of the most famous literary societies west of the mountains, the Semi-Colon Club. The name did not simply refer to the punctuation mark; these were witty New Englanders, not backwoodsmen. "Colon" is Spanish for Columbus, and the members felt that in their role as literary pioneers in a new land they were partial Columbuses. Almost immediately the literary lights of the area, along with those who aspired to literary greatness or simply enjoyed good conversation, sought to join. The membership was large: twenty-one-year-old Harriet, her sister Catharine, and Calvin Stowe were, of course, members, but in addition there were Judge James Hall; Professor Hentz, the naturalist, and his novelist wife, Caroline Lee Hentz; C. P. Cranch, the poet; U. T. Howe, the newspaper wit; Professor O. M. Mitchel, the astronomer; Charles W. Elliott, the historian of New England; Doctor Daniel Drake, physician and author, and his brother Benjamin, author of biographies of Tecumseh and Black Hawk, and of other works of Western history; Edward D. Mansfield, author and editor; Professor James W. Ward, poet and naturalist; James H. Perkins, poet, essayist, and editor; William Greene, political writer; Charles D. Drake and C. B. Brush, both poets; and many others.[1] Aside from the bonds of literary interest, several members of the group had other ties. The Footes, as previously indicated, were cousins to the Beechers. James H. Perkins later married Sarah H. Elliott, sister of Mrs. Samuel Foote.[2] Calvin Stowe married Harriet Beecher. E. E. Mansfield's wife, Mary Wallace Peck, was from Harriet's former hometown, Litchfield.[3]

At the meetings held variously at the homes of Sam Foote, Charles Stetson, and William Greene, Harriet made contacts which encouraged her to write and also helped her publish what she wrote.[4] Before and after they went to Cincinnati, Lyman, Charles, Edward, George, and Catharine Beecher, as well as Calvin Stowe, contributed to many periodicals.

Lyman Beecher wrote seven articles for the *Christian Spectator* from 1819 to 1823; in addition, many of his published works were reviewed here and his sermons reprinted. Catharine contributed to the fifth volume (1823) a poem entitled "Peace I Leave with You."[5] Lyman, his sons, and Calvin Stowe also contributed to the *Spirit of the Pilgrims,* the *Biblical Repository and Theological Review,* the *Bibliotheca Sacra,* and the *New York Independent,* the last of which printed Henry Ward Beecher's famous Star Papers, but these articles and journals were either

---

[1] The list is taken from John P. Foote, *Samuel E. Foote*, 177–79, with corrections and additions from W. H. Venable, *Beginnings of Literary Culture*, 417–18.

[2] Venable, 417.

[3] *Ibid.*, 430.

[4] Foote, 177; Venable, 419.

[5] In the biographical sketch of Catharine which Harriet wrote for her anthology, *Our Famous Women*, 81, Harriet identified Lyman's six contributions to the *Spectator* over the initials "D. D." and Catharine's over the initials "C. D. D." An examination of the journal reveals pieces by D. D. at 1:53–60 and 557–62; 2:119–24 and 129–75; 3:451–55 and 617–22; and 5:523–29. Catharine's single contribution is at 5:540. The reviews appeared in 2:193–99; 9:587–604, 645–55; 7:n.s. 481–503. The sermons may be found at 1:625–29; 2:358–67; 9:62–71.

religious and dealt with matters theological and textual or, if somewhat political, took a conservative, Congregational, colonizationist stand. There was little or nothing in them that Harriet would have found either stimulating or disturbing, nothing that would markedly shape the writing of *Uncle Tom's Cabin.*

Of the Cincinnati magazines, Harriet read at least one with regularity, and its influence upon her was great. Judge Hall, the Semi-Colon Club member, moved his *Western Monthly Magazine* to Cincinnati from Illinois in 1832. Hall was an antiabolitionist, a defender of Catholics, and an espouser of an American literature that was chiefly profrontier and moneymaking. Once the magazine was successful enough for him to become just editor and not editor and chief contributor, he took pains to include as many local writers as possible. In the June 1833 number he gave favorable if brief notice to a *Primary Geography . . . by C. & H. Beecher, Principals of the Western Female Institute.* Although this was the first time Harriet's name appeared in print, it was not her first publication in the magazine: "Modern Uses of Language" had come out in March.[6] Her first published fiction, however, was printed the following year in the February 1834 number. It was "Isabelle and Her Sister Kate," written under the pseudonym "May." Although this first piece of fiction was never reprinted in any of her books, it did appear under her name five years later, in a Kentucky newspaper and again the next month in the Cincinnati *Chronicle.*[7]

Then, in its April 1834 issue, the *Western Monthly Magazine* published Harriet's first signed fictional piece. "A New England

[6] Review of *Primary Geography for Children*, *Western Monthly Magazine* 1 (1833), 287. John R. Adams was the first to identify the piece. All previous biographers had missed the connection. John R. Adams, *Harriet Beecher Stowe*, 36; *Western Monthly Magazine* 1 (1833), 121–35. Charles Stowe, 68; Charles and Lyman Stowe, 85; Lyman Stowe, 162; Catharine Gilbertson, *Harriet Beecher Stowe*, 67; Fields, 82.

[7] Adams, 37; *Western Monthly Magazine* 2 (1834), 72–75; Lexington (Ky.) *Observer and Reporter*, Aug. 3, 1839; Cincinnati *Chronicle,* Sept. 28, 1839.

Sketch by Miss Harriet E. Beecher" had as its hero Timothy Griswold, the first of many New England types she was to portray with such great accuracy.[8] Uncle Tim not only prefigured Mr. Sinclair, Miss Ophelia's Vermont father in *Uncle Tom's Cabin,* still seventeen years away, but also the local-color genre which Harriet was to take from Mrs. Sigourney and her school and bring to full fruition forty years later. The following month saw the appearance of "Frankness," a brief sketch signed "by a Lady." It would reappear under Harriet's name in later years when she collected many of these early pieces. Two months afterward, "Aunt Mary" appeared, signed "H. E. B."[9] Having found her domestic, sentimental tune, Harriet was to play it with slight variations for the next seventeen years and to expand it into a bass chord that ran throughout *Uncle Tom's Cabin.*

But the *Western Monthly Magazine* published pieces less sentimental and more controversial than those Harriet wrote. In January 1834 it printed "The Moral Emancipation of the Negro," which argued for gradual emancipation and colonization. The slaves should be freed if possible when they deserved it. In May 1834, "Education and Slavery" appeared in the same issue with Harriet's "Frankness." The writer had obviously been moved to write by the antislavery turmoil at Lane Seminary, for he spoke of having seen the "constitution of the Anti-Slavery Society of——Seminary" which stated that the group stood for immediate emancipation. The students who subscribed to this philosophy, he said, were children "dreaming themselves into

---

[8] Apparently based on recollections of a real uncle, Benton, the story had its title changed to "Uncle Tim" in Harriet's 1843 *Mayflower*, 165–209. He retained his new name in the 1853 English edition, 3–26, but was rebaptized "Lot" in the expanded 1855 *May Flower*, 9–42. Gilbertson, 69. In addition to the above-named appearances, the tale was published separately as *Prize Tale: A New England Sketch*, and was given its original title, "A New England Sketch" in *The Family Visitor*, ed. John Hayward, 29–47, and in *The Boston Book*, 100–39.

[9] "Frankness, by a Lady," *Western Monthly Magazine* 2 (1834), 263–66; H. E. B., "Aunt Mary," *ibid.*, 362–67.

full-grown patriots." Their course was impolitic, for it lessened public confidence in the school and decreased the value of the institution. Nothing should be permitted inside a school which might disturb the harmony of the institution. As to the problem of slavery, colonization was the best answer. [10]

Before its death in 1837, the *Western Monthly Magazine* printed another piece which perhaps influenced Harriet on her way to 1851 and *Uncle Tom's Cabin*. In August and September of 1836, the "Life of Isaac Shelby," Revolutionary colonel, later governor of Kentucky, appeared in the pages of the magazine which had given Harriet her literary birth. [11] It is not unlikely that Harriet first encountered here the name of that illustrious Kentucky hero for whom Shelby County, Kentucky, was named and that she remembered the Shelby name fifteen years later and 972 miles away in Brunswick, Maine, when she sat down to write her greatest book. But in August of 1836, Harriet had been married only seven months, was pregnant with the twins, and thus had her mind on lives other than Isaac Shelby's.

The role of the *Philanthropist* has already been discussed at some length; the other Cincinnati paper, the *Journal and Western Luminary,* has been described by Forrest Wilson as "one of Cincinnati's best newspapers . . . the leading Presbyterian newspaper in the West." Edited by Thomas Brainerd, "an intense admirer of Lyman Beecher and . . . Dr. Beecher's pastoral assistant in the Second Presbyterian Church," the paper was "virtually the family organ of the Beechers." That Harriet read it "there can be little doubt." It was here that Calvin debated John Rankin over the student revolt at Lane; here that Eliza Tyler Stowe's affectionate obituary, probably written by Calvin, was published; here that "H," who, according to Forrest

[10] P., "Moral Emancipation of the Negro," *Western Monthly Magazine* 2 (1834), 26–30; "Education and Slavery," *ibid.*, 266–73.
[11] "The Life of Isaac Shelby," *Western Monthly Magazine* 5 (1836), 462–70, 516–63.

Wilson, was Harriet, reported on Calvin's series of Sunday evening sermons in 1835;[12] here that Calvin's series of travel letters from Europe was published beginning in the September 1, 1836, issue; and here, as has been mentioned, that Henry Ward Beecher got his first editorial experience during the Birney riots of 1836.

The pages of the *Luminary*, therefore, can give us the best contemporary account of the activities of the Beechers and the Stowes and a good account of events in Cincinnati in 1836, a year of great importance to all.

January saw a reprint of Calvin's address on the education of immigrants in Cincinnati (January 7) and of a section entitled "Atheism" from Lyman's *Lectures on Scepticism* (January 14). Part of Lyman's speech, "Plea for Colleges," given at Miami University the previous fall, was printed on February 25. Colonization in Indiana, the state where both Henry Ward and Charles were to go, was discussed in the March 10 number. Another extract from Lyman's "Plea" appeared the following week. On the twenty-fourth, the editor reported that Lyman had furnished him with the proof sheets of his new book, *Views on Theology*, and had given him permission to extract. In April, the Synod of Kentucky's discussion of slavery ran for two issues (April 14 and 21). The following month, an article treating gradual emancipation was published.

On the twelfth of May, the editor announced that he would be leaving town the next Monday and that a substitute would take his place. He did not leave as planned. On the nineteenth, editor Brainerd said that his substitute had decided against taking the job, but that now another had accepted; the replacement's replacement was Henry Ward Beecher. Just when Henry Ward took over is not clear, but he was certainly in control by the June 2 issue, for he signed himself "Editor-pro-tem" to the

[12] Forrest Wilson, 116, 140–41, 149–50.

editorial attacking a Mississippi postmaster who had canceled all subscriptions to the paper which went through his office.

How much Harriet aided Henry Ward that summer, her biographers cannot decide. Among her contemporaries, Annie Fields said simply that Harriet "lived at her father's home in Cincinnati, writing busily for a local paper, of which Henry Ward has accepted the temporary editorship." Harriet's son, Charles, writing with his mother's aid, said she "assisted her brother Henry Ward, who had accepted a temporary position as editor of the 'Journal,' a small daily paper published in the city." Essentially the same statement is made in the later biography which Charles did with his son Lyman Beecher Stowe. John R. Adams openly questions what the earlier biographies hinted at: "How much she assisted him [Henry Ward] is a question, since her writing for the paper was without by-line and not personal enough to reveal her authorship."[13]

On June 16, an extract from Catharine Beecher's *Letters on the Difficulties of Religion* appeared. On July 7, "Dr. Beecher on the Sabbath" was reprinted from the New York *Observer;* on July 12, 1836, Birney's press was mobbed. Sometime about the twenty-first, Harriet wrote to Calvin in Europe,

> Yesterday evening I spent scribbling for Henry's newspaper in this wise; "Birney's printing-press has been mobbed, and many of the respectable citizens are moving in the line of their prejudices."
>
> I wrote a conversational sketch, in which I rather satirized this inconsistent spirit, and brought out the effects of patronizing *any* violation of private rights. It was in a light, sketch style, designed to draw attention to a long editorial of Henry's in which he considers the subject fully and seriously . . . . Both our pieces have gone to press today, with Charles's article on music, and we have not a little diversion about our family *newspaper.*

[13] Fields, 94; Charles Stowe, 81; Charles and Lyman Stowe, 99; Adams, 39.

I thought, when I was writing last night, that I was, like a good wife, defending one of your principles in your absence, and wanted you to see how manfully I talked about it.[14]

The piece was presented as a letter imbedded in Henry's editorial, which had the title "SPIRIT OF THE TIMES." Reputedly received from one Franklin, the letter took the form of a debate between Mr. L——, an anti-Birney man who rejoiced at the destruction of the press, and Franklin, who condemned the action of the mob and, with Socratic insistence pushed L——'s argument to its logical extremes and forced him into a position which he found logically inevitable but morally untenable. Although Franklin denied abolitionist sympathies and insisted that "he" was only seeking the protection of constitutional freedoms from mob rule, Forrest Wilson is right in finding here Harriet's "first published utterance on the slavery question."[15] Henry, on the other hand, carefully avoided defending abolition in any form; he said that there was an evil abroad in the land, a moral decay which "haunts our liberty and inspires mobs." The source of this evil was "foreign and domestic miscreants" like Robert Dale Owen, Wright Kneeland, "and the locust-swarm of their followers." No Garrisons, no Welds, no Birneys, no Phillipses were mentioned.

The rest of Henry's period of editorial tenure produced nothing extraordinarily exciting. Beechers and Stowes continued to write and be published. Calvin's travel letters appeared sporadically beginning with the issue of September 1. Among his observations were that "ultraism" was falling from favor and that George Thompson, the English abolitionist, had made many misstatements of fact concerning American slavery to a small crowd at Exeter Hall. An announcement in the December issue noted that the proprietors had sold the paper to E. W. Chester, who said that "the spirit of Radicalism, so rife in this

---

[14] Charles Stowe, 82.
[15] Forrest Wilson, 184.

age, will, we hope, find no aliment in the Journal and Luminary." The year of 1836 was over, Henry was relieved, and Harriet never published in the *Journal* again.

Joshua Leavitt's New York *Evangelist,* a Congregational paper with abolitionist tendencies, had begun publishing Harriet's sketches in 1835, her "Uncle Enoch" being the first. During the following years, ten more sketches appeared on topics as diverse as mysticism, religion, temperance, education, literary matters, New England life, and Catholicism.[16]

In 1838 Harriet began contributing to gift books, the nineteenth-century coffee-table book, the leather-bound, gilt-edged, seldom-read repository of sentimental verse, bathetic fiction, and copious steel engravings. "Feeling" was the first to appear. Thereafter, over the next ten years, the name "Harriet E. B." or "Harriet B. Stowe" appeared thirteen more times as author of eleven pieces in eight separate publications.[17] The publication of each tale made the sale of the next one easier. As each tale was reprinted, pirated, synopsized, and quoted, the name of Mrs. Harriet Beecher Stowe was spread farther and farther across the country. "The Tea Rose" is representative of what often happened.

[16] "Uncle Enoch" appeared May 30, 1835. The other sketches were as follows: "Heinrich Stilling," Feb. 6, 1851; "On the Ministrations of Departed Spirits in the World," Jan. 25, 1849; "The Unfaithful Steward," Apr. 7, 1842; "Jesus," Feb. 19, 1846; "Old Testament Pictures—No. 1," Nov. 14, 1844; "The Drunkard Reclaimed," Nov. 30, Dec. 7, 1839; "What Will the American People Do?" Jan. 29, Feb. 5, 1846; "Literary Epidemics—No. 1," July 28, 1842; "Literary Epidemics—No. 2," July 13, 1842; "De Rance and Fenelon—a Contrast," July 7, 1842.

[17] Harriet Beecher Stowe, "Feeling," *Religious Souvenir*, ed. Mrs. L. H. Sigourney, 252–60; "Let Every Man Mind His Own Business," *Christian Keepsake*, ed. Rev. John A. Cooke (1839), 239–63; (1848), 98–128; "Cousin William," *Gift*, ed. Miss Eliza Leslie, 207–19; "Uncle Abel and Little Edward," *Gift*, 59–65; "Clara Delafield," *Violet*, 17–56; "The Sabbath," *Christian Keepsake*, ed. Rev. John A. Cooke, 130–57; "Deacon Enos," *Gift*, ed. Miss Eliza Leslie, 144–87; "The Seamstress," *Religious Souvenir*, ed. Mrs. L. H. Sigourney, 99–114; "A New England Sketch," *Boston Book*, ed. George W. Light, 100–39; "The Yankee Girl," *Token and Atlantic Souvenir*, 63–81; "The Coral Ring," *Christian Souvenir*, 265–81; "The Tea Rose," *Bouquet for 1847*, ed. Alfred A. Phillips, 43–50; "The Twelve Months," *Christian Keepsake*, ed. Rev. John A. Cooke, 115–22.

A sentimental story of beauty and incredible coincidence, "The Tea Rose" first appeared in *Godey's Lady's Book* for March of 1842. It was reprinted in the April 27 issue of the *Philanthropist.* The following year, it stood second in Harriet's first collection of sketches, *The Mayflower,* published by Harper. Alfred A. Phillips selected the story for his *Bouquet for 1847,* which was reissued later as *Flora's Gem, or the Bouquet, for All Seasons.* It appeared in the Woodstock, Vermont, *Spirit of the Age* on August 28, 1851. John S. Hart chose the sketch as representative of Harriet's work for his 1852 anthology, *The Female Prose Writers of America.* The same year, Sarah Josepha Hale published portions of the sketch in her article on Harriet for her *Woman's Record; or, Sketches of All Distinguished Women.* When the British edition of *The Mayflower* was issued in 1853, it was included. Harriet did not remove it when she brought out her expanded American edition of *The May Flower* in 1855.[18]

One of the few surviving family letters concerned with Harriet's publishing problems illuminates not only Harriet's struggles to publish but the relationship between Harriet and sister Catharine. In a letter dated April 24, 1838, the year of Harriet's gift-book debut and of the birth of Henry Ellis Stowe, Catharine asked Lydia Huntley Sigourney, a major gift-book editor and an important contributor to the *Mother's Magazine,* for "a little notice" of Catharine's recent work to be published in the magazine. She then went on to say that she was visiting Harriet and that her sister had been ill, but had borne her trouble with "quietness and equanimity."

> She has recovered her health and finds that the labors of her pen may be made available to increasing domestic comforts and this

[18] Harriet Beecher Stowe, "The Tea Rose," *Godey's Lady's Book* 24 (1842), 145–47; *Philanthropist*, Apr. 27, 1842; *Mayflower* (1843), 80–90, republished 1844; *Bouquet for 1847*, ed. Alfred A. Phillips, 43–50; *Flora's Gem*, 43–50; Woodstock (Vt.) *Spirit of the Age*, Aug. 28, 1851; *Female Prose Writers of America*, 246–53; "From 'The Tea Rose,'" *Women's Record*, ed. Sarah Josepha Hale, 837–38; *Mayflower* (1853), 143–48; *May Flower* (1855), 89–97.

is the chief reason why I have been collecting for her diverse fugitive pieces that have strayed or been stolen. Several have applied to us both to write for Annuals and Magazines at the east but it was when we neither of us had leisure to attend to such matters. Since I have been collecting Harriet's pieces it has occurred to me that as everybody who wants such sort of articles comes to you, that you might dispose of these pieces *more profitably* (for it is a money making effort) than she or I could do at this distance from the head quarters of literature. Trusting to your kind interest in a young and literary mother, I commend them to your care and discretion to dispose of as you shall deem best for her interests. I wish to have her name "Mrs. Harriet Beecher Stowe" put to them—for I have taken the credit of much that she has written and entirely against my will—That printed piece, by the way, was put in the Chronicle of this city without leave, but it has been used only in this vicinity.

I shall send in a week or more a copy of the Chronicle in which you will find a passage in the life of a literary lady—That is *literally* a scene that transpired under this roof and when you find a tale entitled 'Let every man mind his own business' you will know how it was "concocted."—Sister Harriet is sitting by writing the finale to old father Morris—in whom you will recognize "old father Mills of Torringford"—This will better fit some religious annual perhaps—tho' you can judge best. She has furnish [*sic*] a tale and some poetry for the Philadelphia Religious annual, now edited by Revd Mr. Todd so that quarter is supplied—it is in that you will find the piece mentioned above.[19]

Harriet was apparently guided onto the annual road by her often overbearing sister, but within less than two years Harriet

[19] Lydia Huntley Sigourney Papers, Connecticut Historical Society. One of the sketches was probably "Feeling," which appeared in Mrs. Sigourney's *Religious Souvenir* the same year; "Let Every Man . . ." came out in the *Christian Keepsake* in 1839. "Old Father Morris" first appeared in the 1843 *Mayflower*, 313–24. As there is no complete run of the Cincinnati *Chronicle* readily available, tracing the latter two sketches has proved impractical. One may very well be the "Cousin William" which Forrest Wilson (p. 191) says appeared in the winter of 1837. I have been able to find no record of either the Rev. Todd or his annual.

herself was writing Carey and Hart questioning their statement of her account. She had published in the *Gift* and *Violet* at the rates of $2.00 and $1.50 per page respectively. They claimed that one hundred dollars was due her for her contributions. She replied that "the article furnished for the Gift covers 43 printed pages and that for the Violet 39 or 40. This would make the sums due to me $144.50"; she asked that they please recheck their accounts.[20] Harriet was on her way to becoming a business woman, a provider, and a well-known authoress, and, within a year, a mother again. Frederick William Stowe would be born in 1840.

The June 1839 issue of *Godey's Lady's Book* contained the first piece by Harriet to be published by that magazine. For the next three years she was to contribute with some regularity: four pieces in 1839, two in 1840, two in 1841, one in 1842.[21]

The *Western Messenger* of Cincinnati was the medium for a view of slavery which was to be basic to a sketch Harriet would later publish in the New York *Evangelist* and to *Uncle Tom's Cabin*. In October of 1839, a series of articles in the *Messenger* began a discussion of Thomas Carlyle's recently published *Chartism* which was to extend into the following May.[22] In the July 1840 number of his *Boston Quarterly Review,* Orestes Brownson began his discussion of Carlyle's work in an article entitled "The Laboring Classes." The November *Messenger* negatively reviewed Brownson, Brownson replied, and the *Messenger* answered in the February 1841 issue.[23]

[20] Historical Society of Pennsylvania. For the sketches she refers to, see note 17 above.

[21] Harriet Beecher Stowe, "Trials of a Housekeeper," *Godey's Lady's Book* 18 (1839), 4–6; "The Only Daughter," 18 (1839), 115–29; "Olympiana," 18 (1839), 241–43; "Art and Nature," 19 (1839), 241–44; "Eliza: From My Aunt Mary's Bureau," 20 (1840), 24–26; "Sketches from the Notebook of an Old Gentleman, Number 1. The Old Musty House," 21 (1840), 61–63; "Mark Meridan," 22 (1841), 242–44; "Canal Boat," 23 (1841), 167–69; "The Tea Rose," 24 (1842), 145–47.

[22] N., "The Chartists," *Western Messenger* 7 (1839), 365–95; "Chartism," *Western Messenger* 8 (1840), 57–90, 108–15, 162–68.

[23] Orestes Brownson, "The Laboring Classes," *Boston Quarterly Review* 3 (1840),

Brownson praised Carlyle's insight into the reasons for the Chartist movement, but found him unsatisfactory as a practical philosopher because he merely exposed problems without offering acceptable solutions: emigration and education were rejected as untenable answers. The villains, said Brownson, were the middle class, for it was they who controlled the division of the fruits of industry and kept the *"proletarii"* from receiving their equal share. It appeared that "men are rewarded in inverse ratio to the amount of actual service they perform." Slavery was evil and should be abolished, but the wage slavery which existed among the free laborers and would therefore replace the existing kind if the slaves were freed, would be no improvement. The end of slavery was near; the wage system would "supplant slavery, and be sustained—for a time." The present job then was "to emancipate the proletaries." "The regeneration of the race," Brownson maintained, would not come from any one individual or group of individuals, but rather from the nature of the system itself. "The only way to get rid of its evils is to change the system, not its managers. *The evils of slavery do not result from the personal characters of slave masters. They are inseparable from the system, let who will be masters.* Make all your rich men good Christians, and you have lessened not the evils of existing inequality in wealth."[24] The corruptive effects of the slavery system constitute the basic theme of *Uncle Tom's Cabin.*

The correspondence that has survived from the 1840s reflects Harriet's growing business acumen. In 1842 she took the initiative in dealing with Isaac Shepard, whose name she misspelled

---

358–95, 420–510; H., "Brownson on the Laboring Classes," *Western Messenger* 3 (1840), 316–30; 8 (1841), 433–49.

[24] Brownson, 367, 317, 373, 375 (italics supplied). The reviewer in the *Messenger* quoted extensively as he enumerated and answered each of Brownson's points. It is interesting to note, however, that he does not deal with the passage italicized above. Thus if Mrs. Stowe did get the concept here, as Charles Foster has asserted (*The Rungless Ladder*, 50–54), she would have had to use the *Messenger* as a springboard to the Brownson article itself or to the article as it was reprinted and distributed in pamphlet form.

"Shepherd"; she promised to write something for his gift book, the *Christian Souvenir,* and asked if he would be so kind as to recall sister Catharine's "The Puritan Hero" from Carey and Hart. Catharine would much prefer Shepard to publish it. Harriet delivered as promised, and "The Coral Ring" appeared in the *Christian Souvenir* in 1843.[25] Later in 1842, Harriet wrote to Calvin from Hartford about advice she had received from her brother-in-law, Thomas C. Perkins, concerning a dispute with "Williams." Perkins advised that, if Williams would "pay equal compensation to North American writers," the matter should be settled.[26]

In 1843, with sister Catharine's help, Harper and Brothers were persuaded to bring out Harriet's *Mayflower* collection, fifteen of her previously published sketches. The subtitle accurately describes the character of the selection: *Sketches of Scenes and Characters among the Descendants of the Pilgrims.* In every case, the "Mayflower" tales dealt with either religious, moral, or temperance matters *per se* or with some anecdote from Harriet's New England past dressed up and filled out both to represent the special character of that quaint region and to point out a moral principle: Christian charity opposed to snobbishness in "Clara Delafield," proper Sunday diversions and their improper counterparts in "The Sabbath," tithing in "So Many Calls," Christian old age in "Uncle Enoch," the power of the flower in "The Tea Rose," an old man's acceptance of the death of a beautiful young boy in "Uncle Abel and Little Edward," and so on through story after story. There is no mention of slavery or any other controversial, unorthodox topic.

Calvin was visiting his family in South Natick, Massachusetts, in 1844 when a letter dated May 23 arrived from Harriet in Cincinnati. "By the bye," she said,

[25] American Antiquarian Society; *Christian Souvenir*, ed. Isaac Shepard, 265–81. Catharine's story begins on p. 150 of the same volume.

[26] This may be Samuel Williams, the founder of the *Ladies Repository*; see Frank Luther Mott, *American Magazines*, II (1850–1865), 301; folder 67, Beecher-Stowe Papers, Radcliffe.

I think the Evangelist owes me something will you inquire about it for me—they sent me Feb 7 1833 $25—after receiving the two dancing school pieces. Those pieces were worth about 17—then there was a short piece worth about $7 Then the Dickens piece was about 12 or thirteen and the last Missionary piece $25 making what they owe me about thirty one or two dollars—I have some more pieces partly written which I shall send on soon—those dancing pieces with which the account begins are sometime after February 11, 1833 . . . . the pieces are the dancing school 2 no. The pilgrim (or some such name)—Dickens—the Western Missionary—I have not got the titles right but the subject matter is so—. . . I intend to write more soon and have three pieces now already planned and shall write more. I sent my preface to Dodd. I think it is a pretty good one considering—and if he will send me a ten dollar bill for it just as a fee I'l [*sic*] say 'Thank ye sir' and take it.[27]

Calvin apparently did not do as he was instructed, for on August 31, 1844, Harriet wrote again and said that the figure was "more nearer $35 than $25." Calvin was told to take the letter she had written on the matter and check; "better see to it," she admonished him.[28]

The brief sketch "Immediate Emancipation" which appeared in the *Evangelist* on January 2, 1845, marked a turning point in the direction of the attitude toward slavery which Harriet had found five years earlier in Brownson's "Laboring Classes." Set in Cincinnati, it concerned a slaveholder named Alfred B——; his slave, Sam; and a Quaker named Simmons. The slave decided to take advantage of his presence in a free state to leave his master. B—— accused Simmons of helping Sam escape, was taken to Sam by Simmons, and was convinced by his former slave that freedom is better than servitude. Promising to help Sam if he should ever want, B—— returned to the South. The moral of

[27] Folder 68, Beecher-Stowe Papers, Radcliffe. The "Introduction" was to *The Works of Charlotte Elizabeth* (New York, 1845), 2nd ed.; M. W. Dodd was the publisher. She obviously means 1843, not 1833.

[28] Folder 70, Beecher-Stowe Papers, Radcliffe.

the sketch was that good men were found "even among those who are born and bred slaveholders" and that the present

> great error of controversy is, that it is ever ready to assail *persons* rather than principles. The slave *system* as a system, perhaps, concentrates more wrong than any other now existing, and yet those who live under and in it may be, as we see, enlightened, generous, and amenable to reason. If the *system* alone is attacked, such minds will be the first to perceive its evils and to turn against it; but if the system be attacked through individuals, self-love, wounded pride, and a thousand natural feelings will be at once enlisted for its perservation.[29]

Harriet lived in Cincinnati for only four more years—to the end of that relatively blank period in her writing career mentioned in chapter 2. At about this time—late in 1849—her life began to change. When Calvin was offered an appointment as Collins Professor of Natural and Revealed Religion at his alma mater, Bowdoin College, he gratefully accepted the better position with its increase in salary. Harriet longed to return to the East. She had visited from time to time, been to the water cures, but to live again in her beloved New England, to escape the poverty of a struggling school and the unbearably hot Cincinnati summers was a dream she had had for years, and now it was about to become real: to escape Cincinnati, the site of the

---

[29] The sketch was reprinted by the *Philanthropist* on Feb. 2, 1845, and later appeared as the title story under a new name in *Uncle Sam's Emancipation; Earthly Care, a Heavenly Discipline; and Other Sketches.* With a slightly altered title, *Uncle Sam's . . . Other Tales and Sketches*, the collection appeared in London in the same year. The "Introduction" to the American edition, written "By an Alabama Man," first appeared under the title "Some Account of Mrs. Beecher Stowe and Her Family" by the same "author" in *Fraser's Magazine* 46 (1852), 518–25, with slightly altered contents. The June 2, 1853, issue of the *National Era* contains a brief note reprinted from the Philadelphia *Daily Register*. In it the editor of the *Register* takes to task the publisher of the Philadelphia edition of Mrs. Stowe's work for not giving him credit for writing the article which the publisher used as the introduction. The editor of the *Register* was William Birney (1819–1907), son of the James G. Birney who visited Catharine Beecher's school in Hartford and published the *Philanthropist* in Cincinnati in the 1830s.

beginning of her literary career, the scene of her marriage, the birthplace of six children and the resting place of the body of her last. She had arrived in Cincinnati an unmarried, twenty-one-year-old teacher; she left a thirty-nine-year-old mother and author.

Part II–*UNCLE TOM'S CABIN:*
SERIAL TO NOVEL

Chapter 4.

BRUNSWICK: 1850-1851

In early April 1850, Harriet set out with her five children from Cincinnati for Brunswick, Maine. Calvin would not assume his new duties at Bowdoin College until fall, but she was going before him to set up housekeeping while he finished his teaching at Lane. It was a hard trip by boat, coach, and railroad. The party passed by Ripley, Ohio, where Harriet had heard John Rankin tell of the slave girl's escape over the frozen Ohio River. Harriet and her children were ejected from a Pennsylvania railroad station in the middle of the night when a stationmaster mistook them in their shoddy clothes for immigrants. But Harriet seemed to gain spiritual strength as she moved toward her beloved New England. When she wrote Calvin from brother Henry's house in Brooklyn on April 29, she was more the businesswoman than the fainting traveler. She inquired after some of her sketches and said she would spend the week in Brooklyn, then move on to Hartford for a week, Boston for a week or so, and be in Brunswick by May or June.[1] She arrived in Boston on the thirteenth of May and wrote Calvin that she expected to leave for Brunswick on the Bath steamer on the twenty-first. A few days later, she again reminded Calvin that

[1] Charles Stowe, 10–31.

61

she had offered some pieces to Wright of the *Evangelist.* If he had accepted them, Calvin was to use the money; if not, he was to bring the pieces when he came east.[2]

The brief stay in Boston offered more opportunities to Harriet than those of buying furniture and seeing her brother Edward and his wife again, for the city was the Eastern center of abolition, and Edward was one of its principal abolitionists. The city was alive with talk of the impending Fugitive Slave Law, which would, in effect, declare open season on all Negroes in the United States. Without benefit of judge or jury, any Negro could be taken into slavery on the word of any man who claimed to be or to represent his master. Harriet behaved here, however, just as she had done on her visit to Kentucky some seventeen years earlier: the others talked while she listened. There is nothing in her letters from Boston to show that what she heard excited her, or even that such talk was taking place, but biographer Forrest Wilson, in the light of later events, correctly analyzed the effect of the Boston visit when he wrote that "when she arrived in Brunswick, her soul was all on fire with indignation at this new indignity and wrong about to be inflicted by the slave owners on the innocent and defenseless."[3]

She arrived in Brunswick May 25 after a rough voyage and a mix-up at the landing in Bath,[4] and wrote Calvin describing her trip in some detail. She had rented the Titcomb house, she said. Located on Federal Street, which ran parallel to and one block east of Main Street, the big yellow house would have ample room for the still growing family (Harriet was seven months pregnant) and was within a ten-minute walk of the campus. It was a rather famous house even in 1850; Henry Wadsworth Longfellow and his brother Stephen had roomed there when

---

[2]*Ibid.*, 131, 132.

[3]Forest Wilson, 240.

[4]Forrest Wilson, 241, and Charles Stowe, 132, date the arrival as May 22. Letters in folders 74 and 94 of the Beecher-Stowe Papers at Radcliffe have May 24 and state the place as Bath.

students at Bowdoin with Calvin in the 1820s. Calvin knew the house and was pleased. The Stowes would live there only a little less than two years, however, for Calvin was already receiving feelers from his other alma mater, Andover.

Despite her expectant motherhood, Harriet went to work making furnishings, hiring workmen for the heavier tasks, and generally setting things in order. But before Calvin arrived in time to see his new son, Charles Edward, born on July 8, sister Catharine came to Brunswick, moved in with the family, and after the birth of the baby, ran the house.[5] The mother did not recover quickly; the nurse was replaced by a governess on the twenty-second,[6] but Harriet still felt sick three days later.[7] In time, however, she was back on her feet and, with Catharine's help, started a private school and installed the governess as a teacher. In addition, of course, she was writing—this time for a new journal, *The National Era,* an abolitionist paper published in Washington, D. C., by Gamaliel Bailey, the man who had taken charge of the *Philanthropist* in Cincinnati when James G. Birney left journalism for politics.

Harriet's first piece in the *Era* was "The Freeman's Dream; A Parable," which appeared in the August 1, 1850, issue. Perhaps taking the title from Longfellow's "The Slave's Dream," she told in Biblical language and cadences the story of a white man who dreamed that he was damned for refusing shelter "to one of the least of these my brethren," namely a fugitive slave and his family. The moral drawn was that obedience was due a higher law than that of man. The next three sketches were more typical of what Harriet had been doing previously. "A Scholar's Adventures in the Country," a gentle satire against city folk who experience problems when they buy a farm, appeared November 7, 1850, and a sentimental Christmas story, "Christmas; or, the Good Fairy," was printed on December 26. The January 30,

---

[5] Folder 223, Beecher Family Papers, Yale; Sklar, 233.
[6] Forrest Wilson, 246.
[7] Folder 264, Beecher-Stowe Papers, Radcliffe.

1851, issue carried "Independence," a story concerning the consequences of late parties. Of the four sketches, the first is of greatest interest because it marked a shift in her writing.

Freemen were a major topic of conversation in Brunswick, as well as in Boston. In addition to being inundated by local opinion, Harriet was deluged with letters from Edward, his wife, and other friends in Boston.[8] Before the end of the year, the Compromise of 1850 with its Fugitive Slave Law was passed, and Edward's wife, Isabella, wrote Harriet, "if I could use a pen as you can, I would write something that would make this whole nation feel what an accursed thing slavery is." Harriet read the letter and then, according to one of her biographers, "rose to her feet, as if in an act of solemn consecration, the crumpled letter in one small, clenched hand. 'I will write something,' she said. 'I will if I live.'"[9] In December, she wrote to Calvin, away at Andover for the winter term.

> As long as the baby sleeps with me nights I can't do much at any thing—but I shall *do it at last*. I shall write that thing if I live. . . .
>
> What do all you folks think about the slave law and about the stand taken by Boston ministers generally except Edward—To me it is incredible—amazing—mournful—I feel as Aunt Mary said—I feel as if I could be willing to sink with it, were all this sin and misery to sink in the sea. . . . I wish Father would come to Boston and preach on the Fugitive Slave law as he once preached on the slave trade when Mrs. Judge Reeves was crying in one pew and I in another. I wish some Martin Luther would arise to set this community right.[10]

In a letter of January 25, 1851, she wrote Calvin she was "projecting a sketch for the Era on the capabilities of liberated blacks to take care of themselves. Can't you find out for me how much Willie Watson has paid for the redemption of his friends,

[8] Charles Stowe, 144.
[9] Forrest Wilson, 252.
[10] Stowe-Day Foundation Library, Hartford; Charles Stowe, 146, misquotes.

and get any items in figures of that kind that you can pick up in Cincinnati?"[11] *Uncle Tom's Cabin* was yet to come, but the days in Boston and the letters from Isabella and others were beginning to produce results. Harriet was starting to write more and more on the question of slavery, and she went about it here just as she would proceed in less than a year when she began the actual book in serial form for the *National Era,* drawing whenever possible upon her personal experiences and her memories of life in Cincinnati.

Sometime after January 8, brother Henry Ward, fresh from a speech at the Tremont Temple in Boston, came to visit his sister in Brunswick. Many years later, in a letter to Alexander Milton Ross, Harriet said that she had memories of Henry Ward coming "to lecture up in the State of Maine, where I was then living, and of our meeting and sitting up at night to ask each other, What can *we* do for a testimony against this wrong. He was going to preach and lecture through the land; and I said, 'I have begun a set of sketches in the National Era, to illustrate the cruelty of slavery: I call it Uncle Tom's Cabin.' 'That's right,' he said, 'write it, and we'll print it, and scatter it "Thick as the Leaves of Vallambrosa."'"[12] Still later, Harriet wrote to George Eliot and repeated essentially the same tale: Henry Ward had ridden until midnight to see her, and they discussed

till near morning, what we could do to make headway against the horrid cruelties that were being practiced against the defenseless blacks. My husband was then away lecturing, and my heart was burning itself out in indignation and anguish. Henry told me then that he meant to fight that battle in New York; that he would have a church that would stand by him to resist the tyrannic dictation of Southern slaveholders. I said: 'I, too, have begun to do something; I have begun a story, trying to set

[11] Stowe-Day Foundation; Charles Stowe, 147, quotes the letter correctly but dates it Dec. 29, 1850.

[12] Alexander Milton Ross, *Recollections*, 3; Forrest Wilson, 254–55, letter dated Hartford, July 22, 1875.

forth the sufferings and wrongs of the slaves.' 'That's right, Hattie,' he said; 'finish it, and I will scatter it thick as the leaves of Vallambrosa,' and so came 'Uncle Tom,' and Plymouth Church became a stronghold where the slave always found refuge and a strong helper.[13]

On February 1, 1851, she wrote to brother Henry and urged him to "strive, pray, labor . . . be the champion of the oppressed and may God defend and bless you. . . . Would to God I could do something even the humblest in this cause—I have actually and really found tears dropping on my pillow when I have thought of the wrongs and sorrows of those oppressed ones."[14]

Five weeks later, on March 9, 1851, Harriet wrote the most important letter of her life. It was to Gamaliel Bailey, editor of the *National Era.*

> I am at present occupied upon a story which will be a much longer one than any I have ever written, embracing a series of sketches which give the lights and shadows of the 'patriarchal institution,' written either from observation, incidents which have occurred in the sphere of my personal knowledge, or in the knowledge of my friends. I shall show the *best side* of the thing, and something *faintly approaching the worst.*
>
> Up to this year I have always felt that I had no particular call to meddle with this subject, and I dreaded to expose even my own mind to the full force of its exciting power. But I feel now that the time is come when even a woman or a child who can speak a word for freedom and humanity is bound to speak. The Carthagenian women in the last peril of their state cut off their hair for bow-strings to give to the defenders of their country; and such peril and shame as now hangs over this country is worse than Roman slavery, and I hope every woman who can write will not be silent. . . . My vocation is simply that of a painter, and

[13] Charles Stowe, 476. Berg Collection, NYPL, has the manuscript dated March 18, 1876. The letter appears in slightly varying states in Charles and Lyman Stowe, 288; Fields, 363; Lyman Stowe, 281.

[14] Beecher Family Papers, Yale, folder 596.

my object will be to hold up in the most lifelike and graphic manner possible Slavery, its reverses, changes, and the negro character, which I have had ample opportunities for studying. There is no arguing with *pictures,* and everybody is impressed by them, whether they mean to be or not.

I wrote beforehand, because I know that you have much matter to arrange, and thought it might not be amiss to give you a hint. The thing may extend through three or four numbers. It will be ready in two to three weeks.[15]

The letter is interesting on a number of counts. Harriet had written a portion of her story, but had no real conception of its eventual length. She was using, at this point anyway, no published sources, relying on her "observation, . . . personal knowledge, or . . . the knowledge of [her] friends," apparently finding these three counts sufficient to feed the stream of her composition.

She intended, even from the first, to present a balanced picture of slavery. The story would not condemn the institution and all slaveholders and portray the enslaved as poor, abused, moral, Christian people—the standard approach in all slave narratives and abolitionist works. As she wrote to Bailey, she planned to show both the *"best side* of the thing, and something *faintly approaching the worst."*

The letter also indicates that she felt the subject of slavery alien to her nature as a writer. She was more accustomed to dealing with home, motherhood, children, love, and the humorous incidents of everyday life. This story would be a sacrifice of her womanhood; she would cease to be a mother and take up arms as a warrior, doing what she could for her country, which was now in a state of both "peril and shame." She feared the "full force" of the "exciting power" of the subject feared what it would do to her as a woman and as a writer but felt that she must write, must do something to save her country.

The next to the last paragraph of the letter is very important

[15] Forrest Wilson, 259-60. Original in Garrison Papers, Boston Public Library.

for an understanding of Harriet's method of composition. Her style, she explained, was that of a painter, not that of a story-teller, because the former, not the latter, was both her view and her method of writing. Prior to the story she was now undertaking, she had composed only sketches, and the word is well chosen in her case, for her sketches were almost literally pictures. In "The Tea Rose," one does not remember the characters' names or the action; the names are unimportant and the actions slight. What is remembered is the picture Harriet painted there, the poor mother and sickly child in a small room brightened only by the lovely rose on the window sill. In "Uncle Abel and Little Edward," it is the deathbed *scene,* not the dying, that comes to mind. In short, as the pictorial method had been her mode of operation in the past, so it would be now. If the weaknesses inherent in such an approach to novel writing are apparent—jerky movement, lack of continuity, sacrifice of character development—so are its advantages, the characteristics of which were to develop into the realistic-local-color genre.

Harriet packed so much minute detail into each scene she drew that her reader had a sense of reality, of being there—she created a *pictoria poesis.* She spoke with the voice of authority. And, more important, because the scenery was so believable, the reader, having accepted the verisimilitude of the background, tended to carry over his trust in the author to the portrayal of character. Early in the novel, everything she spoke of which dealt with the North was accepted by the reader, who said to himself, "Yes, that's what the Ohio roads look like, that's how a bereaved mother would sort through her lost child's clothes." In these early scenes Harriet created a bond of credibility with the reader.

When she shifted to the Deep South in the later scenes, she maintained the same technique of minute detail, even though she had never been there. The description of Eva's bedroom or St. Clare's house or Dinah's kitchen is an example. Because the reader had accepted the pictures of the North, he accepted the pictures of the South; having once given his confidence, he was not inclined to withdraw it. As a result, the scenes, both North and South, furnished a firm foundation of belief upon which she built both the characterizations and the actions of the principal figures.

Again, in these later sections, Harriet skillfully gave the Northern reader a point of reference in Miss Ophelia, who behaved in a manner consistent with her New England upbringing. If he was ever tempted to think that what Harriet had St. Clare say or Dinah do might be contrary to fact, Miss Ophelia's presence reminded the reader of the author's veracity. By the time Legree came upon the scene, the reader had been subtly prepared through what he had learned about slavery and masters from Haley, and thus he was ready to accept as gospel truth almost anything he read about what Legree did or, indeed, might have done. It is doubtful that Legree could have performed an act which the nineteenth-century reader would have found beyond belief: "There is no arguing with *pictures,* and everybody is impressed by them, whether they mean to be or not," Harriet had written.

She had promised that the story would "be ready in two or three weeks." When Bailey accepted it, or how much manuscript he received, we do not know. Three weeks from the date of the letter would have been March 30. Apparently Harriet did not have it done by then, for it was not until May 8 that Bailey inserted the following notice in the *Era:*

A New Story by Mrs. Stowe—

Week after next we propose to commence in the *Era,* the publication of a new story by Mrs. H. B. Stowe, the title of which will be, "UNCLE TOM'S CABIN, OR THE MAN THAT WAS A THING," It will probably be of the length of the Tale by Mrs. Southworth, Entitled Retribution.

Mrs. Stowe is one of the most gifted and popular of American writers. We announce her story in advance, that none of our subscribers, through neglect to renew their subscriptions, may lose the beginning of it, and that those who desire to read the production as it may appear in successive numbers of the *Era,* may send us their names in season.

One possible reason for the delay was Harriet's attempt to obtain copyright. As this was to be a longer story than any she had done, she probably thought that someday she might be able to place it elsewhere, perhaps collect it with a number of her other sketches as she had done in 1843 with *The Mayflower.* She had seen her sketches pirated from the newspapers and annuals and reprinted time after time at little or no monetary advantage to herself; this story she wanted protected against such theft. Whatever her reasons, she filed for copyright May 12, 1851,[16] and probably held off sending the manuscript to Bailey until she had been assured that she controlled the rights.

The sketch on the ability of liberated slaves to care for themselves, which she was projecting in January for the *Era,* appeared in the *Evangelist* on June 12 and 19, 1851.[17] "The Two Altars; or, Two Pictures in One" was a diptych comparing the sacrifices of a family on the Altar of Liberty for the men at Valley Forge during the winter of 1776, with the sacrifice of a respectable, hard-working fugitive slave, who had been free for ten years, on the "Altar of Liberty" by the 1850 Fugitive Slave law. The parallels were skillfully drawn, and much was made of the efforts of the Negro and his family to improve themselves. They were neat, clean, frugal, interested in education—they embodied all the Puritan virtues.

His May 8 letter indicates that editor Bailey sensed that *Uncle Tom's Cabin* would be longer than Harriet had said in her first letter. His suggestion that it would probably be the length of Mrs. Southworth's tale, which had run from January 3 to April 12, 1849, meant some fourteen issues. However, he was probably guessing, for on May 15 he reprinted the notice of the

---

[16] Arthur Hobson Quinn, *American Fiction*, 159.

[17] Harriet Beecher Stowe, "The Two Altars; or, Two Pictures in One," *Evangelist*, June 12, 19, 1851.

The first installment of the story that was to shock the nation occupied most of the front page of the *National Era*, June 5, 1851. *Courtesy of Stowe-Day Memorial Library and Historical Foundation.*

previous issue announcing publication in two weeks: May 29. Not until one week later, May 22, did he mention seeing the manuscript. At that time he said that "the first two chapters had been received," but publication was still two weeks off; the commencement date was now June 5. As Bailey obviously hoped to have the completed manuscript in hand before he began printing, the first notice was either purely a guess on his part, as suggested above, or was based on something Harriet had written about the length of the proffered tale. But by the twenty-ninth he had apparently despaired of getting the manuscript in before he started and announced that "Uncle Tom's Cabin" would appear "next week." The first installment occupied a little more than half of the front page in the issue for June 5, 1851.

In retrospect Harriet was to say over and over again that *Uncle Tom's Cabin* all began with a vision; however, her correspondence contemporary with the first publication of the serial does not mention such an inspiration. Where the vision took place she was not certain. Most of the time she told it as she did in the Introduction she wrote in 1879 for the edition which renewed the copyright. There, referring to herself in the third person, she gave what can be called the "communion table" version.

> The first part of the book ever committed to writing was the death of Uncle Tom. This Scene presented itself almost as a tangible vision to her mind while sitting at the communion table in the little church in Brunswick. She was perfectly overcome by it, and could scarcely restrain the convulsion of tears and sobbings that shook her frame. She hastened home, and wrote it; and, her husband being away, she read it to her two sons of ten and twelve years of age. The little fellows broke out into convulsions of weeping, one of them saying, through his sobs, "O mamma, slavery is the most cursed thing in the world!" From that time the story can less be said to have been composed by her than imposed upon her. Scenes, incidents, conversations, rushed upon her with a vividness and importu-

nity that would not be denied. The book insisted upon getting itself into being, and would take no denial.[18]

Sometimes she gave the "Andover" version. In reply to questions put to her by her close friend Mrs. John Howard, Harriet said that the book came to her in visions, but that the death of Uncle Tom came in the natural course of composition. Mrs. Howard reproduced the conversation.

> 'And did you know,' I [Mrs. Howard] asked, 'that Uncle Tom would die? 'Oh, yes,' she answered, ' I knew that he must die from the first, but I did not know *how*. When I got to that part of the story, I saw no more for some time. I was physically exhausted, too. Mr. Stowe had then accepted a call to Andover, and had to go there to find a house for the family.
>
> 'He urged my going with him for the change, and I went. . . . After dinner we went to our room for a rest. . . suddenly arose before me the death scene of Uncle Tom with what led to it—and George's visit to him. I sat down at the table and wrote nine pages of foolscap paper without pausing, except long enough to dip my pen into the inkstand.[19]

The biographers have assiduously tried to "clarify" matters. Annie Fields, for instance, pointed out that Calvin did not accept the position at Andover until after the book was published. She cited a letter to the Stowes from the committee of trustees in June 1852 which suggested the use of an old carpenter shop, the "old stone house," as the Stowes's residence if they wished to fix it up.[20] Mrs. Fields also cited, but did not identify, a preface which Harriet wrote for a later edition of *Uncle Tom's Cabin,* in which she gave a third account. Harriet wrote "of having many years before written a sketch of the death

[18] *Ibid.*, "Introduction," *Uncle Tom's Cabin* (Boston, 1879), xiii–xiv, hereafter referred to as "1879 Introduction."

[19] Fields, 164.

[20] *Ibid.*, 165. In a letter to the author July 14, 1967, Mr. Ellis E. O'Neal, Jr., librarian, Andover Newton Theological School, confirmed Mrs. Field's statement: the board of visitors elected Calvin professor of sacred literature on May 10, 1852; he accepted on May 15 and was inaugurated on May 31.

of an old slave, and of reading it to her children, who were very much affected by it, this being the original idea (in part) of 'Uncle Tom.'" When Mrs. Howard presented Harriet with the "serious inconsistency" between this and the Andover accounts, she responded that "'both are true, for I had entirely forgotten that I had ever written that sketch, and I suppose that I had unconsciously woven it in with the other.'"[21]

Charles Stowe's biography accepted the communion table vision. When he and his son Lyman Beecher Stowe wrote the joint biography, they changed the details a bit: the vision was "like the unrolling of a picture scroll" and was accompanied by a voice in her ears intoning Matthew 25:40; she wrote a large part of the scene "in pencil on some brown paper in which groceries had been delivered" and read it that evening to her two little boys "of ten and twelve." The two biographers extricated themselves from the contradiction Annie Fields had noted by stating some ten pages later that "part of the concluding chapter" was written "in Andover."[22]

In *Saints Sinners and Beechers,* Lyman Stowe described the scene as he had earlier but added a few more details and changed a few: the resulting chapter was given its proper title, "The Martyr" (in the earlier biography it had been called "The Death of Uncle Tom"), the ages of the two boys were omitted, and the piece was read to "the children." In addition, Stowe took the scene set by Harriet in Andover, moved it to Brunswick, and dated it some time after Calvin's return. The contradictions which so bothered Mrs. Howard and Annie Fields disappeared.[23] Forrest Wilson added some details of his own invention, but accepted Lyman Stowe's reconciliation of the contradictions, going so far as to date Calvin's "discovery" of the forgotten scene as "one day—early in March."[24]

[21] Fields, 165. The author has not been able to identify the preface.
[22] Charles Stowe, 148; Charles and Lyman Stowe, 145, 155.
[23] Lyman Stowe, 181–82.
[24] Forrest Wilson, 257.

The reason for these multiple and contradictory statements is not far to seek. For the rest of her life, Harriet would insist that she had not written the book but that "God wrote it." "God," of course, was her name for Plato's "divine madness," Coleridge's "imagination," Emerson's "Reason." If she had trouble explaining the "how" of *Uncle Tom's Cabin*, it is no wonder that she often confused the details of the much-less-important "when."

The problems facing the author of a serial may account for lapses in technique as well as accuracy. The *National Era* came out on Thursdays in Washington, D. C.; Harriet wrote in Brunswick, Maine, some 545 miles away. It was obviously impossible for Harriet to dash down the street to the printing office to make corrections. It took at least two days by boat for the manuscript to travel from author to publisher, maybe three or four. To get her copy to the *Era,* Harriet sometimes drove to Portland, sometimes sailed to Boston; occasionally she sent it from New York. Never did she visit Washington while the serial was running.[25] It was therefore impossible for her to have overseen its publication. She read no proof for the *Era.* If the story had been printed at the rate of one chapter an issue, the typical serial structure might have appeared: suspense created, sometimes artifically, at the end of the installment to encourage the reader to buy the next issue in order to find out what happened. But the issues varied from part of a single chapter to as many as three complete chapters.

Several forces were at work upon Harriet as she wrote her weekly installments. Some of them she was conscious of; others operated upon her with subtlety. She was writing within more than one literary tradition, especially in her handling of the sentimental and domestic themes which she had employed in

[25] Regis Louise Boyle, *Mrs. E. D. E. N. Southworth*, *Novelist*, 10, maintains that Harriet visited Washington and met with Bailey. There is no evidence that she went to Washington, and when she wrote to Bailey on April 18, 1852, seventeen days after *Uncle Tom's Cabin* had been completed in the *Era*, she opened the letter with "Tho' I have never seen you" (letter in the Houghton Library, Harvard Univ.).

her earlier short fiction and, as numerous scholars have noted, under the influence of the styles and techniques of individual giants of the age.

Much has been said of Harriet's reading as it affected her writing of *Uncle Tom's Cabin*—and particularly of her reading of Sir Walter Scott and Charles Dickens.

Scott had been a favorite of all the Beechers for years, and he remained so for Harriet. Shortly after Charley's birth in July, she had commenced rereading Scott's "historical novels." By December 7, she could tell Calvin that she had finished *The Talisman* and was now reading *The Abbot*.[26] Ten days later, in a long letter to Sarah Beecher, George's widow, she said that she was "reading Scott's historic novels in their order. To night I finish the Abbot—I shall begin Kenilworth next week."[27]

Among specific Scott influences is a parallel which John Erskine found between Cassy and Scott's Flora MacIvor or Norma: "The mystery of her past, her almost superhuman power, her astonishing influence over Legree, the strain of insanity or fanaticism in her are molded from Scott's material by weaker hands."[28] Noting that Scott is not only a romancer but a writer of expanded travel tales, Charles Foster observes, "In making *Uncle Tom's Cabin* a panorama of mid-America, Harriet could easily have been influenced by Scott."[29]

Perry Westbrook finds Scott's influence obvious in Harriet's use of recent history.[30] Edward Wagenknecht sees Scott "worth more to her as a literary influence than all other writers put together. . . . According to him, "the book recalls [Scott] not only in its specific techniques of story-telling but even more in

[26] Folder 75, Beecher-Stowe Papers, Radcliffe.

[27] The original letter, dated Dec. 17, 1850, is in Beecher-Stowe Papers, Radcliffe, folder 94; it is quoted in Charles Stowe, 133–40. Forrest Wilson cites it, 246–47, but says it was written on a Saturday instead of a Tuesday.

[28] John Erskine, *Leading American Novelists*, 294.

[29] Foster, 16.

[30] Perry D. Westbrook, *Acres of Flint*, 24.

its grasp and vision of the life of a people and the sure, easy mastery with which it marshals and controls large masses of disparate materials."[31] Certainly Scott's ability to encompass an age in all social levels, to create a panoramic effect, had its influence on Harriet. Scott taught her how to put her sketches together.

Dickens, too, was a favorite and something of an influence, though not so notably as Scott. In November 1850, Harriet wrote to her sister Isabella Hooker that she was reading *David Copperfield*. Three months later, according to the child's letter to her father, young Hattie, one of the twins, was reading the same novel. Harriet's indebtedness to Dickens was in the realm of the protest or social novel like *Oliver Twist* and *Nicholas Nickleby*. Like him, she wrote sentimental and domestic fiction with both a bite and a message.

Yet the principal influence which led to *Uncle Tom's Cabin* was neither Scott nor Dickens. It was the force of the native tradition, what John R. Adams calls the "pathos and piety" of such writing as Susan Warner's *Wide Wide World,* the story of Ellen Montgomery, who, Adams says, "grew sweeter and more studious through adversity, finally becoming a true Christian of Mrs. Stowe's own model, earnest, charitable, strict with herself but tender towards others,"[32] *Uncle Tom's Cabin* was not a break from Harriet's earlier work: it was of a piece with it. She recognized, as Herbert Ross Brown notes, that "pathetic episodes were inherent in a social order which permitted families to be separated and domestic ties to be violated at the will of a master"[33]; and therefore she treated slavery, as Foster points out, in terms of its effects on the domestic system. She had lost a

---

[31] Wagenknecht, 144. For examples of carelessness with details, also like Scott, see Howard Mumford Jones, "Introduction," *Uncle Tom's Cabin*, ix–x.

[32] Folder 95, Beecher-Stowe Papers, Radcliffe; John R. Adams, "Literary Achievement of Harriet Beecher Stowe," 90.

[33] Herbert Ross Brown, *Sentimental Novel in America*, 257.

child to cholera in Cincinnati; Mrs. Bird loses a child, Cassy has lost children, and Eliza is moved to act by the fear of losing her child. Tom's greatest, indeed only, discomfort at St. Clare's is his separation from his family. Surely Carl Van Doren is right when he contends that she had no "foreign master, not even Scott. . . . Instead, the native tradition, . . . sentimental, pious, instructive narratives written by women chiefly for women and very largely about women," was the controlling influence. "Leave out the merely domestic elements of the book—slave families broken up by sale, ailing and dying children, Negro women at the mercy of their masters, white households which at the best are slovenly and extravagant by reason of irresponsible servants and at most are abodes of brutality and license—and little remains."[34]

In Harriet's taking slavery as her background lies her originality. Were there no Negroes in the book, no Legrees, no St. Clares or Shelbys, no products of the system, it would be just another sentimental novel. But there are, and so it is not.

Besides broad influences in theme or manner, those of a more specific nature have also been cited. Many novels, for example, are said to have been models for or early forerunners of *Uncle Tom's Cabin*. Almost any such writing before 1851 which deals in any way with the South or the Negro or slavery has been offered up at one time or another as a possible or probable source. An examination of two contenders will suffice. Frances Trollope's *Adventures of Jonathan Jefferson Whitlaw* has been called a "feeble forerunner of Uncle Tom's Cabin"[35]; Lucy and Richard Stebbins have found "many points of resemblance" between the two stories.[36] It is true that *Whitlaw* does deal directly with slavery and is set in Mississippi with many scenes in New Orleans, but the points of divergence far exceed the weak parallels. As even the principal defender of the alleged source is

---

[34] Carl Van Doren, *American Novel*, 110.

[35] Ralph Leslie Rusk, *Literature of the Middle Western Frontier*, I, 110.

[36] Lucy Poate and Richard Poate Stebbins, *The Trollopes*, 79.

forced to admit, "neither Mrs. Stowe, nor any other American abolitionist seems to have known of" the existence of the book; there were "no American editions."[37]

Equally unlikely as an important source is Sarah Josepha Hale's *Northwood,* first published in 1827. In his attempt to place *Uncle Tom's Cabin* in the plantation tradition, Francis Pendleton Gaines cited this work among other possible precursors.[38] Originally sub-titled *"A Tale of New England,"* Mrs. Hale's book may well hold some of the honors awarded it, but when Ruth Finley says that it dealt "primarily with the problem of emancipation" or that it represented Mrs. Hale's "early sensing of the menace of slavery,"[39] she reveals a lack of homework. More perceptive critics, such as Isabelle Entrikin and William Taylor, suspected that the change of the subtitle of *Northwood* to *Life North and South; Showing the True Character of Both* in 1852 was to be taken as a hint that other changes were made, and they began comparing the 1827 first edition with the second edition of 1852. Entrikin suggests the extent of the additions when she notes that "some of the discussions of slavery were amplified."[40] That *Northwood* was a source in its revised published state with the new slavery material is impossible, for the new edition was introduced by "A word with the Reader" from Mrs. Hale dated September 2, 1852, six months after Harriet's book appeared, and was, as Forrest Wilson notes, actually a reply to *Uncle Tom's Cabin.*[41]

Edward Wagenknecht states perceptively that "insofar as they furnished Mrs. Stowe with literary models, guided the bent of her genius, and taught her her trade, the importance of the novels mentioned by Professor Foster and others can hardly

---

[37] Harold H. Scudder, "Mrs. Trollope and Slavery in America," *Notes & Queries* 187 (1944), 46.

[38] Francis Pendleton Gaines, *Southern Plantation,* 21.

[39] Ruth E. Finley, *Lady of Godey's,* 266, 269.

[40] Isabelle Webb Entrikin, *Sarah Josepha Hale,* 110; William R. Taylor, *Cavalier and Yankee,* 116–18.

[41] Forrest Wilson, 325, who cites it by its subtitle.

be overestimated; [but] as actual sources of material I think experience was more important."[42] And fortunately she has left us a few guides to some of her source material in her letters and in the *Key to Uncle Tom's Cabin.* The serial began June 5, 1851, and the book appeared March 20, 1852. As the serial ran and after the book was published, the veracity of the story was continually attacked. The *Key,* published in 1853, was the defense of her facts and her book.[43]

As the *Key* has been both misused and misinterpreted more often than *Uncle Tom,* the meaning of which it allegedly unlocks, it is necessary to point out, first of all, that this work is not a compilation of the source material Harriet had on hand when she wrote the novel. The greater part of this material was collected after *Uncle Tom* was published. She brought it together, not to indicate to the doubtful reader that she had been working from pre-assembled facts and drawing on documentary evidence, but rather to corroborate with data from other sources the authenticity of the scenes she had depicted.

Within the *Key,* however, are hints as to what material she did use in writing the novel. Much of the material, both letters and newspaper clippings, is dated. If the date is after March 20, 1852, or after the date of the publication of a specific installment in the *National Era,* it obviously cannot be considered as a source. Once such dated material is eliminated, the remainder may be examined as possible source material. Often Harriet labeled a fact or an incident as a "parallel case" or "further proof" that her statements were true, clearly labeling it as not being a source. On the other hand, when talking about a true source, she used a phrase such as "it was known to the author" or "some years before, the author read" or "heard" or "saw." But even these two caveats must be supplemented. Harriet had legal advice, probably from her brother-in-law John Hooker, when

---

[42] Wagenknecht, 156.

[43] Harriet Beecher Stowe, *Key to Uncle Tom's Cabin;* hereafter, references to this work will be given as *Key* and incorporated into the text.

she wrote the *Key*. It must have been read in manuscript by other members of the family who corrected her memory here or added a fact or two there. She was angry when she wrote it. Her letters throughout 1851 and 1852 reflect her annoyance at not being believed, at being challenged by the defenders of the hateful system, at being unjustifiably criticized by those who misread her book as an attack upon the South. The preface sums up her attitude toward the *Key* and the material found in it.

> The work which the writer here presents to the public is one which has been written with no pleasure, and with much pain. . . . The author desires to express her thanks particularly to those legal gentlemen who have given her their assistance and support in the legal part of the discussion. She also desires to thank those, at the North and at the South, who have kindly furnished materials for her use. Many more have been supplied than could possibly be used. The book is actually selected out of a mountain of materials. (*Key*, p. iii)

If, then, the *Key* is used with care and an attempt is made to reinforce its statements with data drawn from letters and other outside sources, it will be valuable. To disregard such caution is to invite error.

The first installment of *Uncle Tom's Cabin* in the *National Era* on June 5, 1851, opened in a Kentucky plantation house where Mr. Arthur Shelby was in the process of closing a slave sale with Dan Haley, slave trader. Sources for both characters are not difficult to find. Because Cincinnati was an important center for the underground railroad, Harriet could not have avoided receiving at least secondhand knowledge of escaped slaves and their pursuing masters. In fact, firsthand knowledge was available to her when she began to write her novel. In her description in the *Key* of the sources for the character of Haley she told of a personal observation. A Negro woman came to her for help: her child had been seized by the heirs of her former owner. A collection taken at Lane Seminary purchased the child's freedom (*Key*, pp. 5–6). In addition to this cited source, there were, of course, the innumerable instances of the activities of slave dealers available to Harriet in earlier years in the Cincinnati newspapers and, more recently, in the *National Era*. Haley was not a difficult man to create; materials were plentiful.

The Shelbys were drawn with a little more care. Some of the local detail surely came from the 1833 visit to Kentucky with Mary Dutton. For the character of Mrs. Shelby, as indicated in the *Key* (p. 12), Harriet drew upon the conversations of "some pious ladies" she met on her trip to Kentucky and the statements of "a venerable friend . . . born and educated a slaveholder." Also in the *Key*, Harriet cited as sources for her account of this fairest side of slavery "Mr. J. K. Paulding's Letters on Slavery," and "Ingraham's Travels in the Southwest" (pp. 8–12). It should be noted here that published sources are used for background; character is sketched from personal experience.

George Harris, introduced in chapter 2, the second issue in the serial, came from many sources. In the *Key*, Harriet cited facts from lives of people she knew which paralleled incidents in the novel. Lewis Clarke, an escaped slave, had lived with the family of Harriet's sister-in-law, was educated while there, and was "an acquaintance of the writer." She "frequently heard him spoken of in the highest terms" *(Key,* pp. 13–14). She then listed a series of incidents from his life, "part of which he related personally to the author," and invited the reader to compare them with "the incidents of the life of George Harris." She then drew parallels between Harris and the published lives of escaped slaves Frederick Douglass and Josiah Henson to show that such events as she pictured in the novel were "by no means so uncommon as might be supposed" and pointed out that the examples given from the lives of the two men were *"real* incidents of slavery, related by those who knew slavery by the best of all tests—experience" (*Key,* p. 19). She did not speak of knowing either Henson or Douglass personally; she had read their books but apparently had not met the men. Beginning sometime after publication of the *Key* in 1853, Lewis Clarke maintained until his death that he was the model for George Harris.

Harriet's comments on Clarke's influence are illuminating and predictably contradictory. In a letter to Rev. J. C. Webster of Hopkinton, Massachusetts, written from Brunswick on September 25, probably 1852, Harriet said of the model for George Harris that while in Kentucky "several years ago" she was told "of a young mulatto man of fine talents whose master had hired him out to a bagging factory and that he had invented a machine for cleaning hemp as I stated."[44] There is no reference to Clarke or to his book. The following year, however, in the *Key* (pp. 13–14), she cited Clarke as a source.

Harriet said nothing about Clarke in her introduction to the 1879 edition of *Uncle Tom's Cabin*. Later, in a letter dated 1885, written to the editor of the *Brooklyn Magazine,* she mentioned Clarke by name, but defined his influence. She said:

> In reply to yr inquiry I would say that none of the characters in Uncle Tom's Cabin are portraits—I knew of several colored men who showed the piety honesty & faithfulness of Uncle Tom—but none of them had a history like that I have created for him. Some events in the life of Lewis Clark are somewhat like some in the story of George Harris. I read his history while writing the story merely to see that I was keeping within the limits of probability. It is not surprising therefore that your informant cannot tell you where the originals of Uncle Tom & George Harris are—I know of no such persons.[45]

Inspired by the brief identification in the *Key,* Lewis Clarke built a vocation. In 1882 he told Young E. Allison, writing under the pen name of "Picador," that he spoke to Harriet at her brother-in-law's house in Cambridge, Massachusetts, before 1845 and that "she took full notes of all he said," which information "made the entire republic tremble when 'Uncle Tom's Cabin' made its appearance in 1853 [*sic*]." Clarke told his story thus in this way: Gamaliel Bailey moved to Washington,

[44] St. John's Seminary, Camarillo, Calif.; cf. *Key*, 13.
[45] Barrett Collection, Univ. of Virginia.

D. C. "about 1848 or 1850" and founded the *National Era.* After the passage of the Fugitive Slave law, the paper steadily lost circulation "and was on the point of extinction." Bailey went to New York to talk with leading abolitionists

> as to what course he should pursue. He thought that if he could get some woman of literary reputation and ability to write a series of articles for the paper every week on the subject of slavery and its violation of the finest sentiments, that it would revive public interest and carry the paper to people it had never reached before. The names of Mrs. Lydia M. Child and others were proposed, but not accepted. Lewis Tappan who was one of the counselors, finally said that he knew of one woman who could do the work successfully, that she was poor and must be paid for it, but would succeed. He then mentioned Mrs. Stowe and advised Dr. Bailey to write her, and, by way of earnest, inclose a draft for $100. The letter was written and the draft sent. The next week there appeared in the columns of the National Era, not the first of a series of articles on slavery, but the first chapters of a story called 'Uncle Tom's Cabin.'

According to Clarke, Bailey later sent her $300 more. She then copyrighted the story. She wove into her book all that Clarke had told her plus material from other sources. Allison concluded that nobody who read [Clarke's] narrative can doubt where Mrs. Stowe got most of her facts and suggestions."[46]

In May of 1888, Clarke was in Minneapolis billing himself as "Old Man Harris" with an even better story. He claimed that he spent six years with Deacon Safford, Harriet's brother-in-law,[47] at a place he called Cambridgeport, Massachusetts, where he

---

[46] "Picador" [Young E. Allison], "Uncle Tom's Cabin," Louisville *Courier Journal*, May 16, 1881; see also "Uncle Tom's Cabin," New York *Tribune*, July 22, 1870; Lewis and Milton Clarke, *Narratives of the Sufferings of Lewis and Milton Clarke*, 61.

[47] Safford was not Harriet's brother-in-law; he was in fact no relation. Aaron H. Safford was the husband of Lyman Beecher's third wife's former husband's sister, or Harriet's second stepmother's sister-in-law's husband. Mr. Joseph Van Why, curator of the Stowe-Day Foundation, contributed this genealogical information.

met Mrs. Stowe. "She would talk to me for hours about life among the slaves, and each day she would write down what I had told her. Then she had never been south, and, without vanity I can say that had it not been for me 'Uncle Tom's Cabin' would never have been written. Nearly all the incidents in the book I told her."[48] Both accounts are rife with minor errors of date, place, and names, but Clarke did meet Harriet and talk with her. She did read his story. His character and adventures helped to create George Harris, but he created something better for himself, a legend and a career.

Unfortunately, the legends breed legends. On the Kennedy plantation in Kentucky where Clarke said he had lived, Anna Burnside Brown, writing in the *Kentucky Progress Magazine* in 1930, found the original for the Shelby house and the originals for George Harris and other characters in the book. According to her, Thomas Kennedy, Jr., and his wife were the Shelbys; their daughters, Nancy, "who married a Letcher and lived in the State," and Polly, "very frail and beautiful," who "only lived a short time after her marriage," dying "like Little Eva . . . of tuberculosis, were interwoven . . . to create the character of the beloved Little Eva." The article was illustrated with a sketch of the cabin where Uncle Tom lived. Brown then asserted that Harriet visited the Spillman place in Paint Lick, Kentucky, just a few miles from the Kennedy place. "She also visited her relatives in Massachusetts every summer and took a deep interest in Lewis Clarke and his stories of slave life. . . . From his own lips and information gleaned elsewhere, Mrs. Stowe gathered together the background, scenes and some of the characters from the Kennedy place that were woven into her book."[49] J. Winston Coleman brought together previous mate-

---

[48] "A Gray Old Man Now," Minneapolis *Evening Journal*, May 30, 1888; see also "The Original George Harris," New York *Tribune*, July 22, 1870.

[49] Anna Burnside Brown, "Where Uncle Tom's Cabin Stood," *Kentucky Progress Magazine* 3, no. 12 (Sept. 1930), 20.

rial and made some additions of his own. He asserted that Harriet visited Kentucky several times with Mary Dutton and went to the Spillman home, Kennedy's plantation, and the Marshall home in Washington, Mason County.[50] In spite of these writers, however, no strong evidence remains of frequent trips to Massachusetts and extensive travels in Kentucky.

Brown, Coleman, and others, though seemingly confident in their assertions, lacked the perspicacity of one who had gone before them in the attempt to find "originals." In the mid-1880s, James Lane Allen had spent a great deal of time in Kentucky researching an article on the models of *Uncle Tom's Cabin*. In a letter to Richard Watson Gilder, editor of *The Century Monthly Magazine,* on October 1, 1886, he said that his search had turned up only an extensive collection of Kentucky legends, and he had therefore given it up. He had changed the approach of his article and would write about the typical Uncle Tom. In reply to a request to Mrs. Stowe for help, he had received only the advice to consult the *Key* and the "red line" edition of *Uncle Tom.* His article, "Mrs. Stowe's 'Uncle Tom' at Home in Kentucky," appeared in the *Century* for October 1887; it contains no attempted identifications.[51]

The character of Eliza, wife of George Harris and mother of little Harry, apparently came from a single source. In the *Key,* Harriet explained that on the Kentucky trip she saw "a beautiful quadroon girl" and that, on discovering that she was owned by "Mr. So-and-so," she had remarked that she hoped the girl was treated well and would not be sold. "A person in the company" said that she need not worry; the girl's owner had turned down an offer of one thousand dollars and had told the prospective purchaser that "she was too good to be his wife, and he certainly should not have her for a mistress" (*Key,* p. 22). In the letter to

[50] J. Winston Coleman, Jr., "Mrs. Stowe, Kentucky, and Uncle Tom's Cabin," *Lincoln Herald* 48, no. 2 (1946), 8.

[51] Letter in Barrett Collection, Univ. of Virginia; James Lane Allen, "Mrs. Stowe's 'Uncle Tom' at Home in Kentucky," *Century Monthly Magazine* 34 (1887), 852–67.

the Rev. Webster, quoted above, Harriet told of the same incident.

The sources for Uncle Tom, who was introduced in chapter 4, "An Evening in Uncle Tom's Cabin," are perhaps more difficult to trace than those for any other character in the novel. In the *Era,* the chapter appeared on June 19, the fourth week of the once-a-week serial. It would seem to the modern researcher that every kindly Christian Negro who lived prior to 1851 has at some time or other put himself forth as the "original" Uncle Tom.[52] A desire for wealth and fame motivated many to claim more of a share of the honor than they could rightfully support. Again, the *Key* is a good place to initiate the search.

Harriet began by saying, again in the third person, that Uncle Tom was not an improbable character: "Many people have said to her, 'I knew an Uncle Tom in such and such a Southern State.' All the histories of this kind which have thus been related to her would themselves, if collected, make a small volume. The author will relate a few of them" (*Key,* p. 23). She then printed a number of tales of Uncle Tomish Negroes. The problem concerns which of these stories, if any, were known to her before the publication of the serial. She introduced the first story with the phrase "While visiting in an obscure town in Maine." There is no indication of the date. Although it must have been later than the spring of 1850, when she arrived in Brunswick, and before October 1852, when she was closing the Brunswick house, we can only suspect that it was prior to the serial, on the grounds that the gentleman she mentions as having told her of an honest Negro did not draw a parallel with Uncle Tom.

The second story she cited was taken from *Sketches of Old*

---

[52] John T. Page, "The Original Uncle Tom," *Notes & Queries,* 11th ser. 6 (1912), 367, and Jacob Piatt Dunn, *Greater Indianapolis,* I, 242–44, cited Thomas Magruder as the original. W. B. S., "The Original Uncle Tom," *Notes & Queries,* 11th ser. 6 (1912), 436, said the model was Josiah Henson. Herbert Clayton, "The Original Uncle Tom," *Notes & Queries,* 9th ser. 11 (1903), 445, put forth Norman Argo of Paint Lick, Ky.

Virginia Servants, a book which, she said, "was sent to the writer from the South, through the mail, . . . some time since" (*Key,* p. 24). Published in Philadelphia in 1847, the book could, chronologically, be a source, but as Harriet's copy came from the South, I am inclined to believe that it was sent, as were so many other tracts and books, by a Southerner wishing to help her defend her picture of that region of the country. Furthermore, there is very little in the book that she could have used except for the piety of the slaves.[53]

She next cited various religious tracts which illustrated the "extraordinary piety among negroes" (*Key,* p. 25). The subject of one of these tracts was, "before his conversion, a convict in a state-prison in New York." Harriet apparently learned of him, however, not through his published life, but through "a lady" who "has described to the writer the manner in which he would" conduct a church service. The next tract cited is clearly labeled as having been read by Harriet "when she first went to Brunswick." The subject, a woman named Phebe, was a resident of Brunswick and "so eminent for her piety and loveliness of character, that the writer has never heard her name mentioned except with that degree of awe and respect which one would imagine due to a saint" (*Key,* p. 25). The tract has not been identified, and so we cannot say just how the life of Phebe was used; most probably its function was to supply examples of pious conduct.

At the end of her list Harriet cited a man already named, who was to be very successful in palming himself off as the original Uncle Tom. She wrote, the "last instance parallel with that of Uncle Tom is to be found in the published memoirs of the venerable Josiah Henson, now a clergyman in Canada" (*Key,* p. 26). Neither in this passage nor in the earlier one in the *Key* (p. 19) did Harriet say of Henson, as she did of Clarke, that he was a personal friend or acquaintance. On the other hand, it is perfectly obvious that she was familiar with his *Life,* which had

[53]*Sketches of Old Virginia Family Servants,* 24, 60–70.

Josiah Henson claimed to be the original Uncle Tom. *Courtesy of Stowe-Day Memorial Library and Historical Foundation.*

been published in Boston in 1849. She quoted from the book extensively in the *Key*.[54]

When Henson issued an expanded edition of his life, he asked Harriet to write an introduction, and she complied. In 1858 appeared *Truth Stranger than Fiction: Father Henson's Story of His Own Life* with an introduction dated Andover, Massachusetts, April 5, 1858, and signed "H. B. Stowe." In her introductory essay, Harriet highly recommended the book but gave no indication that Henson was the model for Uncle Tom. Her reference to the author as "our excellent friend" is probably a conventional phrase only. Although Henson added six new chapters (some forty pages) covering his life from 1849 to 1858, and told the reader much about his adventures after 1849 in great detail, nowhere in this expanded edition did he mention meeting Harriet. Certainly, if he had met her, he would have mentioned the fact, since she had written the introduction. Up until 1858, it seems not to have occurred to Henson that he was the model for Uncle Tom.

Twenty-one years later there appeared yet another expansion, *An Autobiography of the Rev. Josiah Henson (Mrs. Harriet Beecher Stowe's 'Uncle Tom') from 1789 to 1879 with a Preface by Mrs. Harriet Beecher Stowe, Introductory Notes by Wendell Phillips and John G. Whittier and an Appendix on the Exodus by Bishop Gilbert Haven.* Harriet's 1858 introduction was reprinted without the date and minus a concluding sentence which concerned Henson's brother still in slavery at the time of the 1849 edition. The early years were depicted essentially as they were in the preceding editions. In new material covering the years 1853–1879, however, were a number of rather startling claims. On page 303 Henson said:

> When I was in England before,—some twenty-five years ago,—the people generally did not know my history. . . . The Rev. Thomas Binney, now deceased, astonished me one day,

[54] Josiah Henson, *Life*, 3–4, 42–43; cf. *Key*, 19, 26–27.

just before I left England, by saying that a lady in America had written a book about me! . . . 'Well,' he then said, 'do you know a lady in Massachusetts named Mrs. Stowe? . . . Did you ever see her and talk with her about yourself?' 'I called on her at her home not long before coming to England, and we talked a long time. She seemed much interested in my story, and I told her all I could think of.' . . . 'She has written a book about you which will make you famous. I recognized the character as yours at once.'

From other sections of the book, it can be determined that Henson was in England at the World's Industrial Exhibition in 1851 and set out for home in early September 1852. He therefore must have met Harriet in late 1850 or early 1851, before his departure for the Exhibition. Yet, in the 1858 edition, there was no mention of the meeting.

At the beginning of the new section, Henson stated:

I was once in the vicinity of Andover, Massachusetts, where Mrs. Harriet Beecher Stowe resided. She sent for me and my traveling companion, Mr. George Clarke, a white gentleman, who had a fine voice for singing. . . . We went to Mrs. Stowe's house, and she was deeply interested in the story of my life and misfortunes, and had me narrate its details to her. She said she was glad it had been published. . . . She manifested so much interest in me, that I told her about the peculiarities of many slaveholders, and the slaves in the region where I had lived for forty-five years. . . . Soon after, Mrs. Stowe's remarkable book 'Uncle Tom's Cabin' was published, and circulated in all parts of America. . . . Many thought that her statements were exaggerations. She then published the Key to the book, to prove that it was impossible to exaggerate the enormities of slavery, and she therein gave many parallel cases and referred to my published life-story, as an exemplification of the truth of the character of her Uncle Tom.

The main discrepancy here is that Harriet did not move to Andover until July 1852, four months after *Uncle Tom's Cabin* was finished.

Henson went on to say that George Harris and his wife Eliza were his "particular friends." According to Henson, George's real name was Lewis Clarke, and he had "travelled and lectured with me in the New England States." The models for Topsy, St. Clare, Eva, and Simon Legree were all people Henson had known and presumably told Harriet of during his visit with her.[55] Surprisingly, he had forgotten to mention these facts in 1858. In short, it appears that Henson's memory, unlike most mortals', improved with age to the degree that he could remember at a distance of twenty-five years the specific meetings and details that had escaped him after only seven years.

Harriet read Henson's biography in the 1849 edition. She alluded to it in the *Key,* and she cited it as one of her sources in the "1879 Introduction" to *Uncle Tom's Cabin.* Further, in a letter to an unknown correspondent dated May 19, 1875, she said that incidents of Uncle Tom's character "were added by reading the life of Father Henson in Canada." Nowhere in either published sources or unpublished correspondence does she mention meeting Henson before the publication of *Uncle Tom's Cabin;* however, Lyman Stowe cites a letter to a Rev. W. H. Gilley, in which she said that Henson was a " 'noble black man' " and that she drew " 'many of the finest conceptions and incidents of Uncle Tom's character' " from his life. Most important, the letter told "of a visit he paid her in Andover, after the publication meeting Henson before the publication of *Uncle Tom's* had for him.' "[56]

But the biographers, influenced by Henson's career-making claims, have ignored the lack of supporting evidence and the presence of contradictory facts.

In their nineteenth-century "lives" both Annie Fields and Charles Stowe failed to mention Henson, although Charles and Lyman Stowe's 1911 work alluded to him, alleging that Harriet

[55] Josiah Henson, *Autobiography*, 217–20, 225–26.

[56] Harriet Beecher Stowe, "1879 Introduction," xiv; letter in Cincinnati Historical Society; Lyman Stowe, 180–81.

met him at Edward Beecher's in Boston "about the last of January, 1850." They undoubtedly meant 1851, not 1850, as Harriet was still in Cincinnati in January of 1850, but there is no evidence to substantiate their statement. Lyman Stowe apparently had second thoughts about the dating, for in his 1934 family biography he generalized the time of the meeting to "not long after" December 1850.[57]

In 1918 W. B. Hartgrove added to the growing tradition of errors, omissions, and halftruths in an article published in *The Journal of Negro History*. Drawing indiscriminately from the various editions of Henson's biography, he produced a biographical sketch that repeats at some length the story of Henson's visit to Harriet in Andover, although it acknowledges, "It has been denied tht he was this hero," before hurrying on to consider other aspects of Henson's life.[58]

Vernon Loggins's study in 1931 pointed out that "the publication of his autobiography became a profitable pursuit for" Henson; that, as early as 1858, he was "trying to live up to the ideal of the fictional hero whose creation he had helped to inspire"; that "no one of the versions of Henson's life supports Mrs. Stowe's declaration regarding his interest and singularity"; that, although it was unlikely that Henson knew the model for Eliza, he might have known Lewis Clarke, but at any rate Clarke was "too bitter and ungoverned a hater to have found a true portrayal for the Christian and womanly pen of Mrs. Stowe." He is far removed in Character from the gentlemanly George Harris.[59]

Catherine Gilbertson's 1937 biography says only that Harriet read Henson's book; she mentions no meeting. Four years later, however, Forrest Wilson defended the meeting, dating it "some

---

[57] Charles and Lyman Stowe, 144; Lyman Stowe, 180–81.

[58] W. B. Hartgrove, "The Story of Josiah Henson," *Journal of Negro History* 3 (1918), 18.

[59] Vernon Loggins, *Negro Author*, 216–17; see also the balanced account by Newton MacTavish, "The Original Uncle Tom," *Canadian Magazine* 30 (1907), 25–29.

time before she wrote *Uncle Tom's Cabin*" and placing it "at her brother Edward's home."[60] Wilson's statement, although not footnoted, is undoubtedly based on the tradition begun in the earlier biographies without additional proof, as an examination of his sources for the chapter shows.

Brion Gysin elaborated in *To Master—A Long Goodnight,* mostly with inaccuracies. Gysin's work has Harriet reading Henson's life in the 1849 edition.[61] To the identification of Bryce Litton, Henson's master, with Legree, it adds the rather odd fact that the Riley brothers, one of whom owned Henson, became the Shelbys, although there are two St. Clares, not two Shelbys.[62] Gysin went on to say of Henson's early years, "It is essentially the reminiscences of this period of his life which he recounted to Mrs. Stowe in Andover, Massachusetts, in 1849, some time after she had seen the account of the first years of his life which had been published in Boston that same year." Without identifying the document, Gysin then referred to "a private letter" which, he stated, shows "that at the time of writing her famous book she relied very extensively on Henson's verbatim account of his experiences."[63] Although two unrelated paragraphs intervene, Gysin may have been referring to the letter reproduced on the following page. Allegedly from Harriet to "Reverend William H. Tilley of Canada" written "May 15, 1876," it appears to be the letter of which Lyman Stowe had a copy and which has been referred to above. Although the names of the recipients do not agree exactly and the texts vary slightly (Stowe quotes only a few lines), this letter gives little support to Gysin's argument. Harriet endorsed Henson and stated that "a sketch of his life" furnished her with much material for Uncle Tom, "in particular the scene where he refuses to free himself by the murder of a brutal master. . . . He once visited me in

---

[60]Gilbertson, 143; Forrest Wilson, 249.
[61]Brion Gysin, *To Master—A Long Goodnight,* 15.
[62]*Ibid.,* 27–28.   [63]*Ibid.,* 45–46.

Andover, and personal intercourse confirmed my high esteem I had for him."[64] Gysin's version of the meeting took place after the reading of the book, the book is considered the principal source, and the meeting is not dated. Gysin produced no support for his argument for a pre-*Uncle Tom* meeting, but, undismayed, continued to misstate and draw conclusions. Henson had been in Cincinnati between 1829 and 1830. "It is just possible that he may have heard of Mrs. Stowe for the first time" while there.[65] (Harriet arrived in the city in 1832.) Harriet married "in 1837."[66] (The date was 1836.) "In 1849, he [Henson] happened to be in the neighborhood of Andover, Massachusetts. There he met Mrs. Stowe. She had just come from Cincinnati to prepare a home for her husband, who had been appointed to the chair of Biblical literature at Andover Theological Seminary. Mrs. Stowe had begun to write in order to earn enough for the family needs, as her husband was ill paid."[67] In refutation of these statements, Harriet actually went to Brunswick (not Andover) in 1850 (not 1849), where Calvin had been appointed to the chair of Collins Professor at Bowdoin (not Andover Theological Seminary). Harriet "had begun to write" in 1834, not later, as Gysin implied. Calvin took both the Bowdoin and the Andover jobs because the pay was good; at neither place was he "ill paid." Gysin stated that, when Harriet "had come North," apparently some time prior to 1849 by his reckoning, "she had traveled to Boston to join the Anti-Slavery Society."[68] Harriet a Garrisonian? In addition, Gysin misquoted Levi Coffin, indicating that Coffin knew that the models for Eliza and George Harris were from Amos Riley's plantation.[69] And lastly, Gysin had George Harris becoming a

---

[64] *Ibid.*, 47; cf. Lyman Stowe, p. 181. The author has been unable to locate the original. Gysin does not remember where he saw it, and a survey of Canadian libraries has failed to identify Tilley/Gilley or locate the letter. Letter to the author April 14, 1970, from Gysin.

[65] Gysin, 114, 53. [67] *Ibid.*, 132. [69] *Ibid.*, 48.
[66] *Ibid.*, 115. [68] *Ibid.*, 133.

member of the legislative assembly of North Carolina during Reconstruction; he never held such an office.[70]

Gysin's basic critical fault, aside from his neglect of such research as that of Loggins and his apparent lack of concern for the accuracy of his information, was his lack of perception in regard to Henson's character.

A 1958 article by Charles Nichols points out that Harriet's first meeting with Henson took place after the publication of *Uncle Tom's Cabin* and that "it was not until 1858 that she propagated the legend that Henson was the 'original Uncle Tom.'" But the legend, abetted by Gysin's shoddy scholarship, has continued. J. C. Furnas wrote in 1956 that Edward Beecher introduced Henson to Harriet in Boston early in the year 1850, and Walter Fisher stated in his introduction to the 1962 reprint of the 1858 edition of Henson's life that Henson met Harriet "in 1849 at her home in Andover and again in 1850 at the Boston home of her brother, Edward Beecher. . . . His story of slavery made her 'Beecher blood boil' and fortified the account which had already appeared in the first edition (1849) of Henson's autobiography." In 1965 Herbert Hill said that Henson met Harriet "when he was preaching throughout New England."[71] And so it will probably go. All but a few have chosen to forget how Harriet began that paragraph in the *Key* in 1853 in which she introduced her discussion of Josiah Henson: "A last instance parallel with that of Uncle Tom. . . ." The book as an influence, yes; the 1853 or later meeting as a source, no.

One of the reasons why Charles Nichols sought to demolish Henson's claim is that Nichols had a contender of his own to put

---

[70] *Ibid.*, 184. William S. Powell, former curator of the North Carolina Collection, Univ. of North Carolina at Chapel Hill, informs me that there was no George Harris in the North Carolina legislature during Reconstruction.

[71] Charles Nichols, "The Origins of Uncle Tom's Cabin," *Phylon Quarterly* 19 (1958), 330; J. C. Furnas, *Goodbye to Uncle Tom*, 22; Walter Fisher, "Introduction," *Father Henson's Story*, vi–vii; Herbert Hill, "Uncle Tom, an Enduring American Myth," *Crisis* 72 (1965), 290; "Uncle Tom Lived in Daviess County, Kentucky," Owensboro (Ky.) *Messenger-Register*, Oct. 22, 1967.

forth: Archy Moore. According to Nichols, Richard Hildreth's novel *The Slave: or, the Memoirs of Archy Moore,* published in 1840, was the "real source" of *Uncle Tom's Cabin,* which was "primarily a derivative piece of hack work. . . . Hildreth's book supplied not only the setting and some of the incidents of *Uncle Tom's Cabin* and *Dred,* but the characters who appear in them." Nichols states that Uncle Tom was the Thomas of Hildreth's book; George Harris was a "mere replica" of Archy; Eliza was Cassy.[72]

But Nichols's proof for these identifications is self-contradictory. Although both Hildreth's Thomas and Uncle Tom are religious, says Nichols, Thomas "is not so long-suffering. He interferes when the overseer attempts to whip the slave's wife and then runs away. Later, tracked down by bloodhounds, Thomas shoots the overseer while the latter begs for mercy." Truly Thomas is "far more three-dimensional" than Tom. One might add that he is so "dimensional" as to be unrecognizable. Nichols proceeds to find models for St. Clare, Eliza, Cassy, and other characters. But he unwittingly weakens his case for Hildreth's book as the source when, for example, he states that Hildreth's Cassy and Harriet's Cassy, "like Pamela," remained virtuous to the end, thereby pointing to the Richardsonian heroine as the more probable common source of both authors; and he further weakens his case when he comments that the minor characters "fall into recognizable types." He concludes that *"Archy Moore* furnished striking incidents and personalities."[73] Yet the only candidate in Hildreth's novel who might have a parallel character in Harriet's is the aforementioned Thomas, and Thomas loses his Tom-like attributes two pages after he is introduced. There are no incidents in Hildreth's story which Harriet could not have found in any one of the other

[72] Nichols, "Origins," 328–30. An interesting approach to the Archy/Tom relationship is taken by Evan Brandstater, "Uncle Tom and Archy Moore: The Antislavery Novel as Ideological Symbol," *American Quarterly* 26 (1974), 160–75.

[73] Nichols, "Origins," 331–32.

sources mentioned earlier. Then too, it does not appear that Harriet read *Archy Moore* before she wrote *Uncle Tom's Cabin* or after; there is no mention of either Archy or Hildreth in any of the biographies or in any of the extant letters. In short, as hard as he has tried, Nichols does not present a convincing case.

It is interesting to note that in a letter cited earlier, written probably in 1852, Harriet said nothing about Henson, Clarke, Hildreth, or any other published source as her inspiration for the various characters. She said this about Uncle Tom:

> I know a man now a slave in Kentucky—a worthy excellent soul a devoted Christian who is the character from which I designed Uncle Tom—His wife lived with me for sometime as cook & I used to write her letters to him—It is true that he had the over-sight of his masters business & the care of his horses & it is true that when he came over to see his wife who is a free woman living in Ohio & she tried to persuade him to run away that he told her 'Master *trusts* me & I cannot' yet his master has promised this man his liberty at Christmas for three years in succession & never kept his promise & I left him still a slave.[74]

It would appear that here and elsewhere it was her experience that Harriet drew upon first; when she needed more background or wished to add a scene, she went to a printed source. She wrote many years later:

> The first conception of the character of Uncle Tom came to me while I was living in Cincinnati. I had a free woman cook whose husband was a slave in Kentucky and had the management of his masters place—I used to write his letters for her to him. She said that he was such a christian she could not get him to run away from his trust tho his master constantly broke his work to him having repeatedly promised to Emancipate him at certain times—but never doing it. Whether he ever got free I never heard—This was the first suggestion of the character—other incidents were added by reading the life of Father Henson in Canada.[75]

[74] To Rev. Mr. Webster, Sept. [?1852], St. John's Seminary, Camarillo, Calif.
[75] Cincinnati Historical Society, dated May 19, 1875.

But, contradictory to the end, in a letter written less than seven months before her death she wrote. "The characters of Uncle Tom and George Harris had no living proto-types but were created by me."[76]

In chapter 5, which appeared in the *Era* on June 26, 1851, Harriet attacked churchmen who defended slavery. The source for her attitude is not hard to find. She had seen slavery firsthand and heard much about it. Her brothers Edward and Charles had both preached against it. If there was self-righteousness in her attacks, there was also a good bit of family pride. Charles had traveled in Louisiana, had given Harriet details about slavery, and was to be asked for more. More recently, he had preached a sermon in New Jersey in which he had argued against obedience to the Fugitive Slave law on the grounds that Christians had a stronger allegiance to a Higher Law.[77] Edward, of course, had been an antislavery combatant in the field even before the riot at Alton and the death of Lovejoy in 1837. Here were two ideal examples for the religious community to emulate: churchmen who knew whereof they spoke and who spoke loudly.

A letter written from Brunswick on July 9 to Frederick Douglass provides evidence that Harriet was planning ahead. She knew that Tom was going to be in the South and that she should probably know more about cotton plantations than she did. She asked Douglass for help.

> You may perhaps have noticed in your editorial readings a series of articles that I am furnishing for the Era under the title of 'Uncle Tom's Cabin, or Life among the lowly,' In the course of my story, the scene will fall upon a cotton plantation. I am very desirous hence to gain information from one who has been an actual labourer on one, and it occurred to me that in the circle of your acquaintance there might be one who would be able to communicate to me some such information as I desire. . . . I will subjoin to this letter a list of questions, which in that case

[76] Berg Collection, NYPL, dated Dec. 8, 1895.
[77] Charles Beecher, *Duty of Disobedience*.

you will do me a favor by enclosing to the individual, with a request that he will at earliest convenience answer them.[78]

Whether Douglass or one of his "acquaintance" ever answered is not known. That Harriet had to delay in getting Tom south until an answer came is doubtful, for a cotton plantation was not presented in any detail until Tom was taken to Legree's in chapter 32, which appeared in the *Era* on February 5, 1852, some seven months after the assumed date of the letter. What seems fairly certain is that, at this point, although Harriet was anticipating a future need, she had no realistic idea of just when the need would occur. True, she did not work without a plan; but as the story unfolded, it became more and more clear why she had declared that it was imposed upon her and not of her making. She was evidently also aware, however, that her pump of experience might need to be primed, if not fed, by other sources. Certainly she needed knowledge of Deep South slavery, and she turned to two types of books to find it: slave narratives and abolition tracts.

Marion Wilson Starling lists 112 authors of slave narratives and remarks that many of the stories went through numerous reissues and editions. There were also literally hundreds of slave biographies left in manuscript or published only in periodicals, antislavery gift books, anthologies of underground railroad experiences, and the like. Charles Nichols sets the number of autobiographies and biographies published after 1831 in the thousands. In some cases, Harriet either knew of the author or had read his book. In the July letter to Frederick Douglass asking for help, she mentioned Henry Bibb as a possible source of information. According to Vernon Loggins, she probably never met Bibb but did know his book published in 1849. Some parallels between Bibb's life, as recorded in his autobiography, and *Uncle Tom's Cabin* are interesting. Bibb was born in Shelby

---

[78] Charles Stowe, 149–50, dates it July 9, 1851. The manuscript is in the Stowe-Day Foundation Library and is not dated. Stowe's text varies from the manuscript.

County, Kentucky, escaped to Cincinnati, returned for his wife, was caught, and was sold down river to New Orleans. Sold again, he was taken to a plantation some fifty miles up the Red River, the location of Simon Legree's fictitious plantation, where the slaves were poor, ragged, stupid, and half-starved. The owner employed "one of the most cruel overseers to be found in that section of the country."[79] Henry made friends with a mulatto girl, whom he refused to whip when the owner gave him the order. The parallels with Harriet's book are obvious, but parallels are easy to find in slave narratives.

William Wells Brown published his *Narrative* also in 1849. When he was a slave in St. Louis, his overseer, he wrote, "was a regular Yankee from New England. The Yankees are noted for making the most cruel overseers."[80] Brown was hired out to Elijah Lovejoy, the Alton editor whose martyrdom was commemorated in Edward Beecher's book. Eventually sold down river to New Orleans, he met a beautiful mulatto girl and watched helplessly as a white man attempted to seduce her on the riverboat. Similar incidents are found in narrative after narrative. The selling down river, the religious slave forbidden by a cruel master to read his Bible, the lecherous overseer's attempted or successful seduction of the beautiful mulatto girl, the noble slave refusing to flog the girl, the cruel Yankee overseer can be found in various combination in almost every slave narrative.

But for her examples of the cruelty and the viciousness of slavery, Harriet turned to a book compiled in 1839 by one of her father's former students, the volume which, according to Gilbert Hobbes Barnes, became the "handbook of the anti-slavery impulse for more than a decade," the publication which Henrietta Buckmaster says "shocked the country as it would not be

[79] Marion Wilson Starling, "The Slave Narrative," Ph.D. diss., New York Univ., 1946, 492–512; Charles Nichols, *Many Thousands Gone*, xii; Loggins, 213, 215; Henry Bibb, *Life and Adventures*, 110.
[80] William W. Brown, *An American Slave*, 20.

shocked again until *Uncle Tom's Cabin* broke upon them [*sic*]."[81] This was Theodore Weld's anonymous *American Slavery as It Is: Testimony of a Thousand Witnesses.* In 224 pages of small type set in double columns, Weld presented statements by former and present slaveholders, advertisements from newspapers, and extracts from legal documents to illustrate the evils of slavery. Sections of the book were devoted to "Personal narrative," "Privations of the slaves," "Punishments," and "Tortures of slaves (the last subdivided into "iron-collars, chains, fetters," "slaves burned alive," "slaves roasted and flogged," "brandings, maimings, and gun-shot wounds," "a slave chopped piece-meal and burnt," "slaves murdered," and other tortures). Finally, the seven principal objections to the criticism of slavery by abolitionists were examined and proved false. Although anti-slavery papers often printed advertisements for runaways as proof of the bestiality of the system, Weld was the first to compile long lists of such material, and the effect on the reader was and still is devastating.

Harriet later told Weld's wife, Angelina Grimké Weld, that she slept with *American Slavery* under her pillow as she wrote *Uncle Tom's Cabin.* If this statement seems to be an exaggeration, and perhaps it is, there can be no doubt that she knew the book well, for she cited it twenty-one times in the *Key.* As Benjamin Thomas points out, "Only a small part of the material in the *Key* influenced her in writing *Uncle Tom's Cabin,*" but Weld's book is a major exception: "She drew upon it as she wrote."[82] Any one of the whip-scarred, bent-backed women might have been a model for Old Prue, who sold bread to the St. Clare kitchen. Any or all of the many descriptions of vicious whippings could have given her the necessary details for Tom's death. George Harris's account of a beating at the hands of his master's son will be found, says Thomas (as well as Harriet), on page 51 of Weld's book. Yet Thomas concludes by saying that

---

[81] Barnes, 139; Henrietta Buckmaster, *Let My People Go*, 91–92.
[82] Benjamin Thomas, 223.

neither Weld nor his wife suspected the influence of the book on Harriet until years afterward.[83]

In an early July installment, Harriet enjoyed writing of slave trader Haley's discomfiture at the hands of the Shelby slaves Sam and Andy and of Sam's sermon on "principle" and "conscience." Mary Dutton later remembered that the slaves had performed funny antics in their efforts to entertain the two Ohio teachers visiting in Kentucky in 1833. Forrest Wilson suggests that Sam was drawn from the actions of a Negro employed by Lyman Beecher at Walnut Hills. When he returned to his job after an absence of some two years, the man told Dr. Beecher that he "had been working for the Government up at Columbus. [The family] found out afterwards that Sam had been in the State prison."[84] Perhaps traveling minstrel shows had contributed to Harriet's knowledge of Negro pranks, but if the source of the character and actions of Andy is somewhat indefinite, Harriet would not have had to dig very deep to be able to parody a sermon.

[83]*Ibid.*, 222–224; *Key*, 16.
[84]Forrest Wilson, 270.

Chapter 5.

BRUNSWICK: 1851-1852

The summer of 1851 found Harriet in circumstances much different from those of 1850. She was settled in her new home and not pregnant. Her only baby this year would be her book, and it was developing nicely. The six chapters she had finished exceeded the three or four numbers she had estimated in her original proposal to Bailey, but she certainly had no idea that there would eventually be forty-five chapters and that fall and winter would pass and spring come again before she would finally be delivered of her paper child. July in Brunswick is hot, and household chores, the baby, and the demands of her growing family added to the tension created by the Damoclean deadline of the weekly installment.

On July 10, in chapter 7, Eliza crossed the ice and the book divided. Henceforth there would be two plots, two sets of characters, two series of actions and adventures to develop and maintain, for Harriet had sent Eliza and little Harry north and would soon have George follow them. Tom, on the other hand, was doomed to travel south. At first Harriet attempted to balance the two plots. Chapters 9, 11, and 13 are devoted to Eliza and George, and Tom is presented in chapters 10, 12, and 14. But Tom is also the principal in chapters 15 and 16. In fact, George and Eliza appear again only in chapters 17 and 37. From chapter 18 through his death in chapter 40, Tom has center stage. Harriet interrupted the flow in chapter 36 only because she became aware that George and Eliza had been stranded just short of Canada's shores for nineteen chapters. But these problems were many months away from the July heat.

As the reader has come to expect, conflicting reports, even from Harriet herself, make the sources of Eliza's crossing the ice difficult to trace. The testimony can be grouped into two schools: one maintains that Harriet drew her account from personal experience either with "Eliza" herself or with the person or persons who knew or helped such a slave; the opposing view asserts that she drew on published accounts printed some years after the event. Unfortunately, Harriet's statements on various occasions put her into both schools.

In support of the personal-experience school, Harriet remarked in a postscript to an 1852 letter that "the crossing of the slave mother on the ice is a well known fact—a missionary told me that the woman is now living at Toronto, Canada." In the *Key,* she said, "Last spring, while the author was in New York, a Presbyterian clergyman, of Ohio, came to her and said, 'I understand they dispute that fact about the woman's crossing the river. Now, I know all about that, for I got the story from the very man that helped her up the bank. I know it is true, for she is now living in Canada'" (*Key,* p. 22). Yet in the "1879 Introduction" Harriet stated that the source was in print: "She was one day turning over a little bound volume of an anti-slavery magazine, edited by Mrs. Dr. Bailey, of Washington, and there she read the account of the escape of a woman with her child on the ice of the Ohio River from Kentucky. The incident was given by an eye-witness, one who had helped the woman to the Ohio shore."[1]

There is no doubt, however, that a slave girl once escaped across the Ohio River on the ice. The Reverend W. M. Mitchell

[1] To J. C. Webster, Sept. [1852], St. John's Seminary, Camarillo, Calif.; Harriet Beecher Stowe, "1879 Introduction," xiii.

in his 1860 book, *The Underground Railroad,* stated categorically
that Mrs. Stowe had not exaggerated. "The person who she
. . . denominates Eliza is a living character. I lived on the Ohio
River over which she crossed, and have been to the spot more
than once, not however till after she became the subject of the
story which Mrs. Stowe tells so well." He continued: "Eliza,
whose real name was Mary, ran away from Kentucky; her child
was truly sold, but not delivered to the purchaser . . . she
passed many sleepless nights in her humble cottage" while
debating whether or not to escape. She decided to go, came to
the Ohio, which was "frozen over, though melting very rapidly," successfully crossed, and "was sheltered by J. R————, a
well-known abolitionist, and the following night came to my
house. . . . The circumstances of this young woman crossing
the river at that time was [*sic*] published in the leading Anti-
Slavery papers of the North, and no doubt but many Anti-
Slavery people here [England], who read American Anti-Slavery
newspapers, have read it."[2] Later writers have found a number
of published accounts, any of which could have been a printed
source for Eliza.[3]

Charles and Lyman Stowe thought that Harriet erred in
ascribing her source to the magazine article. In the twenty-seven
years between the composition of the novel and the writing of
the later Introduction, they suggested, she perhaps made a

[2] Rev. W. M. Mitchell, *Underground Railroad,* 100–3.

[3] Russell B. Nye, "Eliza Crossing the Ice: A Reappraisal of Sources," *Bulletin of the
Historical and Philosophical Society of Ohio* (April 1950), 106–12. Nye cites *A Friend of
Youth* 2 (Feb. 1851), 28; "Thrilling Incident near Cincinnati," *The Antislavery Bugle*,
Nov. 26, 1847. The latter was reprinted in *Liberty Almanac for 1848*, 42, with the
Bugle title. John C. Crandall has found an even earlier account of crossing the Ohio on
the ice in "Moral Bravery," *The Youth's Cabinet* 1, n.s. 5 (May 1846), 135, which in
turn was reprinted from the *True American*, a periodical which the author has not been
able to identify. Crandall, "Patriotism and Humanitarian Reform in Children's
Literature 1825–1860," *AQ* 21 (1969), 3–22. Nye errs when he ascribes the "1879
Introduction" to *Uncle Tom's Cabin* to "the editor" and when he says that Harriet was
living in "New Brunswick," Maine (p. 105).

This British view of "Eliza Crossing the Ice" appeared in that country's illustrated edition of *Uncle Tom's Cabin. Courtesy of Stowe-Day Memorial Library and Historical Foundation.*

mistake.[4] She heard the story from John Rankin, clergyman of Ripley, Ohio, the man who met "Eliza" at the Ohio shore. An anonymous biography of him, published in Cincinnati about 1868, describes the event in some detail, but does not mention Mrs. Stowe.[5] S. G. W. Rankin, a son of John Rankin, told the Eliza tale to a group in Hartford, Connecticut, on November 22, 1895. He said that the incidents of the crossing came within his father's personal knowledge and "that he gave them to Mrs. Stowe and that she used a younger woman, who escaped at nearly the same time, to complete the picture and make it more dramatic."[6] In addition, in the library of the Ohio Historical Society at Columbus are three manuscript papers on the subject of the underground railway station at Ripley, written by the sons of John Rankin. All three papers discuss "Eliza," but only one mentions the Stowes. It states that the crossing took place in 1838, and that the author's father had written a pamphlet against slavery (*Letters on Slavery*), in 1826.

> My brother Rev. A. L. Rankin was at Lane Theological Seminary on Walnut Hills Ohio in his first year, 1838. He gave the pamphlet to Mr. Stow my father and the Beacher wear quite intimate as will as the younger professor Calvin Stowe and his wife and they weare particularly kind and friendly with our This Brother of the class of 1840 . . . My older brother gave this pamphlet to Mrs. Stow Thanks kinder she said that she had heard of it and as she was thinking of writing something on that subject she was happy to have it.[7]

[4] Charles and Lyman Stowe, 146.

[5] *The Soldier, The Battle, and The Victory.*

[6] "The Story of Eliza," Hartford *Daily Courant*, Nov. 23, 1895; rpt. in the Boston *Evening Transcript*, Nov. 30, 1895.

[7] Rankin Papers, Ohio Historical Society. As the manuscripts are in pencil and irregularly paged, it is difficult to tell which son is writing which account. To compound the problem, someone has attempted to make a composite narrative by drawing on all three sources, and in doing so has supplied information not included in the original; e.g., the revisionist supplied a wrong middle name for one of Lyman Beecher's sons where only the first name is used in the original. The original

Harriet's memory of the event that had been described to her by John Rankin was probably sparked by her reading the later account. It is doubtful that she encountered the incident for the first time in the abolitionist press.

In chapter 8, in the July 17 *Era,* the reader was introduced to Loker and Marks, slave catchers. Marks told with great relish how he used the provisions of the Fugitive Slave law to his own ends. He was accomplished at passing himself off as the master of escaped slaves. "I come in all dressed up . . . One day, I'm Mr. Twickem from New Orleans; 'nother day, I'm just up from my plantation on Pearl river . . . if thar's a feller in the country that can swear to any thing and everything, and put in all the circumstances and flourishes with a longer face; . . . I'd like to see him." After all, Harriet reminded her readers, "The catching business . . . is rising to the dignity of a lawful and patriotic profession."

There was apparently more difficulty and less joy in writing the next chapter than previous ones; it was longer than any preceding chapter and arrived at the press a bit late. Bailey told the readers that "the installment of Mrs. Stowe's story, 'Uncle Tom's Cabin,' for this week, reached us at so late an hour that we were compelled to divide it. It increases in interest as it progresses. We trust that no one will omit to read it" (*Era,* July 24, 1851). It had been easy to get Eliza across the ice and move her into the home of Senator and Mrs. Burr. The discussion of slavery in the abstract by the senator and his wife was skillfully contrasted with actuality when Eliza sought refuge with them. The senator rose to the occasion, safety was promised, and a bed was made up. Then Harriet opened an old wound.

Samuel Charles Stowe died of cholera in Cincinnati July 24, 1849; Charles Edward Stowe was born July 8, 1850. Harriet's letters in the two years following the death of the child were full

---

manuscripts have been cited because, in spite of the spelling, grammar, and style, they appear to be more authentic.

of references to him. In a letter of January 1, 1850, she said, "My fair my sweet my loving and glorious boy has lived and died."[8] On October 29, 1850, she wrote her stepmother that the new baby, Charles, "grows so exactly like him I have lost that I feel almost sad when I look at him."[9] On December 17, 1850, she wrote to Sarah, brother George's wife, that little Charley (Charles Edward) was "as like the one I lost as a twin brother—so like some days that I almost feel sad."[10] It is clear that Harriet was deeply affected by the loss of her baby son.

Eliza asked Mrs. Burr if she had ever lost a child, and Mrs. Burr dissolved in tears. As it turned out, her youngest was only one month in the grave. When she decided that Eliza and Harry must have dry clothes to continue their journey, Mrs. Burr went to the "little bed-room," put a key into "the lock of a drawer, and made a sudden pause." Harriet then interrupted to ask:

> oh! mother that reads this, has there never been in your house a drawer, or a closet, the opening of which has been to you like the opening again of a little grave? Ah! happy mother that you are, if it has not been so!
>
> Mrs. Burr slowly opened the drawer; there were little coats of many a form and pattern, piles of aprons, and rows of small stockings; and even a pair of little shoes, worn and rubbed at the toes, were peeping from the folds of a paper. There was a toy horse and wagon, a top, a ball—memorials gathered with many a tear, and many a heartbreak! She sat down by the drawer, and leaning her head on her hands over it, wept till the tears fell through her fingers into the drawer.

Of all the correspondence in which Harriet compared the living with the dead baby, an unpublished letter from her to Mrs. Allen in Walnut Hills written from Brunswick, December 2, 1850, is the most poignant and most pertinent here.

> My little seignior—the 'reigning baby'—is as much like the

---

[8] Stowe-Day Foundation.

[9] Beecher-Stowe Papers, Radcliffe, folder 96.

[10] *Ibid.*, folder 94.

departed as one mould of clay can be to another—only of his age
he is larger & he is a little fairer—I often think what you said to
me—that another child would not fill the place of the old one
that it would be a separate another interest & another love—so I
find it—for tho he is so like I do not feel him the same nor do I
feel for him that same love which I felt for Charley—It is a
different kind—I shall never love another as I did him—he was
my *'summer child'*—I cannot open his little drawer of clothes
now without feeling it thro my very heart—Is there a peculiar
love given us for those that God wills to take from us—Is there
not some thing brighter & better around them than around
those who live—Why else in so many households is there a
tradition of one brighter more beautiful more promising than all
the rest, laid early low—[11]

Lyman Beecher and Roxanna Foote Beecher had had two
Harriets; the Harriet that lived had had two Charleys. Death
came often to small children in both real and fictional families,
but it never came easily or departed without leaving a scar, and
in some cases the scar never completely healed. Long after
Harriet had become famous, she still thought of her first Charley. (She lost another son by drowning in 1857, one whom she
had named for the brother she loved most. Like Mrs. Burr's dead
child, he was named Henry.)

Eliza's flight from Senator Burr's house had as its probable
source an event close to home. Harriet told in the *Key* the story of
the servant girl from Kentucky whom the Stowes hired in 1839
thinking her free. When it appeared that she was a runaway,
"Professor Stowe performed for the fugitive that office which the
senator is represented as performing for Eliza. They drove about
ten miles on a solitary road, crossed the creek at a very dangerous
fording, and presented themselves, at midnight, at the house of
John Van Zandt a noble minded Kentuckian, who had performed the good deed which the author, in her story, ascribes to
Van Tromp" (*Key,* p. 23). In the "1879 Introduction" she again

---

[11] Barrett Collection, Univ. of Virginia.

identified Van Zandt as a man who "received and protected fugitive slaves in the manner narrated in Chapter IX of 'Uncle Tom's Cabin.'"[12] Ten years previously, Harriet had put together an anthology of eighteen biographical sketches entitled *Men of Our Times.* In the essay on Salmon P. Chase, she spoke of the "great Van Zandt case" of 1846, in which Chase was defense attorney. Van Zandt was identified as the man who "figured in Uncle Tom's Cabin under the name of Van Tromp; . . . it was well known that no hungry, wandering fugitive was ever turned away from Van Zandt's door. The writer has still memory of the wild night ride of husband and brother through the woods, and over swelled creeks dangerous enough to cross, which carried a poor slave girl to this safe retreat." Chase lost the case brought by slaveholders against Van Zandt for helping escaped slaves, and "Van Zandt was ruined, 'scot and lot'; by a fine so heavy that all he had in the world would not pay it, and he died brokenhearted."[13]

Charles and Lyman Stowe accepted the model but added that the servant girl was "a young woman whose little boy was the original of the 'little Harry'" of the story, and that the previously nameless brother who helped professor Stowe was Henry Ward. Later, in Lyman Beecher Stowe's biography of the family the helpful brother was identified as Charles Beecher, "then a student at the Seminary," on the basis of "a journal of Charles Beecher, which has recently come to light" but has since been lost. Catherine Gilbertson accepted Charles as the aide and gave the girl's name as "Mina." Forrest Wilson, on the other hand, reverted to Henry Ward as the second party, and said it was he rather than Calvin who "went into action" and initiated the rescue. Jane Elsmere, on the other hand, Henry Ward's most recent biographer, finds him an "unlikely" candidate as he never claimed the identity and he was "seldom reticent in later life

[12] Harriet Beecher Stowe, "1879 Introduction," xii.
[13] "Salmon P. Chase," *Men of Our Time,* ed. Harriet Beecher Stowe, 259, 262.

about his exploits."[14] Whatever the details, whatever the names of the principal models, it would appear that Harriet drew from life, primarily, rather than from her reading, for the characters of Eliza and her helpers, although written accounts might have served to spark her extremely retentive memory.

In the August 7 issue, with Tom in chains, Haley drove to the blacksmith shop to have handcuffs fitted for his captive. Young George Shelby tied his silver dollar onto a string around the slave's neck and told him to remember that some day George would buy him back. Harriet apparently foresaw the scene in chapter 35 in which the silver dollar and the lock of Eva's hair revealed Legree's superstitiousness, and the scene in chapter 41 in which George arrived too late to save Tom. As she wrote, Harriet had some idea of the details of scenes to come. The next week, chapter 11 brought the story back to the Canada-bound fugitives. George Harris performed his little masquerade in the Kentucky tavern and prevailed upon his former employer, whom he happened to meet there, to keep his secret. Among other things, they discussed the nature of freedom, and George mentioned Fourth of July speeches. Many a slave narrative records the confusion of a slave when told it was wrong for him to act upon ideas he might have gotten from Fourth of July speeches that lauded America's founders who broke away from tyrannical British masters and extolled the blessings of freedom. When George used this point in his argument, his former owner was unable to refute him.

On the twenty-first of August, Harriet missed the deadline. Bailey printed a brief note of explanation: "Chapter XII of 'Uncle Tom's Cabin' reached us at too late an hour for insertion this week. Mrs. Stowe having requested that it should not be divided, our readers may look for the entire chapter in the next *Era*." The following week, the installment was back in its usual left-hand column position, and it was, as Bailey had indicated,

---

[14] Charles and Lyman Stowe, 126; Lyman Stowe, 175; Gilbertson, 108; Forrest Wilson, 194; Elsmere, 175n.

rather long, running four and a half columns. A little different from previous parts, it was perhaps the angriest chapter Harriet had written to date. She struck out at slavery in general, of course, but also attacked a number of particular issues and problems.

Haley's business problems were immediately contrasted with Tom's thoughts about a Biblical passage, "some words of an unfashionable old book," a volume "got up principally by 'ignorant and unlearned men.'" Harriet then went on to say that these words "stir up the soul from its depths, and rouse, as with trumpet call, courage, energy, and enthusiasm, when before, was only the blackness of despair." And here there appeared in the *Era* a paragraph which was deleted in the novel: "I mention this, of course, philosophic friend, as a psychological phenomenon. Very likely it would do not such a thing for you, because you are an enlightened man, and have out-grown the old myths of past centuries. But then you have Emerson's Essays and Carlyle's Miscellanies, and other productions of the latter day, suited to your advanced development." Harriet, still a Beecher, fought liberalisms of all kinds. Why she deleted the paragraph six months later is difficult to say. Perhaps Calvin objected, perhaps she had second thoughts about such strong language or felt that the paragraph diverted the reader from her main topic. Whatever the reason, the passage did not appear in the novel.

Next she employed the technique which Theodore Weld had used to such advantage in his book on slavery and she herself was to use extensively in the *Key;* she reprinted a newspaper advertisement for a slave sale. Although it was a borrowed device, its effect was now greatly increased by the fact that the reader could identify with one who was to be sold. Weld had no Tom.

The sale itself fitted nicely into the developing structure. The reader was reminded that this was what would have happened to Eliza and Harry had they not escaped from Haley. Unlike the loss of Mrs. Burr's child, the separation by sale had no comfort in it in the form of belief that the child had gone to a better world. Here it was truly a fate worse than death. It also foreshadowed scenes to come: the suicide on the steamboat of the mother who drowned herself and her child rather than have him sold from her, the division of families in the St. Clare sale, and Cassy's loss of her children through sale. All these scenes helped the reader to understand the power one master had over Cassy through his promise not to sell another son and prepared the reader for Cassy's decision to kill a child with an overdose of laudanum rather than have him grow up to a life of slavery or risk being sold from her. Then, too, the emphasis on separation throughout the novel helped to pave the way for the pleasant if obviously contrived reunion of Cassy and Eliza, and George and Madame de Thoux in the final chapters. That separation is, as Charles Foster has maintained,[15] a major theme in the novel cannot be denied. And that Harriet knew the most terrible aspect of slavery firsthand is demonstrable from her correspondence. In an 1852 letter, she wrote:

Again—In the scene on the boat when a woman is inveighed on board by a trader on false pretenses.

I was on board that boat on the Ohio river some ten years ago when a trader brought a woman on board under exactly the pretext I thus described—the scene that followed—her incredulity—her assertion that her master couldn't have cheated her so & all occurred just as I have related—She was a very decently dressed woman & must have been brought up in some careful respectable family—The only 'difference is' that she had not an infant with her but a boy of eight years—but Mr. Thome I think—a gentleman whom I was acquainted with relates that he has seen an infant taken from the mothers breast & sold for a dollar at the steam boat landing when the mother was to be taken down river—I have seen too a letter from a negro trader to a respectable colored woman—sister of my cook, stating to her that on such a day he would set up at public sale her child three years old, unless before that time she remitted him two hundred dollars—the child was redeemed by subscription in our

[15] Foster, 38.

neighborhood—That heart rending picture of the separation of the old negro woman from her boy of thirteen is taken almost verbatim from the journal of a young southerner—a slaveholder Joseph Cobb & is given as a fact that he witnessed. I am sorry that fiction has nothing to do with that—"[16]

The previous May 15, the *Independent* had published a letter from its European correspondent which quoted an extensive list of proslavery utterances by prominent American clergymen that had appeared in the Bristol, England, *Mercury.* One of the men on the list was the Reverend Joel Parker, D.D., the man whom Edward Beecher blamed "more than any other single man for the death of Lovejoy." Parker had been the leader of the Colonization Society in Alton and president of Union Theological Seminary, and was at the time of the letter pastor of the Clinton Street Presbyterian Church in Philadelphia.[17] The *Independent* quoted Parker as saying, "There are no evils in slavery but such as are inseparable from any other relation in civil and social life." Whatever these ambiguous generalities meant, they certainly were not antislavery.

Here, in chapter 12, as Harriet concluded her description of the slave sale, her anger rose to a peak, and she remembered Parker's words. She began her paragraph with Tom's reaction to the sale, but quickly shifted to biting irony as she noted that he responded as he did only because he was a "poor ignorant black soul" and "had not learned to generalize, to take enlarged views." She sharpened the point by noting that, had Tom been instructed by "a certain minister of Christianity, he might have thought better of it." Pressing onward, she quoted "an American divine" as saying that slavery had " 'no evils but such as are inseparable from any other relations in social and domestic life,' " paused, underlined the passage, and then as a final stroke, drove her shaft home with an asterisk and a footnote attributing the

[16] To J. C. Webster, Sept. [1852], St. John's Seminary, Camarillo, Calif.
[17] Meredith, "Introduction," 186; Forrest Wilson, 261.

quoted statement to "Dr. Joel Parker, of Philadelphia." That footnote would rise to haunt her.

Chapters 13 and 14 flowed smoothly again. Her anger vented, Harriet could relax and return to the type of writing she had been doing for years—descriptive scenes of domestic bliss. The kindly Halliday family was easy to portray with its quaint speech, its men in "Ohio sleeves" (changed to the less regional "shirt-sleeves" in the novel), and its big breakfasts. After Haley and slave sales and suicides, these pleasant, quiet Quakers were a welcome interlude for both reader and author.

Levi Coffin, often called the president of the underground railroad, was probably the Hallidays' real-life counterpart. In his *Reminiscences,* Coffin said that she who "crossed the Ohio River, near Ripley, on the drifting ice with her child in her arms, was sheltered under our roof and fed at our table for several days." On the basis of this fact, he went on, "it was generally believed among those acquainted with the circumstances that I and my wife were the veritable Simeon and Rachel Halliday, the Quaker couple alluded to in 'Uncle Tom's Cabin.'" Although Harriet said in the *Key* (p. 54) that she had in mind Thomas Garret of Wilmington, Delaware, who hired a hack to help slaves escape, Coffin's self-identification has never been disputed. Coffin went on to say that Eliza and her child were sent "by the Greenville branch of the Underground Railroad, to Sandusky, Ohio, . . . crossed the lake to Canada, locating finally at Chatham, Canada West." It should not be surprising that the fictional Eliza and George went by way of Sandusky, although, as Coffin's book appeared in 1876, there remains the question of who borrowed from whom. [18]

[18] Levi Coffin, *Reminiscences*, 148–51. In the Manuscripts Section of the NYPL there is a letter from Mrs. Lunette A. D. Chamberlin of Oklahoma City dated Oct. 12, 1930, in which she offers for sale a watch which had belonged to Eliza Harris. Eliza and George had lived in Oberlin, Ohio, and had been members of the Second Congregational Church. When Eliza, whose real name was Clark, died in 1877, her

Even when the story shifted back to Tom in chapter 14, the tone and content remained pleasant, for it was here, in the issue for September 11, 1851, that the reader first met the unbelievably good, wise-beyond-her-years, scripture-and-platitude-spouting daughter of Augustine St. Clare: "Little Eva." Literary models for Eva are plentiful. Moral little girls are legion in the religious and didactic literature of the age, but one is moved to wonder whether Eva is not, at least in part, an idealized portrait of Harriet's "summer child," her first "Charley." If so, the creation is obviously tinged by the character of the mother who, as a religious woman by both conviction and family ties, would have wished her son to grow up in the faith. Perhaps, too, there is a bit of self-idealization here: Harriet had almost no unpleasant memories of her childhood, or if they were there, she never spoke of them. Could she be drawing here a picture of herself as she then thought she had been or would like to have been? If, on the other hand, the reader can assume that Harriet knew the picture of Eva was overdrawn and found it almost as unbelievable as many do today, can he also assume that she intended it to represent a slightly satiric portrait of her older sister Catharine, her father's first and favorite daughter, the girl who always did everything right and was, at this time, much more famous and popular than her quieter, less successful sister? Eva never made a mistake, never said the wrong thing, was always ready with the perfect answer.

On September 18 (chapter 15), the story was again on the front page, running over for two and a half columns onto the second page. It was a long chapter, perhaps longer than Harriet had planned. Sister Catharine was doing all she could to help. She wrote her sister Mary in September of 1851: "At eight o'clock we are through with breakfast and prayers and then we send off Mr. Stowe and Harriet both to his room in the college. There is no other way to keep her out of family cares and quietly

---

husband sold the watch to Alan Drew, Mrs. Chamberlin's father. Fountain City, once Newport, Ind., is the site of Levi Coffin's house.

at work and since this plan is adopted, she goes ahead finely."[19] Harriet was thus provided with free time to work and to visit both in town and out. Her biographers have maintained that she made occasional trips to Boston to visit the antislavery rooms for material and her brother Edward's house for companionship. But she had been busy at other tasks in late August and early September, for in this September 18 issue Bailey inserted an announcement: "We learn through a private source that Mrs. H. B. Stowe has just completed an engagement with Messrs. Jewett & Co., of Boston, for the publication of her story, now appearing in our columns. The stereotyping commences this week; and it will be corrected, complete, from the press, immediately after its close in the Era." In actual fact, publication was almost exactly six months off, but Harriet did have a publisher, even if neither she nor Bailey nor "Messrs. Jewett & Co." had any idea as to the length of the book they were dealing with.

In this fifteenth chapter, Harriet paused to introduce her new characters in some detail. She began with the early life of Augustine St. Clare, employing the well-worn theme of the suitor who is rejected by his sweetheart's parents without her knowledge to explain why Augustine married Eva's mother. As trite as it may appear now, it was undoubtedly accepted with tongue-clucking and head-shaking by Harriet's readers who had become accustomed to such misfortunes in the works of Susan Warner, Mrs. E. D. E. N. Southworth, Sarah Josepha Hale, and the early novels and tales of Timothy Shay Arthur. Harriet carried this part off rather well, but when she shifted to Vermont and Ophelia Sinclair, she shone.

Certainly the "large farm-house, with its cleanswept grassy yard, shaded by the dense and massive foliage of the sugar maple" was the Beecher house in Litchfield. The entire paragraph is reminiscent of the opening section of Harriet's "Prize Tale," written eighteen years earlier. There she described her

[19] Sklar, 232.

fictional "Newbury, in Connecticut" as a place where "nobody ever seemed to be sick or to die. . . . The natives grew old, till they could not grow any older, and then they stood still and lasted from generation to generation. There was, too, an unchangeability about all the externals of Newbury."[20] In the *Era* in 1851 she said there was an "air of order and stillness, of perpetuity and unchanging repose, that seemed to breathe over the whole place. Nothing lost, or out of order; not a picket loose in the fence, not a particle of litter in the turfy yard, with its clumps of lilac-bushes growing up under the windows."

The books in "the respectable old book-case, with its glass doors . . . in the family 'keeping room'" were certainly those which Harriet had known for many years; she quoted from a number of them repeatedly: "Rollin's History, Milton's Paradise Lost, Bunyan's Pilgrim's Progress, . . . Scott's Family Bible, . . . Morse's Atlas, . . . Flint's Travels in the South and West."[21] The names of the milliner and her assistant—Miss

[20] Harriet Beecher Stowe, "A New England Sketch," *Western Monthly Magazine* 2 (1834), 170.

[21] Cf. the following passage from an early sketch by Harriet entitled "Cousin William": "She had read, too, everything she could find: Rollin's History, and Scott's Family Bible, that stood in the glass bookcase in the best room" (*Mayflower* [1843], 149–50). The sketch, according to Forrest Wilson, p. 191, appeared in the Cincinnati *Chronicle* before the end of the winter of 1836–1837. Wilson's notes refer to only one issue of the *Chronicle*, Feb. 11, 1837. The issues covering this period at the Wisconsin Historical Society have been read for the author; no story has been discovered. The sketch was, however, printed (or reprinted) in *The Gift . . . for 1839*, ed. Miss Eliza Leslie, 207–19, and later in the 1843 *Mayflower*, 146–64. "Morse's Atlas" is *An Atlas of the United States on an Improved Plan* by Sidney Edward Morse, printed first in New Haven in 1823. "Rollin's History" is Charles Rollin's *The Ancient History of the Egyptians, Carthaginians, Assyrians, Babylonians, Medes and Persians, Macedonians, and Grecians* published in French in Paris, 1730–1738; in English in London, 1738–1740; in America, 1805; and often reissued. "Flint's Travels in the South and West" may refer either to Timothy Flint's *Recollections of the Last Ten Years in the Valley of the Mississippi* (Boston, 1826) or to his *History and Geography of the Mississippi Valley to Which Is Appended a Condensed Physical Geography of the Atlantic United States and the Whole American Continent* (Cincinnati, 1827). Kenneth Lynn, in the notes to his edition of *Uncle Tom's Cabin*, 162, states that "Scott's Family Bible" (1789–1792) is named for Thomas Scott, the English editor and commentator.

Peabody and Miss Moseley—probably had basis in fact; the characters certainly have. Harriet did in these few pages what she had been doing for years and doing well: drawing from life, the life of the land she never really left, her New England.

It was personal experience that provided the data for Miss Ophelia. The New England drive for tidiness and order were a part of Harriet's life. Her father was untidy; sermons, pamphlets, notes, books, and bits and pieces of most everything cluttered the floor of his study. Wife after wife and daughter after daughter attempted to do to his study what Miss Ophelia attempted in Dinah's kitchen. Here Harriet needed no books for ideas. The hypocritical stand the old maid took with regard to Topsy—improvement without involvement—had been part and parcel of every Ladies Missionary Society since the founding of such work. Here, too, Harriet knew whereof she spoke. As daughter, sister, and wife to ministers, she had met such attitudes face to face for years. It was not by accident that she gave no published source for Miss Ophelia in the *Key* (pp. 30–33).

Marie St. Clare also had her living models. Invalids were common then as now. Some bore their afflictions well. In Litchfield, Judge Tapping Reeve's first wife, a sister of Aaron Burr, was described by Catharine Beecher as "a delicate invalid, confined to her bed for many years, and various interesting stories were told of [Reeve's] tender watching and unwearied care."[22] Calvin Stowe was, by his own account, always near death's door. When he was in Cincinnati, he wrote to his mother on February 8, 1850: "My health has not been good this winter, and I do not suppose that I should live long were I to stay here."[23] He was not to die for another thirty-six years, but he worried about his health constantly. Writing to her sister-in-law from Brunswick in December 1850, Harriet described what she had been through trying to get the house organized without

[22] Lyman Beecher, *Autobiography*, 162.
[23] Charles Stowe, 128.

121

Calvin. Amid all the confusion "comes a letter from my husband saying he is sick abed, and all but dead; don't ever expect to see his family again; wants to know how I shall manage in case I am left a widow; knows we shall get in debt and never get out; wonders at my courage; . . . warns me to be prudent, as there won't be much to live on in case of his death, etc., etc., etc. I read the letter and poke it into the stove, and proceed."[24] Again, without the aid of books, Harriet had her models. But then, too, perhaps there was more of the author herself in Marie St. Clare than Harriet would ever admit. Perhaps she saw herself under such circumstances and pictured what she might become, for she, too, was something of a hypochondriac. Although she had more cause for self-concern than Calvin, having more often been seriously ill, still her fear that the sickle of death hung constantly over her occurs over and over throughout her letters. Her response to Sarah Beecher's urging that she write something about this slavery business is an example. Harriet's resolve in the letter was tempered by her awareness of the transitoriness of her life: "I will, if I live," she said. She outlived her husband by ten years.

For the other New Orleans scenes and characters, Harriet also had a fund of personal experience to draw upon. Cincinnati was a major stopping place on the trip north and east. The Beecher parlor had been repeatedly graced by visiting clergymen or old friends traveling to or from the South, often New Orleans. In the middle of August 1838, for example, while Harriet was still living at home, George W. Perkins stopped with the Beecher family for a few days. He remembered Harriet from Hartford and wrote his wife that he "had a pleasant chat for an hour." That night at the Beechers he met a pleasant young man from New Orleans, "brother to an old classmate," who told the group, Perkins reported, that slavery "does not exhibit its worst features, in the city, and among the house servants. Its appro-

[24]*Ibid.*, 135; Dec. 17, [1850], original in Beecher-Stowe papers, Radcliffe, folder 94.

priate fruits are fully developed on the plantations, where licentiousness and cruelty, having no fear of exposure, reign and triumph. There are several laws against teaching the slaves to read, and very few of them consequently are ever taught. But there is no hindrance whatever to their receiving religious instruction, orally, from any one not suspected of abolition."[25] How many more reports Harriet heard from how many more visitors can only be a matter of conjecture, but Lyman Beecher's stature in the religious life of the West would certainly have attracted many visitors. Few clergymen would have missed an opportunity to stop off and chat with the defender of the faith west of the Alleghenies.

The story seems to have flowed freely during these early fall weeks. On September 25, Harriet filled four columns on the front page and ran over to another column and a half on the second. Chapter 16 described a debate between St. Clare, Marie, and Miss Ophelia. Harriet had heard and participated in arguments since childhood; Beechers were seldom silent when it came to opinions. Marie, whom the reader had already been taught to dislike, presented the first position on the question of slavery, and Harriet undercut her with heavy irony. Marie maintained that "we mistresses are the slaves," that slaves were "the plague of [her] life," that selfishness is "the fault of the whole race," that the "servants [were] over-indulged," and that the owners must *"put them down,* and keep them down. . . make 'em know their place," for "these [were] a degraded race" "who couldn't have the feelings" she had. Just when the reader was settling back into a cushion of self-righteous indignation in response to Marie's views, Harriet pricked him with a short exchange between Miss Ophelia and St. Clare, who had been drawn from the room by the sound of Eva's laughter.

They found Eva sitting on Tom's knee. Miss Ophelia asked how her cousin could permit such intimacy: "It seems so dreadful." St. Clare then attacked the hypocrisy of the Northerner

[25] Stowe-Day Foundation.

who could condemn slavery in the abstract, but who wanted nothing to do with Negroes personally. "You loathe them as you would a snake or toad, yet you are indignant at their wrongs. You would not have them abused; but you don't want to have anything to do with them yourselves. You would send them to Africa, out of your sight and smell, and then send a missionary or two to do up all the self-denial of elevating them compendiously." The ambivalent attitude was no doubt common among the Beecher acquaintances; Harriet had touched on it earlier in the Senator Burr episode, but there the characters were less fully developed and the commitment for moral good over legal evil was less involved. Her reintroduction of the subject here and in succeeding chapters was to develop it into the major problem Miss Ophelia must face, and to symbolize what Harriet felt to be the most significant contradiction in the antislavery attitude. It will be noticed here that St. Clare, in his exposure of the contradictory positions of the Yankee, struck hard at colonization, the solution to the problem of slavery which Lyman Beecher had defended for years.

The chapter concluded with a discussion of a question that had been paramount in the minds of both pro- and antislavery forces for years: Does the Bible justify slavery? Harriet had St. Clare cogently argue that it does not. In his presentation, he used points that were widely circulated, but can be traced to at least two sources positively known to the author. James G. Birney had founded the *Philanthropist* in Cincinnati, had run for office on the Liberty party ticket, and had been generally active in the abolition movement. In 1842 he anonymously published *The American Churches, the Bulwarks of American Slavery,* in which he attacked organized religion as perpetuating the institution in direct contrast to the fundamental principles of Christianity. Harriet quoted extensively from this book in the *Key* (p. 193) after asking Birney for permission to cite his work and for verification of the material he used as sources.[26] In

---

[26] James G. Birney, *Letters*, 1158–63.

addition to Birney, both here and throughout the novel Harriet used a source much closer to home whenever she dealt with the conflict of organized religion and true faith or Christianity and law. On November 11, 1850, her brother Charles delivered a sermon in Newark, New Jersey, entitled "The Duty of Disobedience to Wicked Laws: A Sermon on the Fugitive Slave Law" and published it the following year. Citing both Old and New Testament passages, Charles proved that God's Law is superior to any and all laws made by man.

There were, no doubt, other influences at work here and elsewhere in the story when Harriet discussed government and the church in relation to man in general and slavery in particular. She knew the writings of Carlyle, Emerson, Godwin, and Brownson, and what she had not read directly, she had heard discussed in innumerable debates at dinner and after, both at home and at the houses of friends. There can be no doubt that she knew Birney's and her own brother's works. Yet it would be intemperate to try to identify the source of each and every philosophical position her characters took, for Harriet was eclectic in the extreme. Essentially, however, she was a Golden Rule Christian, a fundamentalist in the sense that she took the Bible for her text without the trimmings of sectarian hair-splitting.

As her writing progressed, Harriet drew again on her reading and experience. In chapter 17, October 2, she had the Harris party take refuge among some high rocks, a topographical formation all but unknown to the region through which they were passing. It seems likely that her rocks came not from Indiana, where thirty-foot chasms are scarce, but from either Scott's *Rob Roy*, in which the most memorable scene pictures Helen Campbell MacGregor stopping the soldiers in a narrow defile, or Cooper's *Prairie*, in which Ishmael Bush and party take refuge atop a rock formation of equal topological improbability. More contemporary heroics were alluded to in this chapter and elsewhere throughout the story when repeatedly Harriet mentioned Louis Kossuth, the Hungarian revolutionary whose name had been mentioned in the *Era* and other papers for some time. The following installment, chapter 18, on October 9, occupied four columns and began the debate between St. Clare and Miss Ophelia about slavery. During the discussion, St. Clare remarked that "all the world over . . . it's the same story—the lower class used up, body, soul and spirit, for the good of the upper," a statement reminiscent of Orestes Brownson's "Laboring Classes" article. Later in the same chapter, for another remark from St. Clare, Harriet drew upon the family story of Aunt Mary Hubbard, who had lived in Jamaica: "There have been times when I have thought, if the whole country would sink, and hide all this injustice and misery from the light, I would willingly sink with it." Shortly after, the description of St. Clare's mother was a portrayal, idealized perhaps, of Roxanna Foote, Lyman Beecher's first wife and Harriet's mother.[27] The story of Prue, the alcoholic bread lady, Harriet identified as "related by a brother and sister of the writer," (*Key,* pp. 48–49).

This chapter was so long that, despite Harriet's earlier requests, Bailey divided it, completing it the following week. The topic was still the debate between St. Clare and Miss Ophelia about slavery. Harriet had a wealth of material which she had been storing up for almost twenty years, beginning with the debates at Lane in the thirties, moving through the abolitionist articles in the *Philanthropist* and the proslavery essays in other Cincinnati papers, and topped off by the reiteration of what had proved to be the best responses in the newspapers of the day to the Fugitive Slave law.

Along with the end of chapter 18, which would conclude the first volume when the book was published, Bailey ran the beginning of chapter 19. The two fragments filled a little more than three columns. In the issue of October 23, however, someone lost count, for the conclusion to chapter 19 was num-

---

[27] Lyman Beecher, *Autobiography*, 226.

bered "18"; the error would never be corrected in the pages of
the *Era*.

Week by week the installments had been appearing steadily
since late August, and Harriet seems to have been able to keep
up with the demanding pace. But then what Bailey continually
feared happened again; Harriet missed an installment. The
following notice appeared in the issue for October 30: "MRS.
STOWE'S STORY—We regret exceedingly that the nineteenth
chapter of Mrs. Stowe's Story did not reach us till the morning of
the day on which the *Era* goes to press, and after all its matter,
except one column, was set up. It shall appear next week."

Chapter 19, when it did appear, filled four and one half
columns and introduced Topsy. There are some clues as to the
sources for the little girl who just growed. Although Harriet
gave neither name nor date, she did say in the *Key* that one of her
friends, married to a gentleman in Louisiana who owned "some
eight hundred slaves," told her anecdotes of the thievishness of
the blacks and of the attempts she had made to educate them
(*Key,* pp. 52–53). Charles and Lyman Stowe provided a little
more detail: "About this time a wealthy and cultivated family
came from Louisiana to Ohio, and settled near Cincinnati. They
brought with them a number of slaves whom they set at liberty,
and among them was a quaint little Jim Crow of a Negro girl
who was the original of 'Topsy.' It was in attempting to give this
wild little savage some religious instruction, in a little mission
Sunday-school, that Mrs. Stowe got her material for the celebrated dialogue between Miss Ophelia and Topsy in which
Topsy 'spected she just grow'd." Lyman Stowe repeated the
story in his family biography, but Forrest Wilson supplied the
girl's name: Celeste.[28]

The work moved smoothly again. Aware that her dichoto-
mous story was becoming unbalanced, Harriet attempted to put
a little weight on the Kentucky side with chapter 20, "Ken-

[28] Charles and Lyman Stowe, 80–81; Lyman Stowe, 174–75; Forrest Wilson,
270.

tuck," in which Chloe decided to go to work at a "perfectioners" to earn money for her husband's freedom. The change of scene lasted for only a column and a half; having done what she apparently felt was required, Harriet returned to the South. The progress of George and Eliza was not noted.

In chapter 22 Harriet continued with two devices, the debate and the black-white contrast, which she was beginning to overuse. In order to give another perspective of slavery—she had already contrasted the kindly and orderly Shelbys with the kindly but inefficient St. Clares—she introduced Augustine's brother Alfred, the efficient but neither kindly nor yet cruel master. As the brothers were to be compared, so were their children, Eva and Henrique. Softhearted, religious, wise beyond her years, sickly but brave in the face of death, Eva was constrasted with her stern, non-humanitarian, impetuously youthful, power-corrupted, healthy cousin. Here again was the Eva-Topsy contrast on another level, reinforcing the Dinah-Chloe, George-Adolph, Mrs. Shelby-Marie St. Clare contrasts already presented, and preparing the reader for the further complications of the mother figures Eliza, Rosa, Cassy, Emmeline, and Madame de Thoux, the owners St. Clare, Legree, and George Shelby, and the "low mechanicals" Sam/Andy/Adolph/Sambo/Quimbo to come. Harriet seemed to function smoothly only when she could get one against one, whether it be in debate or in character.

After Eliza's crossing of the ice, the most memorable scene in *Uncle Tom's Cabin* is that of Little Eva's death. For some unaccountable reason, Forrest Wilson not only got the date of her death wrong—he said Eva died in the Christmas Day issue—but also misnumbered the installment.[29] Eva actually "passed from death unto life" on December 4, 1851, in the twenty-fifth chapter. Her passing was a shock to the *Era*'s readers, but it was not a surprise; to Harriet it was a relief. If Mrs. Burr's trip to the bureau full of child's clothes had been a dart struck deep into the

[29] Forrest Wilson, 265.

WASHINGTON, D. C.

THURSDAY, DECEMBER 18, 1851.

☞ WANTED—An efficient and responsible agent, to canvass the city of New York for subscribers to this paper.

☞ AN APOLOGY.—We regret, as much as any of our readers can regret, that Mrs. Stowe has no chapter in this week's *Era.* It is not our fault, for up to this hour we have nothing from her. As she is generally so punctual, we fear that sickness may have prevented. We feel constrained to make this apology, so profound is the interest taken in her story by nearly all our readers.

We have also to ask the forbearance of those whose patience is apt to be wearied with long articles. The proceedings of Congress are deeply interesting, and we felt it our duty to give up much space to some of the best speeches of our friends in the Senate. Then comes the long speech of Kossuth at the great Banquet at New York : its non-appearance in our columns would have been unpardonable. It is a magnificent effort—cogent, comprehensive, original, eloquent, overpowering.

As to our own articles, it was proper to present an abstract of a correspondence which has excited much interest in the public mind; and we felt anxious to bring to a conclusion the series of articles on our "Foreign Policy," commenced a month ago.

THE SIXTH VOLUME OF THE ERA

ator received with m

TUESDAY

The House did not were called several reached of any impo

The Senate, by a passed a resolution three, to wait upon gary, on his arriva Senate.

The Compromise and Mr. Rhett del favor of Secession, t ern wrongs.

THE TR

Last week was a Conservatism of th blow in the passage and the doctrine o ceived its quietus in and abandonment o son in Philadelphia has failed in its ef country the bloody c

" Tuesday last, in Court, David Paul B tion for the discha charged with treaso ner Hanaway.

" Mr. Read also discharge of Jacksc he being engaged fo

" Mr. District Att all the prisoners nar the minor charge of

" One of the pri then admitted to be

As this notice in the *National Era* reveals, the weekly installments of Mrs. Stowe's novel did not always arrive on time for publication. *Courtesy of Stowe-Day Memorial Library and Historical Foundation.*

heart of the memory of her summer's child, Eva's parting must have been a spear. Harriet's deathbed words some forty-five years later would be "I love you";[30] they might well have been those of Emerson, "Oh, that beautiful boy," for Harriet never forgot the death of her son.

Harriet got through Eva's funeral, as she had survived Charley's, and then she collapsed. There was no installment for December 18; Bailey printed "AN APOLOGY—We regret, as much as any of our readers can regret, that Mrs. Stowe has no chapter in this week's *Era*. It is not our fault, for up to this hour we have nothing from her. As she is generally so punctual, we fear that sickness may have prevented. We feel constrained to make this apology, so profound is the interest taken in her story by nearly all our readers."

When the story returned to the *Era* in the Christmas Day issue, Tom's hopes were raised as St. Clare, finding religion and a purpose in life after his daughter's death, promised to free him. Miss Ophelia procured a bill of sale for Topsy. The author seemed to be tidying things up either to end her story on a happy note with Tom free, St. Clare's soul saved, and Topsy in a Vermont finishing school, or to end on a more serious note.

On January 1, St. Clare was killed. Harriet could have disposed of him in myriad ways: drowning, an overdose of laudanum, a riding accident, a steamboat explosion. It is therefore both interesting and significant that she chose to kill him the way she did. In attempting to separate two brawling drunks, St. Clare received a "bowie-knife" in the side for his pains. Harriet's disapproval of strong drink is notable both in her earlier works and in the novel. The other aspect of St. Clare's death may well go back almost forty-six years to the pulpit of a Presbyterian Church in Aquebogue, New York, where a thirty-year-old minister from East Hampton delivered a sermon on the topic "Remedy for Duelling" before the opening session

[30]*Ibid.*, 636.

of the Presbytery.[31] His name was Lyman Beecher, and this sermon made him sufficiently famous to call his name to the attention of the Litchfield congregation when they were looking for a new pastor. More recently, the sermon had been parodied, "Slavery" being substituted for "Duelling," and published in a number of antislavery papers.[32]

With the coming of the new year Harriet picked up speed. She would miss no more deadlines and would be finished by early March. On January 15, 1852, Tom was sold to Simon Legree and started his final journey up the Red River to death and immortality. Although no mention is made of Theodore Weld in her section on Legree in the *Key*—most of Harriet's instances are drawn from Weld's antislavery book—his influence is acknowledged elsewhere. Harriet's knowledge of Louisiana had been expanded by what her brother Charles had had to tell after his return in 1839 from Louisiana, where he had worked for a cotton factor. Her brother had sent her a transcription of some shorthand notes he had taken on board after hearing a Yankee slave driver brandish his fist and say: "Well, I tell ye this yer fist has got hard as iron knocking down niggers. I never see the nigger yet I couldn't bring down with one crack. . . . You see, I just put 'em straight through sick or well. When one nigger's dead, I buy another; and I find it comes cheaper and easier, every way."[33]

Some of her information may have come from even more immediate firsthand sources. In the manuscript reminiscences of the Stowes written by the sons of John Rankin, quoted earlier in conjunction with the character of Eliza, there is a passage which deals with the character of Legree:

> My brother Rev S. G. W. Rankin had the prevalege holdings over an old Nigrous who had been sent down from the blue

[31] Lyman Beecher, *Remedy*.

[32] *Philanthropist*, Sept. 18, 1838, notes that the parody appeared in the *Emancipator*.

[33] Lyman Stowe, 174.

grass region of Ky to Neworleans and solde to a planter on the Read River of Louisiana After many years had made his escape by foot all the way to Cincinnati and was turned ovr to my bro by Levi Coffin. He was kept in one of the Roomes of the old dormatory which had plentia of such as any one knew who was ever there in those days for 8 or ten day and highed down to professor Stowes as often as circumstances under such a dangirus and adventureous times would permit and there was just how Mrs. Stowe got her Lagre Trageades.[34]

Among other matters of interest concerning Legree is a small body of popular legend which deals with Harriet's knowledge of Louisiana. It had its origin in a self-serving pamphlet written by D. B. Corley, a former mayor of Abilene, Texas. Corley wandered about Natchitoches Parish, Louisiana, in the early 1890s asking old people the following rather leading question: "You must have known something of the cruel slave-holder, 'Simon Legree' who was written up in a little book called 'Uncle Tom's Cabin.' The book appeared about 1852 I believe. And the whole scene was laid on the Red River here in your parish. Do you remember such a man?"[35] Not surprisingly, Corley turned up some interesting "facts." He "discovered" that a slave owner named Robert McAlpin, who lived in the parish, was cruel to his slaves. According to Corley, Mrs. Stowe was at Robert McAlpin's house in 1850 or 1851, or at least the woman who told Mrs. Stowe about McAlpin was. Eva was modeled, he said, on Eugénie Chopin, who had long golden hair or whose picture reminded him of Eva.

With these clues, Corley obviously had no trouble in finding Uncle Tom's genuine, original cabin, which he then had disassembled and shipped to Chicago for the 1893 World's Fair. On page 40 of his pamphlet Corley urged the reader to see the cabin there, purchase a souvenir "for the dear ones at home," and admire a fine picture of Simon Legree "kept by a lady living in

---

[34] Rankin Papers, Ohio Historical Society.
[35] D. B. Corley, *A Visit to Uncle Tom's Cabin*, 11–12.

the parish ever since his death." As further evidence of the authenticity of his find, Corley published a letter from Charles Beecher written in answer to a letter of inquiry from Corley. Charles said that he was in the parish in 1837 or 1838, and remembered "incidents, but not names or dates. I cannot remember where the plantation was, nor the name of its owner, which gave my sister a hint for the character of Legree. I have no records of any kind of that Red River trip, and do not recognize the names you mention."[36]

Following Charles's letter in the pamphlet were a number of sworn testimonials from individuals who all said that they had "always heard" or "generally known and believed" that "Mrs. Stowe wrote her work 'Uncle Tom's Cabin' whilst on a visit to McAlpin, and that McAlpin owned a slave Tom," or that "the book of Mrs. Stowe was written whilst on a visit to McAlpin."[37]

Corley concluded with one very bold statement of identification, which has a neat little qualifying clause—"in just so far as this portion of the novel are [sic] founded on fact"[38]—and one even more bold—"the cabin which Mr. Corley is about to ship to Chicago is an historic relic in that it is without doubt the veritable cabin in which the prototype of Mrs. Stowe's hero lived when on the plantation of the planter whom she called Simon Legree."[39]

The Chicago *Tribune* sent a reporter to see the cabin; his report was headlined "Not His Real Home." A 1924 article by Phanor Brazeale states that the Chopin family, owners of the land after McAlpin, denied the identification and that he himself could find no support for Corley's arguments. Lyle Saxon's 1929 book on Louisiana mentions the two sides of the arguments, but takes no stand; yet, the next year, Anna Burnside Brown wrote that Saxon had "given much time and thought to gathering facts" and supported the "McAlpine" identification. In his biography of Kate Chopin, daughter-in-law of the owner of the plantation, Daniel S. Rankin took no sides. Kate had

[36]*Ibid.*, 41.   [37]*Ibid.*, 45–47.   [38]*Ibid.*, 60.   [39]*Ibid.*, 73.

introduced the problem in her novel *At Fault,* published in 1890, but had one of her characters say only "I wonder if it could be true." The reply was "that's w'at they all say: ask any body."[40]

Of recent critics, I can find only Edmund Wilson who accepts the source. It was the McAlpin plantation, he states, which furnished "the stories of this place of horror . . . that Harriet Beecher Stowe's brother brought back to her from Louisiana and which inspired the final episode of *Uncle Tom's Cabin.*" On the other hand, Per Seyersted "found no McAlpin-Legree material of any kind in the matter" and concludes that the identification "belongs in the realm of conjecture."[41]

The name of the arch-villain of her tale Harriet probably took from an old South Carolina family who spelled it "Legaré." One member of the family, Hugh Swinton Legaré, was a famous editor, congressman from South Carolina, chargé d'affaires to Belgium, and attorney general and secretary of state under President Tyler. He defended slavery and states rights. He visited New England every summer from 1836 to his death in 1843, and died July 21, 1843, after attending the Bunker Hill monument celebration in Boston. Although Linda Rhea says nothing about the supposed connection in her biography of Hugh Swinton Legaré, Curtis Carroll Davis in his biography of James M. Legaré, Hugh Swinton's third cousin, proposes the family as a source for the name.[42]

---

[40] "Not His Real Home," Chicago *Tribune,* Nov. 20, 1892. I am indebted to Arlin Turner for calling my attention to "Uncle Tom's Cabin," New Orleans *Times-Democrat,* Dec. 4, 1892, which accepts the McAlpin-Legree identification but furnishes no additional information; Phanor Brazeale, "Uncle Tom's Cabin and the Spanish Post of the Adaias," *Louisiana Historical Society Quarterly* 7 (1924), 305; Lyle Saxon, *Old Louisiana,* 254–66; Anna Burnside Brown, 21; Daniel S. Rankin, *Kate Chopin,* 119–21; Kate Chopin, *At Fault,* 21.

[41] Edmund Wilson, *Patriotic Gore,* 588; letter to the author, Jan. 21, 1968. In his 1969 book, *Kate Chopin,* Per Seyersted notes (p. 203, n. 4) that the Natchitoches Parish chamber of commerce decided in 1960 not to declare the plantation an historic site "because of the lack of evidence to back up the legend."

[42] Linda Rhea, *Hugh Swinton Legaré,* 225, n. 1; Curtis Carroll Davis, 3.

Either the copy arrived a little late or far in advance for both the January 15 and 29 issues, for Bailey put the story on page 3 on both dates. It was more likely the former than the latter, for Harriet was entering upon the more distasteful section of the book—the sale of Tom and the introduction of Simon Legree, and she wanted to check her facts. Checking meant time and travel. No letters are extant from Harriet from January 1, 1852, until after the publication of the novel, and the secondary sources are, as usual, contradictory. In the Portland *Sunday Telegram,* July 19, 1931, Louise Littlefield told of Harriet's frequent visits to the Luther Dana family of Portland while she was writing *Uncle Tom's Cabin.* Mr. Dana had come originally from Natick, Massachusetts, Calvin Stowe's birthplace, and the boyhood acquaintances had kept track of each other over the years. As Harriet "set down the story of Uncle Tom," said Littlefield, "it became her habit to take with her to Portland the chapters written since her last visit and read them aloud to the assembled circle of Danas." That Harriet knew the Danas and thought much of them can be authenticated; one of the earliest presentation copies of *Uncle Tom's Cabin,* dated March 31, 1852, was inscribed to this family.[43]

More directly important in tracing the sources of the novel is Benjamin Thomas's assertion that "Mrs. Stowe visited the rooms of the American Anti-slavery Society, now located in Boston."[44] Mrs. Edward Beecher wrote of this period to Charles Stowe: "When we lived in Boston your mother often visited us. . . . Several numbers of 'Uncle Tom's Cabin' were written in your Uncle Edward's study at these times, and read to us from the manuscripts."[45] Still later, Charles and Lyman Stowe asserted that "it was written mostly in Brunswick, Maine. Some of the chapters were written in Boston, while she was visiting

[43] Louise Littlefield, "Letter," Portland (Me.) *Sunday Telegram*, July 19, 1931; Chester E. Jorgenson, *Uncle Tom's Cabin*, 15.

[44] Benjamin Thomas, 22.

[45] Charles Stowe, 145.

her brother, Edward Beecher, and part of the concluding chapter in Andover."[46]

The impulse upon which Harriet drew for the portraits of Cassy and Emmeline could have come from any of a number of slave narratives. The stories of Henson, Clarke, Douglass, and others told of sisters or wives sold South into lives of sin. But a more reliable source seems to have been in the Stowe household itself.

In a letter to Mrs. Eliza Lee Cabot Follen, written in December of 1852, Harriet told of information given her by Eliza Buck, her cook.

> My Cook, poor Eliza Buck, (how she would stare to think of her name's going to England) was a regular epitome of slave life in herself, fat, gentle, easy, loving and loveable, always calling my very modest house & door yard "The Place" as if it had been a plantation with 700 hands on it. —Her way of arranging her kitchen was at first somewhat like Dinah's though she imbibed our ideas more rapidly, & seemed more ready to listen to suggestions, than did that dignitary. She had lived through the whole sad story of a Virginia-raised slave's life. In her youth she must have been a very handsome mulatto girl. Her voice was sweet & her manners refined and agreeable. She was raised in a good family, as nurse & sempstress, When the family became embarrassed, she was suddenly sold on to a plantation in Louisiana; She has often told me how without any warning, she was suddenly forced into a carriage, & saw her little mistress screaming & stretching her arms from the window towards her, as she was driven away. She has told me of scenes on the Louisiana plantations & how she has often been out in the night by stealth, ministering to poor slaves, who had been mangled & lacerated by the whip. Thence she was sold again into Kentucky, & her last Master was the father of all her children. On this point she always maintained a delicacy & reserve, which, though it is not at all uncommon among slave women, always appeared to me remarkable. She always called him her husband, & spoke of him

---

[46] Charles and Lyman Stowe, 155.

with the same apparent feeling with which any woman regards her husband, & it was not till after she had lived with me some years, that I discovered, accidentally, the real nature of the connexion. I shall never forget how sorry I felt for her, nor my feelings at her humble apology "You know, Mrs. Stowe, slave-women can't help themselves." She had two very pretty quadroon daughters, with beautiful hair & eyes interesting children, whom I had instructed in the family school with my children. Time would fail me to tell you all that I learnt incidentally of the working of the slave system, in the history of various slaves, who came into my family & of the *underground railway* which I may say ran through the barn.[47]

Eliza Buck obviously made a strong impression on Harriet. In 1892 when Houghton Mifflin brought out a new edition of *Uncle Tom's Cabin,* Harriet said in a thank-you note to the company that the illustrations were "excellent particularly that of Aunt Chloe pleases me. It reminds me strongly in the expression & attitude of my faithful friend and servant Eliza Buck of many years ago, whom I believe is now in Heaven."[48] It would be difficult to trace all the possible hints and suggestions supplied by Eliza and equally impossible to underestimate her influence. In this single letter to Mrs. Follen, however, can be seen the germs of many characters and incidents: Aunt Chloe; Dinah and her kitchen; Tom's parting from George Shelby; Cassy's youth and her relationship to Legree; Eliza as Cassy's

[47] The letter exists in many different printed states and four manuscripts, versions which vary significantly from one another both in date and in content. The four manuscript versions are in the Houghton Library, Harvard; the Massachusetts Historical Society Library; Dr. Williams' Library, London; and the Vassar College Library. Only the Vassar ms. is labeled "copy." The author has used the Dr. Williams text as it is labeled "not to be copied" and appears to be closest to Harriet's hand. Of the versions published in the standard biographies, Fields, pp. 172–78, is closest to the text used here. Shorter versions will be found in the *London Weekly Chronicle,* April 28, 1855, p. 265; Salem (Mass.) *Register,* May 24, 1855; the Swanton (Vt.) *American Journal,* June 8, 1855; Lawrence (Kan.) *Herald of Freedom,* July 14, 1855; Wallace Brookway and Bart K. Winer, *Second Treasury,* 414–19; Charles Stowe, 197–204; Charles and Lyman Stowe, 152–54; Forrest Wilson, 337–39.

[48] American Antiquarian Society.

long-lost daughter. Eliza Buck was a rich mine of information.

Harriet moved her story along rapidly during February. She not only missed no issues; she never left page one of the *Era*. But in the weeks leading up to the end of the serial, Bailey was less and less inclined to heed her earlier stricture not to divide chapters. It may well be that she was supplying him with more copy than he could conveniently use. Whatever the reason, on February 5 he printed chapter 31 and part of 32; on the twelfth he concluded 32 and printed all of 33. Chapters 34 and 35 both had their own issues, but on March 4 two chapters, 36 and 37, appeared; on March 11, 38 and half of 39; on March 18 the conclusion to 39, all of 40, and part of 41; on March 25 the conclusion of 41 and part of 42; and on April 1 the end of 42, all of 43, and the final chapter, 44.

After the death of Uncle Tom on March 18, the story began to draw to a close. Cassy prepared Legree by playing on his superstitious mind the tricks which effected her escape with Emmeline. The reunions on the boat, although stretching credibility more than a little, were well done, even if the reader expected the captain of the boat to be Tom Loker's good-hearted brother or Haley's second son by his first wife. The scene in George Harris's house in Canada was practically ready-made. It had appeared, complete in its essentials of respectability, in the "Two Altars" piece Harriet had done just before she started the serial. Tying up was about all she had to do. George Harris stated the colonizationist position that had been barely covered anywhere in the story, and once she had the loose ends of lives accounted for, she could not resist an overt demonstration of what she had been doing perhaps more subtly throughout: in her "Concluding Remarks" she mounted the pulpit and, in best Beecher fashion, preached.

The sources for two parts of her sermon are easy to trace. The story of Nathan, the escaped slave, is paraphrased from one of her stories, "Immediate Emancipation," which had appeared in the New York *Evangelist,* January 2, 1845. In the *Era* Harriet had written that a "young southern gentlemen," in "Cincinnati with a favorite slave," was "exceedingly indignant" to find that the Negro had "fled to the protection of a Quaker." When the young slave, Nathan, was asked if he had been mistreated, he and his owner engaged in the following dialogue:

"No, Mas'r," said Nathan "you've always been good to me."
"Well, then, why do you want to leave me?"
"Mas'r may die, and then who get me?—I'd rather be a free man."

After some deliberation, the young master replied,

"Nathan, in your place, I think I should feel very much so, myself. You are free."

The *Evangelist* version had read:

". . . has not my father always been good to you?"
"Oh, yes, master; very good." . . .
"Well, then, why do you wish to leave me?". . .
"Oh, massa may die; then nobody knows who get me . . . I'd rather be free man . . . "
Alfred turned to the window, and thought a few moments, and then said, turning about, "Well, Sam, I believe you are right. I think, on the whole, I'd like best to be a free man myself, and I must not wonder that you do. So, for aught I see, you must go. . . ."

Also in the last chapter, Harriet mentioned the capture of the schooner *Pearl* and the fate of two girls, Emily and Mary Edmundson, whom she cited as counterparts to Emmeline and Cassy. More important to Harriet than the political implications of attempts to aid the escape of slaves from a ship in 1848 was the fate of these two passengers on the ship.[49] She became

---

[49] For the political side see John H. Paynter, "The Fugitives of the *Pearl*," *Journal of Negro History* 1 (1915), 243–64; Daniel Drayton, *Personal Memoirs*; James W. C. Pennington, *The Fugitive Blacksmith*; "Slave Raid," Cincinnati *Enquirer*, Sept. 14, 1895; E. Bruce Kirkham, "Two Abolitionists and a Pearl," *Journal of Negro History* 50 (1965), 123–25.

personally interested in the family and aided in the education of
the two girls at Oberlin College. Although the events occurred
from about 1848 to 1850, Charles Stowe dated Harriet's interest in the matter as beginning later, "very soon after the
publication of *'Uncle Tom's Cabin.'*" He said that "Mrs. Stowe
had first known of the liberated girls in 1851" and that she met
the mother, Milly Edmundson, "during her visit to New York
in the spring of 1852." By "spring," Charles apparently meant
about May 1852, for the letter to Calvin in which Harriet said
that she had met Milly is dated May 29. Yet in the letter she
simply noted that "the mother of the Edmundson girls, now
aged and feeble, is in the city";[50] no further explanation or
identification was apparently needed. She must have known of
the family earlier, for Henry Ward had undertaken to help them
in early 1849. By April 18, 1852, Harriet had turned her
attention to the fate of the two officers of the *Pearl*, asking about
them in a letter to Gamaliel Bailey.[51] In July of the same year,
the Edmundson girls were already enrolled at Oberlin, and
Harriet had instructed Calvin to send thirty dollars toward their
expenses.[52] In November, Harriet sent another one hundred
and ten dollars. The girls are mentioned again in letters of
January 7, June 2, and December 12, 1853.[53] Despite Charles
Stowe's confusion on dates—neither Charles and Lyman nor
Lyman alone nor Forrest Wilson straightened it out—it is
apparent that Harriet had considerable knowledge of the Edmundson girls prior to the beginning of her writing.

The story was finished, as noted earlier, probably sometime
in late February or early March. Between the time Harriet
concluded the writing of the manuscript and the book was
published, she revised. As already mentioned, she had selected a
publisher the previous September, and the choice had been

[50] Charles Stowe, 179–80.
[51] Houghton Library, Harvard.
[52] Cowles Papers, Oberlin.
[53] First two letters in Barrett Collection, Univ. of Virginia; third in Cowles
Papers, Oberlin.

entirely her own. At first others tried to help. Sister Catharine had asked her own publisher, Phillips, Sampson, & Co., to accept the growing story, but they had turned it down, fearing that an antislavery book by a woman would be a poor risk and might alienate a sizable portion of their Southern trade.

Harriet had then turned to a publisher with whom both she and the family were familiar. John Punchard Jewett, born in Lebanon, Maine, in 1814, began in the book business in Salem, Massachusetts, where, before long, he owned his own store. He moved in 1847 to Boston and there became both a bookseller and a publisher, at first specializing in texts and graded readers, but soon concentrating on religious books.[54] In 1846 he brought out a collection of sermons and essays called *Lectures to Young Men on Various Important Subjects* by youthful Indiana minister named Henry Ward Beecher. In December 1851, Jewett announced the first volume of a projected six-volume edition of the *Works* of the minister's father, Lyman Beecher. The name "Jewett" must have been in Harriet's mind as she sought someone to publish her serial in book form, but just how they came together was not clear to the biographers.

Mrs. Fields did not attempt to explain how Jewett became acquainted with Harriet's story; she merely reprinted Harriet's explanation from the "1879 Introduction" to *Uncle Tom's Cabin:* "As the story progressed, a young publisher, J. P. Jewett, of Boston, set his eye upon it, and made overtures for the publication of it in book form, to which she consented." Charles Stowe simply stated that the story "had attracted the attention of Mr. John P. Jewett, Boston publisher, who promptly made overtures for its publication in book form." In the later biography which Charles did with his son Lyman, the two accounts were combined and altered to read "John P. Jewett, a young publisher of Boston, made overtures for the publication of 'Uncle Tom's Cabin' in book form long before it was finished as a serial in the *National Era*." When Lyman Stowe treated the topic in

[54] *Dictionary of American Biography*, s.v. "Jewett, John Punchard."

his family biography, he omitted the "long before" and added the assertion that Jewett's firm was "a predecessor of the present house of Houghton Mifflin Company."[55] All accounts agree that the contract with Jewett was signed March 13, 1852.

Although Jewett himself never gave a specific date, on two separate occasions he attempted to explain the relationship. In an interview appearing in the first volume of a New York magazine, *The Manhattan,* published in 1883, Jewett said that he was "a rabid anti-slavery man," that he had published a book by Henry Ward Beecher, and that it was the Stowes who, having been unsuccessful elsewhere, had approached him "after about one half of the story had been published in the *Era.*" He continued: Mrs. Jewett "had read the story as it had appeared in the *Era, . . .* had highly praised the portions she had read, and declared that 'Uncle Tom' would make a book that would sell largely. She had urged me to read the parts as they were published, but I had declined, preferring to wait and read the complete story." After he had been approached by the Stowes, however, he apparently changed his mind, for he said that he "read the portion which had been printed and the remainder of the manuscript as far as it was written, for it had not yet been finished," and "expressed a willingness to publish it."[56]

In 1947, the East Orange (New Jersey) *Record* published a manuscript account written by Jewett himself of the facts surrounding the publication of the book. Jewett indicated that he had been very active in antislavery circles, had known Bailey in Cincinnati and defended him from antiabolition mobs, and had

---

[55] Fields, 148; Charles Stowe, 158; Charles and Lyman Stowe, 155–56; Lyman Stowe, 183. In a letter to the author from Ellen (Mrs. Norman V.) Ballou, Jan. 19, 1968, Mrs. Ballou, compiler of a history of Houghton Mifflin, denies that Jewett was a predecessor of that company. In his history of American publishers (*History of Book Publishing: Volume I*), John Tebbell explains that William Lee of Phillips, Sampson told Jewett of the decision not to publish, whereupon Jewett then "made an offer to Mrs. Stowe" (p. 426).

[56] "Uncle Tom's Cabin," *The Manhattan: An Illustrated Literary Magazine* I (1883), 28.

been an agent for the *National Era,* procuring many subscriptions: "It was during the winter of 1851–52 that my attention was called to this story by my noble wife, to whom the entire credit is due for its publication in book form. . . . On a cold morning in January, 1852, my wife sat by my side reading from the last number of the *Era* the touching death scene of Little Eva, having more than once urged me to write to Mrs. Stowe soliciting the story for publication in book form." The next morning, he continued, he wrote to Harriet and by "return mail . . . received her reply, informing [him] that she and her husband would be in Boston in three weeks and would be pleased to make arrangements with [him] for publishing the story." The Stowes apparently arrived on time, negotiations proceeded, the contract was signed, and Jewett set to work. "Next in order after the contract with the author came the contract for stereotyping, printing and binding."[57] As has been mentioned, Jewett did not date the signing of the contract, but if he first wrote to the Stowes in January, waited three weeks for their arrival, and then worked over the contract with them, it would appear that the signing took place after mid-February.

A number of major inconsistencies appear when all these accounts are compared. The Jewett versions seem to place the contract signing much earlier than the March 13 date given by Stowe biographers. The "after about one half of the story" of the *Manhattan* article would make it October or November of 1851; the manuscript account that appeared in the East Orange *Record,* indicates that Jewett began to take action on the day after "a cold morning in January, 1852," on which the Jewetts had in hand the December 4, 1851, *Era* installment, which dealt with Little Eva's death. The initial overture probably, therefore, took place as early as January. Upon close inspection, the March 13 date seems even more improbable if we assume that Jewett did

[57] East Orange *Record*, Nov. 13, 1947. The manuscript, not on deposit in the East Orange Historical Society, the Free Public Library of East Orange, the New Jersey Historical Society, or at Rutgers Univ. or Princeton Univ., has apparently been lost.

not negotiate with stereotypers, printers, and binders until after the contract with the author was signed. March 13 fell on a Saturday; the book appeared March 20, the following Saturday. Jewett could have done nothing in Boston on the fourteenth, a Sunday. He would have had to delay any activity until Monday. He therefore had five days, March 15 through 19, to have plates cast for 634 pages of text and six illustrations, to have galleys run and corrected, sheets printed for 5,000 sets (10,000 copies of the two-volume format), the 10,000 copies bound in three formats—paper, cloth, and gilt-edged cloth—and the sets delivered to his stores in Boston and Cleveland, Ohio, in time for the March 20 sale date. There must be another answer.

After the September 18 notice stating that Jewett was to be the publisher, the *Era* remained silent until October 30, when the following advertisement appeared in its pages.

New Book Establishment
Jewett, Proctor and Worthington, Publishers, Booksellers and Stationers, 136 Superior Street, Cleveland, Ohio, respectfully announce that they have commenced business as above, and have become the Western Publishers of all the works issued by J. P. Jewett & Co., of Boston, among which are the following, to which attention is solicited:
The Works of Leonard Woods, D. D. 5 vols 8vo
The Works of Lyman Beecher, D. D. 6 vols 12mo, in press—1st volume out
Commentary on the Book of Acts, by Prof. H. B. Hackett, 1 vol 8vo
Grote's History of Greece, 1st Am. ed., 10 vols, 12mo
Also, the thrilling tale, by Mrs. Harriet Beecher Stowe, called,

UNCLE TOM'S CABIN
published in the columns of the National Era. All orders from the West for this interesting book should be directed to us.

The notice went on to describe various services the firm was willing and able to perform for clergymen and others in their

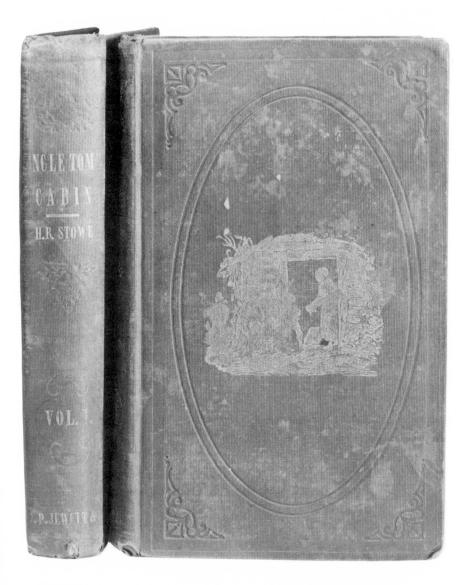

The first edition of *Uncle Tom's Cabin* was bound in dull colored cloth with gold-leaf overlays, a modest appearance for the book that, as Abraham Lincoln said, "started this great war." *Courtesy of Stowe-Day Memorial Library and Historical Foundation.*

search for moral and pious works. The same advertisement appeared in the *Era* on November 6, 13, and 20.[58]

The Jewetts bought space again in the number for December 25 to announce that the first volume of Lyman Beecher's *Works, Lectures on Political-Atheism . . .* was "ready for sale" and promised the second volume about February first, the other four volumes to appear at approximately two-month intervals. The same notice ran in the following three numbers. *Uncle Tom's Cabin* was not mentioned.

On January 1, Bailey inserted a paragraph which read: "Mrs. Stowe's Story: This story is to be published in a separate form by Jewett & Co., of Boston. Orders for it should be sent to them. They are stereotyping it, as it appears in the Era, so that it will be issued by them, so soon as completed in our paper." In the last issue for the month, January 29, 1852, Bailey again mentioned Harriet's forthcoming book: "A correspondent asks whether Mrs. Stowe's story and the 'Mother in Law' and 'Retribution' of Mrs. Southworth can be published so as to be bound in one volume. The last two novels have been already published, and are for sale at the principal book stores. As to Mrs. Stowe's story, the Jewetts of Boston are stereotyping it as fast as it appears in the Era, and they will have it out the moment it is completed in our paper."

When Jewett next made an announcement, the date was March 4. He said:

> Will Be Ready March 20
> *Mrs. H. Beecher Stowe's Great American Tale*
> Entitled
> Uncle Tom's Cabin; or, Life Among the Lowly
> This great work, which has been long expected, is now so nearly completed that we can promise its appearance on the 20th of March.
> By all who have read it it is pronounced to be

---

[58] Wilson first discovered the advertisement in the Nov. 6 issue. See Forrest Wilson, 275.

THE STORY OF THE AGE

For power of description and thrilling delineation of character it is unrivaled, and will add fresh laurels to the reputation of the talented Authoress. It will be published in two volumes, 12mo, 312 pages in each vol, with six elegant designs by Billings engraved by Baker—in three styles of binding: Paper covers for $1; Cloth, $1.50; Cloth, full gilt, $2—with discount to the Trade. Early orders solicited.

JOHN P. JEWETT & CO, Publishers, Boston, and JEWETT, PROCTOR, & WORTHINGTON, Cleveland, Ohio. For sale by the principal Booksellers in the United States.

The notice was repeated March 11, 25, April 1, 8, and 15.

Forrest Wilson is the only one of the biographers to have traced the publication record through the *Era* pages, but in doing so he made mistakes and left gaps. He reprinted the September 18 announcement of the selection of Jewett as publisher, but noted only that it indicated "how little Harriet as yet understood the scope of her masterpiece" and said that Harriet told "Jewett to begin setting it up in type."[59] According to Wilson, the "first public advertisement for *Uncle Tom's Cabin*" was bought by "the Cleveland, Ohio, house of Proctor & Worthington" on "November 6";[60] the date was October 30, and the firm was Jewett, Proctor & Worthington. He missed Bailey's notes of January 1 and 29, caught Jewett's advertisement of March 4—dating it only as "early in March"—but failed to say that in addition to "the Boston and New York newspapers" it was published in the *Era*.[61]

In evaluating the two versions of the prepublication activities, one must remember that all of the Stowe biographers —Mrs. Fields, Charles Stowe, Lyman Stowe, and indeed, Harriet herself—were working many years after the fact, that the Jewett interview took place less than a year before the pub-

[59] Forrest Wilson, 269.

[60] *Ibid.*, 275.

[61] *Ibid.*, 278. Tebbel, 427, says that there were three woodcuts and the two volumes sold for $2.50; he read no ads.

lisher's death in 1884, and that the Jewett manuscript, although not dated, was also probably written many years after the fact. Although Jewett's holograph and Harriet's introduction are primary sources, they are not primary in point of time. Bailey's account, or rather the data furnished by Bailey's paper, are contemporary with the events they describe and must be taken as the most authoritative. That Wilson recognized the importance of the notices and advertisements in the *National Era* is to his credit, but more conclusions may be drawn.

First, it is clear now why Jewett contacted Harriet or vice versa: they had known of each other for some time. Jewett had published and repeatedly reissued Henry Ward's book and was publishing Lyman's *Works.* If Harriet sought him out or suggested Jewett's name to her husband, it was because she knew something of the man. The only other Eastern publisher she had had dealings with was the Harper Brothers, who had done the 1843 *Mayflower.* Catharine had tried to interest Phillips, Sampson, her own most recent publishers, but they had declined. What would have been more natural than for Harriet to turn to the man who was publishing both her favorite brother and her father? Jewett, on the other hand, may have contacted Harriet on his wife's suggestion—as he stated in the East Orange *Record*—but whether or not Mrs. Jewett was the stimulus, the relationship with Harriet even from the first could not have been that of a stranger.

Secondly, that very relationship appears to have been the motivation for Jewett to act on the basis of what was certainly an informal agreement. If no contract was signed until one week before publication, Jewett had had nothing but Harriet's (or Calvin's) word that the book would not go to another publisher after the contract for the stereotyping of the entire work had been made. This was, of course, a most unbusinesslike arrangement. Indeed, it may be because of his later doubts about what people would think of a man who would indulge in such a caprice that Jewett insisted in the manuscript account—which, as he himself says, is a defense of his actions—that he did not commit himself to stereotyper, printer, or binder until after the contract was signed, when, in point of fact, he had been stereotyping since the previous September. It is undoubtedly this very lack of a contract which inspired his often-cited worry about the length of the novel. Had he only informally agreed to publish the work and done nothing more, he could have adjusted his terms or backed out to save himself, but, as it was, he had stereotypers to pay whether the book sold or not. The length worried him for a reason which none of the biographers have noted.

In addition, of course, he had another cause for concern. He had advertised himself as the sole publisher of the book ever since the preceding October. If Harriet changed her mind, someone else, the new publisher, would reap the benefit of all his advertising and possibly go ahead and put out the book without even buying his plates. He had also, of course, arranged for the illustrations to be drawn and the engravings cut. *Uncle Tom's Cabin* was rapidly becoming an all-or-nothing venture. It is amazing that he did not demand a contract earlier than he did.

Furthermore, the March 4 advertisement announcing the publication date as March 20 certainly means that Jewett had either seen the last pages of manuscript or had been told that they would be forthcoming shortly; but it cannot mean that the story was completely stereotyped, for the work is described as "312 pages in each vol" when, in actuality, the first volume has 312 pages and the second, 322. By March 4, perhaps a bit earlier, Harriet was already working on revisions, and the foundry was busy chipping off the old lines and casting new. As a number of paragraphs were both added and deleted, the activity must have been chaotic at the Hobart and Robbins New England Type and Stereotype Foundry.

Chapter 6.

THE MANUSCRIPTS

All but one of the scholars who have commented on the process of composition of *Uncle Tom's Cabin* have judged it both careless and hasty. One of Mrs. Stowe's earliest biographers, Florine Thayer McCray, said that the book "was not written like any other successful story that the world ever saw; it had no re-writing, scarcely a revision; it was dashed off at a white heat, and sent forthwith to the printer."[1] According to Constance Rourke, too, Harriet began writing "without premonition or plan" and wrote "installment after hasty installment for publi-cation in the National Era."[2] Lyman Stowe suggested the same unchanged state of succeeding texts when he stated that the scene of Uncle Tom's death was first composed "practically as it stands today."[3] Among more recent scholars Forrest Wilson, after noting that Harriet left details such as punctuation and capitalization to Bailey's printer, has said that "as she filled each sheet, she pushed it aside, never to look at it again with revisionary eye."[4] J. C. Furnas, in his unsympathetic study, comments, "Mrs. Stowe always wrote hastily, seldom revised,

---

[1] Florine Thayer McCray, *Life-work*, 74.
[2] Constance Mayfield Rourke, *Trumpets of Jubilee*, 104.
[3] Lyman Stowe, 182.
[4] Forrest Wilson, 271.

usually left punctuation to the printer. With sounder technical habits she might have written fairly well."[5] Lawrence Lader seems to echo Lyman Stowe when he states that "she wrote the book at breakneck speed, dashing off the chapter on Uncle Tom's death in one sitting, hardly making a correction later in the original manuscript."[6] In his introduction to the John Harvard Library edition of *Uncle Tom's Cabin,* Kenneth Lynn notes that some revisions were made, but "aside from changing the name 'Senator Burr' to 'Senator Bird' and correcting a number of minor errors, Mrs. Stowe made no alterations between the magazine version and the book version of her text. The only really significant change was in the nature of her audience."[7] Howard Mumford Jones agrees with Lynn, but calls attention to an added preface and shorter final paragraph which replaced the "Concluding Remarks" of the *Era.*[8] Philip Van Doren Stern goes so far as to imply that the type for the novel was set from *National Era* tear sheets.[9]

Although in the "1879 Introduction" Harriet mentioned reading proof[10]—a statement cited by three of the biographers[11]—and Forrest Wilson expands upon it when he says that she sent a list of corrections to the printer,[12] no one of these biographers checked the manuscripts against the newspaper text or the newspaper against the first edition of the novel. In his 1886 sketch entitled "Harriet Beecher Stowe in Hartford," Joseph H. Twitchell noted that in her Hartford house was "Mrs. Stowe's copy of the first American edition, with the first sheet of the original manuscripts . . . pasted on the fly leaf, showing that three several beginnings were made before the setting of the

---

[5] Furnas, 55.
[6] Lader, 172–73.
[7] Kenneth S. Lynn, ed., *Uncle Tom's Cabin*, xxvi.
[8] Jones, xvii.
[9] Philip Van Doren Stern, ed., *Uncle Tom's Cabin*, 22.
[10] Harriet Beecher Stowe, "1879 Introduction," xvi.
[11] Fields, 136; McCray, 104; Charles Stowe, 159.
[12] Forrest Wilson, 279. The list is not extant.

introductory scene was fixed upon."[13] Apparently no one but Chester Jorgenson has heeded that clue, and even he pursues the topic no farther than to note that the *National Era* and first edition texts differ.[14] Had he and the others investigated, they would have discovered that the process of the composition of *Uncle Tom's Cabin* was more complex than they have stated and revealed more about Harriet as an author than any one of them was prepared to accept.

Nine leaves of the original manuscript have survived. Some leaves have writing on both sides, some on only one side.

Of these twelve pages of text, ten are preserved in holograph original and two in facsimile.[15] All are in Harriet's hand. An examination of these leaves (Appendix I below, pp. 157, 197–99) reveals, first that, Harriet's handwriting is not difficult to read. Her few characteristic oddities include forming the second of a double "l" shorter than the first, often but not consistently using the older form for double "*s*," and usually writing a truncated number "2" instead of "&" for the word "and." Aside from these easily learned peculiarities, her hand should have offered few chances for misreading by the typesetter.

Second, the niceties of punctuation are ignored. Dashes serve for periods, semicolons, question marks, and exclamation points. Quotation marks, apostrophes, and hyphens are omitted. Paragraphing is rather haphazard, sometimes indicated by a dash at the beginning of a line, sometimes by indentation.

A closer examination and a comparison of the leaves with the newspaper and novel texts suggest some interesting facts and conclusions. When leaves A and B are collated with the corresponding text in the *National Era* (pp. 199–211), a large number

---

[13] Joseph H. Twitchell, "Authors at Home, XXIII: Mrs. Harriet Beecher Stowe in Hartford," *The Critic* 9 (Dec. 18, 1886), 301–2. The article was later reprinted in *Authors at Home*, ed. J. L. Gilder (New York, 1889), 319–20. See also Twitchell's "Reminiscences of Mrs. Stowe," Litchfield (Conn.) *Enquirer*, Oct. 29, 1908.

[14] Jorgenson, 13.

[15] These manuscript pages, designated as leaves A through I, are discussed individually in Appendix I as to their form, condition, and history.

of variants appear, both substantive and accidental, including the addition in the *Era* of fifty-eight consecutive lines not found in leaf B. When the *Era* text is compared with that of the novel (pp. 211–13), ninety-four variants emerge, but eighty of those are accidentals, and of the fifteen that are substantive, thirteen are probably typographical errors in the *Era:* omission of "and," "in," "that," "then," and "a"; "places" for "palaces," "screachin" for "scrachin," "article" for "articles," "arm" for "arms," "great" for "greatest," "get" for "gets," "further" for "farther," and "quietly" for "quickly." Out of the ninety-four variants, therefore, only two may be authorial: "he" of line 100 in the *Era* is changed to "Haley" in the novel, and the "gentlemen" of line 98 is changed to "gentleman" in the novel.

What is most important about these variants as a whole is that they clearly demonstrate two highly significant points and hint at a third. First, the manuscript preceded the *Era* text since the two do not agree and the newspaper does agree, generally, with the novel. In addition, the lack of agreement between the holograph and the *Era* text indicates that it was not the version Harriet sent to the paper, but that another version, incorporating the changes found in the newspaper, was written after the holograph. She could not have proofread the *Era* text in galleys before it went to press. It thus must be that at least two versions of this passage were written before the episode was published in the *Era*.

Second, the collation reveals that, generally, Harriet is not to be held responsible for variants in punctuation and often not in spelling. She may have read proof for the novel, as she says, but even if she did, she was content throughout her life to let printers and publishing-house workers attend to her punctuation and her spelling, unless they corrected or changed her text when she was attempting to render dialect.[16]

[16] In the extensive collection of Harriet's correspondence with James T. and Annie A. Fields in the Henry Huntington Library, there are many references to Harriet's dependence on her printer for accidentals. See her letter to JTF, Andover, Jan. 16,

Third and finally, the "gentlemen/-man, he/Haley" changes may be instances, unsupportable from this evidence but demonstrable from sources which will be cited presently, that Harriet did revise, often extensively, before the novel went to press.

When leaves C and D and the corresponding *Era* passages are compared (pp. 213–18), one finds again, a large number of variants between the manuscript and the newspaper; on the other hand, comparison between the newspaper and the novel (I, 38–39) texts shows them to be identical except at seven points, mostly of minor significance: "par excellence" of the *Era* is italicized in the novel; "where every summer strawberries" becomes "where, every summer, strawberries"; "here also in summer various" becomes "Here, also, in summer, various"; and "four o'clocks" becomes "four-o'clocks."

Results are very similar in regard to leaf D. A long list of variants appears in the comparison with the appropriate *Era* text (p. 273), but when the *Era* and the novel (I, 41) texts are compared, they are found to be all but identical. The book corrects "laboriously; brought" of the *Era* to "laboriously brought," restoring the manuscript reading, but wrongly changes the *Era*'s "out 'that'" at line four to "out; 'that.'" Aside from some other minor spelling and punctuation changes, the only further change is that of George's *Era* "aint" at line seventeen to a more proper "Isn't" in the novel. Thus it can be

---

1861: "My manuscripts are always left at the printer for punctuation—as you will observe—I have no time for copying"; and to [JTF], Aug. 16, 1867: "My printers always inform me that I know nothing of punctuation & give thanks that I have no responsibility for any of its absurdities. Further than beginning my sentences with a capital I go not—so I hope my friend Mr. Begelow who is a direct and lineal descendant of 'my Grandmother' will put those things all right." But see also the letter to JTF, Mandarin, Fla., Mar. 2, 1869, in which she takes Begelow to task for regularizing her dialect spellings: "Let me have it my way." Howard Ticknor, assistant editor for the *Atlantic*, summed up her attitude: her "manuscripts required special editing as she regarded spelling and punctuation as something quite outside the author's field, to be supplied by editor and printer." Caroline Ticknor, *Glimpses of Authors*, 81.

deduced that leaves C and D were both written prior to the version submitted to the *Era*.

The texts of the *Era* for June 26, 1851, and the novel at I, 64–65, are much closer to one another than leaf E is to either. The substantive and accidental variants between the *Era* and leaf E texts appear on pages 218–22. Only fifteen variants, all accidental, occur between the *Era* and the novel at this point.

On the other hand, leaves F, G, H, and I resemble the novel text much more closely than they do that of *Era*. This fact suggests that these leaves were part of the drafts for the novel rather than for the newspaper.

All these comparisons point to the conclusion that there were at least three distinct, though possibly partial, manuscript versions of *Uncle Tom's Cabin:* two prior to the *National Era* text and one subsequent to it but prior to the novel text.

All four leaves (F, G, H, and I) are approximately the same size except for F, which has been trimmed at the top and has a mutilated top line. Because of their similar size and their numbering, "2," "3," and "7" respectively, it seems probable that the four leaves, F, G, H, and I are part of a package of at least seven sent with a cover letter, the beginning of which has survived in rough draft on the verso of I, indicating the changes Harriet wanted made in the text which Jewett was setting in type. Although no date can be placed on these leaves, they do show that Jewett did not set his type exclusively from *Era* tear sheets.

Mrs. Stowe's story was not "dashed off at a white heat" with "scarcely a revision" as McCray and others have suggested. The text sent the *Era* was the result of considerable rewriting, and further revisions, often extensive, were made by the author between the publication of the story in the *Era* and its appearance in novel form.

The effects of the changes Harriet made when revising for Jewett will be discussed in chapter 7. The changes prior to publication in the *Era* are not, however, without significance. These emendations indicate Harriet's compositional technique and developing aesthetic sensibility, and the growth and development of characters and plot in the mind of the author.

The variants between leaves A and B and the *Era* text pp. 207–11 provide a logical starting point. At line 2 of the *Era* text, Eliza is described as a "quadroon"; in the manuscript version she had been a "mulatto." The change is important because, whereas a mulatto is either a Negro with one white parent or merely a Negro with some white blood, the term "quadroon" is applied only to a Negro with three white grandparents. Eliza's blood line and therefore, to some degree, her color, education, and social background are more clearly defined by "quadroon" than "mulatto"; she is made whiter. The change from "the complexion" to "her complexion" at line 7 tends to humanize the description of Eliza. Originally Eliza "caught the eye of the stranger," but Mrs. Stowe emended the sentimental cliché with its overtones of coquetry to read "saw the gaze of the strange man" (line 9), a phrase which has no hint of flirtation in it. Likewise, the fit of Eliza's dress, changed from "closest" to "neatest" (line 11), seems to make her more respectable; perhaps the change from "form" to "shape" (line 12) has the same motivation.

The revisions in Haley's speech are more significant. As the story progresses, he and his cronies are pictured as ignorant, semi-literate, cunning, hypocritical men. Four paragraphs previous to his first speech, Haley is described as one who regarded Eliza not as a human being, but as a "fine female article" (line 15). Having already been condemned by the author, Haley confirms her judgment by repeating the word "article" in his evaluation of Eliza, not as a beautiful woman, but as a piece of merchandise which will bring a good price (line 24). The change from "that girl" to "that ar gal" and the contraction of "New Orleans" to "Orleans" reveal both Haley's education and his social class (line 25): all his protestations notwithstanding,

                                                            Massr
thing I cant feel it right to do — &, I never shall
do it — never!

        Tom had a remarkably smooth
soft voice & habitually respectful manner that had
given Legree an idea that he would be cowardly
& easily subdued — when he spoke these last
words a thrill of amazement went thro every
one — ~~the poor w~~ ~~there was a general drawing~~
~~in of breath~~ the poor woman clasped her hands
& said "Oh Lord!" & every one involuntarily looked at
each other and drew in their breath as if to prepare
for the storm that was about to burst

        Legree looked stupified & confounded but
at last burst forth

        What' ye blasted black beast! tell
me ye dont think it right to do what I tell ye —
what have any of you cussed cattle to do
with thinking whats right! — Il put a stop to
it   Why what do ye think ye are ?   may be
ye think ye'r a gentleman master Tom to be
a telling your master whats right, & what aint
So you pretend its wrong to flog the gal

        "I think so Massr", said Tom the poor
critter, sick & feeble — 'Twould be down right cruel
& its what I never will do nor begin to — Massr
if you mean ~~to think~~ kill me, kill me — but as
to my raising my hand agin any one here I never

Only nine leaves of the original manuscript of *Uncle Tom's Cabin* have
survived. The page shown is leaf H, published here for the first time.
Courtesy of Stowe-Day Memorial Library and Historical Foundation.

Haley is basically no better than his fellow dealers and Marks.

In his attempt to persuade Shelby to sell Eliza, Haley points out the price Shelby could get for her. The emended version changes the "a thousand—two thousand" paid for "girl not half so handsome," to "over a thousand . . . for gals not a bit handsomer" (lines 26–27). How much over "a thousand" Haley leaves to Shelby's imagination. The hyperbole "half so handsome," changed to "not a bit handsomer" makes the comment more believable and less grammatical. Bit by bit, Haley's character is being attacked. The change at line 32 from the slave trader's description of Shelby's wine as being "excellent—first rate" to "capital, sir—first chop" again puts into Haley's mouth idiomatic expressions more in keeping with his character and background. He now slaps Shelby on the shoulder (line 33) instead of clapping him, as in the earlier version. The familiar tone and jocose behavior are intensified by the addition of "what'll you take?" at line 36.

Shelby's reaction is toned down by the deletion of intensifying italics at line 37. His tone of voice is more even, less excited, although it is perfectly apparent that he is annoyed by Haley's speech and actions and evaluation of his character. The more Haley talks, the more laconic Shelby becomes. The owner is forced by his financial straits to deal with a man he dislikes both as a type and as an individual, but he tries at all times to maintain control of himself.

Haley, of course, does not see his own offensiveness even when he is momentarily stopped by Shelby's decided "I say no, and I mean no" at line 44. Unabashed, the trader quickly shifts his strategy and tries for Harry. Shelby's reaction is one of curiosity. Haley has mentioned earlier that he would be willing to take a boy or a girl with Tom to make up a package worthy of the price Shelby is asking. Harriet's addition of Shelby's question at this point justifies Haley's explanation of the how small children were employed in Louisiana slave society and, by implication, elsewhere. In his explanation, Haley's character is more effectively pointed up by the changes, which involve both idiom and pronunciation: "line" to "yer branch," "rich folks" to "rich 'uns," "handsome article" to "handsome 'uns," "these stylish establishments you know" to "yr great palaces" (lines 50–55).

The abbreviated phrasing set off by dashes gives an almost casual tone to Haley's description. His knowledge of the uses to which little boys were put is great; he will be brief in outlining the facts. The addition of the last two clauses is most effective, for it brings the description home to Shelby. It is his Eliza's Harry who is "this little devil, . . . such a comical, musical concern" (lines 56–58). Shelby's response is immediate but qualified as he vacillates between his need for cash and his disinclination to divide families. In his reply, wavering though it is, he supplies Haley with the word which the latter will presently adopt as the leitmotif of an extended self-defense: "humane." But for the moment Haley only indicates that he is sympathetic; the problems arising from dealing with women are often "onpleasant," and in her revision Harriet not only changes to the dialect spelling, but repeats the word (lines 63, 65). Of course, the experienced slave trader has all the answers ready. Get the mother away for a time, sell the child, and then placate her with trinkets. It is all in the management. Haley waxes anecdotal, and Shelby sits back to listen.

In the manuscript Harriet stopped after Haley's first story, but in the *Era* text she added lines 93 to 151, and in so doing gives greater depth to both her characters. Haley, as Harriet indicates, is "as if . . . driven," but not "actually" by the "force of truth" in its usual sense, "to say a few words more" (lines 101–2). He is a man who has solved all his problems and is at peace, having convinced himself that the trade has not hardened him, that he is a humane man, and that he is successful because of his skill at management. His articles are in good condition, "in good case, fat and likely," and he loses "as few as any man in the business" (lines 108–9). He is a man of principles and has "stuck to 'em" (line 116). Others, such as his "good hearted" friend Tom Loker, have been unable to adapt, but his own methods obviously pay off. This "second Wilberforce" (line 97) has found both that "a little humanity thrown in along, goes a heap farther than all your jawin and crackin," and that "it pays better, . . . depend on't" (lines 146–48).

Mr. Shelby has been fascinated by Haley's lecture; he has described himself as a "humane" man only to have Haley unintentionally turn the word on him and define it in a way which is annoyingly close to the manner in which an abolitionist might define Shelby's humanity. That Haley has supplied him with all the rationalizations he needs, even though he refuses to accept them immediately, is a tribute to Mr. Shelby's character. He says that he must think the matter over and will tell Haley in the morning. Had Harriet cut off the conversation as indicated by the deleted section of the manuscript, there would have been more reason for Shelby's delay; both he and Haley are rather straightforward characters. When she continued the conversation in the manuscript, she left the way open for further development of Shelby's predicament. Later, when she added lines 93–151 in the *Era* text, what must have been the common problem of a sensitive man saddled with both humanitarian and monetary responsibilities is developed in such a way as to help the reader both identify with Shelby's conflict and see how much more of a man he really is than would have been perceptible had this addition never been written.

The variants recorded in the comparison of leaf C—the description of Uncle Tom's cabin (pp. 215–16)—and the *Era* text also offer some interesting insights into Harriet's writing technique. The change from "the masters dwelling" to "his master's dwelling" (line 3) and the addition of the phrase "every summer" (line 4) to the description of the garden patch imply a not unhappy relationship of slave to master. The master is regarded personally, not objectively, and there is continuity to a slave's existence on the Shelby place. The change from "the dwelling" to "it" in line 7 seems to have been ill-advised, for the pronoun has a double antecedent until the reader reaches the end of the sentence. On the other hand, the emendation of "with" to "by" (line 7) in the description of the flowers is an improvement, for the change implies activity and vitality on the part of the plants. The change from "building" to "rough logs" (line 10) presents a more accurate visual image. In the revised version, the concept of vitality is further emphasized by the repetition of the season and the suggestion of an "indulgent" earth which permitted the flowers to "unfold" (perhaps the correction of a typographical error, "enfold," which makes no sense) and display their "splendors" (lines 10–13). All these changes give the cabin and its immediate surroundings a relationship with nature which they did not have in the original.

The last paragraph of the leaf contains a few changes which are either typographical or show the care with which Harriet emended her text. The change in tense from "presides" to "presided" (line 16) plays down the continuity of Chloe's actions in the kitchen and emphasizes the dual role that Chloe plays, that of cook to the Shelbys and wife to Tom. She has finished cooking for others and now will begin cooking for her family. When she is at home, her duties are not limited to just the kitchen; she has many "territories" (line 20), not just one.

The change from "old man" to "ole man" (line 20) is representative of many changes Harriet would make in Chloe's speech and the speech of other Negro characters when she later revised *The National Era* serial text for the 1852 book version. Some fifty-five dialectal variants in Chloe's speech are to be found in the 1852 and 1879 editions of the novel. Here in the manuscript stage can be seen an instance of a problem that was to plague the author, and one which she never really solved: the consistent, accurate representation of Negro speech.

Leaf D (p. 217) again reveals how careless she was with her punctuation. She used the dash liberally and all other marks sparingly. The *Era* editor or typesetter did a respectable job except for the misplaced semicolon in *Era* text, line 3. More important, but still minor, are the substantive changes in the *Era* text. Tom has been working at his slate, practicing his letters. In the manuscript, George takes the slate, dashes off the correct letters, and returns the slate to Tom, who begins again, holding the pencil in his work-hardened hands. The change for the *Era* text is no great improvement. "On his slate" is changed to "for his edification" (lines 7–8), thus accurately describing the manner in which George, young scholar turned teacher, proudly exhibits his knowledge. The emendation at the end of the sentence, "patiently recommenced" (line 9) replacing "began patiently again," is certainly an improvement.

The only two other substantive changes in the passage are the dropping of the "fat" from "bacon fat" (line 12) in the manuscript text—seeming to imply that life is good enough in the cabin for Chloe to use something better than fatback to grease her griddle—and the shifting of George's question in the next paragraph closer to the beginning of the sentence (line 17), an improvement in that the speaker is more quickly identified. The *Era,* or the intermediate manuscript, also corrects the manuscript's "browing" to the intended "browning" (line 19).

Leaf E (p. 220) exhibits the punctuational chaos which recurs many times. Here again the *Era* typesetter brings some order to the passage, but makes two errors, both of which were corrected for the book. At line 20 in the *Era* text, the manuscript reads "'. . . you & the poor'—". The *Era* follows suit, but eliminates the ampersand. The book (I, 64) moves the dash inside the quotation marks to read "'. . . you and the poor—'" and thus more clearly implies the breaking off of the sentence. Tom cannot bring himself to say "children." The other mistake is the placement of a period at the end of line 30. Harriet had been linking clauses with dashes; the *Era* substitutes some semicolons and a period, and in doing so divides a sentence in the middle. Where the *Era* read "jewels. You are" the novel reads "jewels, you" correctly identifying the "jewels" phrase as adverbial. At line 25, however, the *Era* text mistakenly changes the manuscript's "onto" to "on," thus warping the intended meaning.

At lines 10–12 of the *Era* text, the manuscript reads "If I must be sold or all go to rack why let me be sold." The *Era* passage is longer and more explicit: "If I must be sold, or all the people on the place and everything go to rack, why, let me be sold." The general "all" of the manuscript is expanded and personalized to indicate that not only the people but the place that has been their home must be put up for sale if Tom does not agree to be sold. The additional information here more than outweighs the deletion in the manuscript a few lines later when the phrase "sell em all" is cut to the *Era*'s sell "all" (line 19). The "all" is still effective, because it functions as an all-inclusive reference.

The major changes in the text take place toward the end of the passage. The manuscript, corresponding to *Era* text lines 31–32, is more extensive. Where the *Era* reads "in life's great straits & mighty griefs you feel but one sorrow," the manuscript reads "in lifes great straits & mighty griefs ye feel all but one anguish—for the heart can feel no more than 'all.'" Both versions are poorly stated. What Harriet meant is that there is one sorrow, one grief in a woman's life in relation to which all other moments of sadness are but pale copies. The *Era* text pares the passage to "one sorrow," as if to say that deep sadness comes only once. The manuscript emphasizes the "all"; once one has felt the great pain, nothing can approach it again and nothing can surpass it. The manuscript version is ineffectually redundant, but that of the *Era* cuts back too much.

The last paragraph, on the other hand, is effectively expanded in the *Era* text. The abruptness of the change in Eliza's life is brought home with the addition of the statement that she did not know as recently as earlier in the day that she would be planning to run off to Canada. A slave family, the wording implies, could be broken up, literally, in a matter of hours. The next sentence in the *Era* text, telling the reader that George is already at the point of running off, stresses the idea that he, unlike docile Tom, has been pushed too far. Eliza, then does not precipitate the running off; in fact, she is helping George by going first. He will not have to worry about her and Harry as all three escape, nor will he have to risk capture by coming back for them later. Her need to get word to him now is not, however, based on her desire to tell George where she has gone so that he will not worry about her, but is rather a declaration that she has gone ahead to prepare a place for him. Yet the uncertainty of the outcome of her decision is emphasized by the unfinished sentence in both texts: "if I never see him again —" which the *Era* text weakens by concluding with a period instead of a dash (lines 41–42).

What, then, can be seen in a comparison of the manuscript leaves and the newspaper text? Most importantly, it reinforces the fact, already stated, that Harriet did revise, in spite of those who have concluded otherwise: she made many changes from the inception of the idea of a fairly short serialized story to the publication of the two-volume novel. Though the changes were both good and poor, in general the newspaper text can be seen as an unquestioned improvement over the earlier drafts.

Chapter 7.

THE NOVEL
AND ITS REVISIONS

Many of the textual variants in the various stages of *Uncle Tom's Cabin* cannot be ascribed to the author's revisionary pen. House rules both at the *National Era* and at Jewett's played important roles in producing the finished product. If Bailey's printer supplied much of the punctuation Harriet omitted, Jewett's printer further increased the formality of the pointing to conform with the practice of his firm. Consistently, the Jewett printer substituted a comma followed by a dash for the *Era's* simple dash. Consistently, this printer used lowercase for the initial letter of "North" and "South" and their derivative adjectives. Consistently he changed the chapter titles from lowercase italic to uppercase roman type; spelled "gaily" with two "*y*'s" "Oh" without the "*h*," "aint" as "ain't"; dropped the " *'s*" from the possessive of "mistress"; capitalized the initial letter of "mass'r" and spelled it "Mas'r"; and tended to hyphenate common noun-noun and adjective-noun combinations such as "barn-yard," "corn-cake," and "drawing-room" which the *Era* printer had left as two words. In addition, he did not feel bound by his predecessor's paragraphing, changing it at will. Thus, although he corrected many of the typographical errors in the *Era* and clarified a good deal of the newspaper's ambiguous punctuation, he also created his own problems and himself set into type some absurdly obvious misprints.

There are, however, literally thousands of significant changes which are not attributable to house rules or printers' corrections but are probably authorial in origin. Some of these involve only a single word or, in the case of an unusual word of a regional or dialectal nature, a single letter, e.g. "de" to "der" or "chirrup" to "cherrup." Many are more extensive, e.g., the addition of chapter titles and head quotations, the addition or deletion of a paragraph or series of paragraphs, the addition of a preface and deletion of an epilogue. If this study were an edition of *Uncle Tom's Cabin,* each and every variant, both substantive and accidental, would be recorded and commented upon. But the purpose here is to chart the migratory pattern, as it were, not to locate the resting place of each bird of the species each night. To that end, the changes that Harriet made in chapter titles and head quotations throughout the story as it moved from newspaper to novel will be discussed first. Then the variants between manuscript leaves F-I and the novel text, further proof of authorial revision of the *Era* text, will be examined. Third, several passages which contain major emendations will be reproduced, as well as a representative passage in which a significant number of single changes appear. Finally, the puzzling events which took place between March 1 and April 1, 1852, will be discussed because, although the novel was published March 20 and revised copy for it was being sent to Jewett well into March, there are significant variations between the text of the *Era* and that of the novel at a time when the story was still being issued in serial form and the *Era* printer could have set his type from the proof sheets or final copy of the book.

As for the chapter titles and headnotes, the *Era* and the novel agree in having titles for chapters 1 through 7, no title for 8, titles for 9 through 23, and titles for 40 and the remaining chapters. Titles for chapters 24 through 39 were lacking in the *Era* but were supplied in revision for the novel as follows:

Chapter

24	Foreshadowings	32	Dark Places
25	The Little Evangelist	33	Cassy
26	Death	34	The Quadroon's Story
27	"This Is the Last of Earth"	35	The Tokens
28	Re-Union	36	Emmeline and Cassy
29	The Unprotected	37	Liberty
30	The Slave Warehouse	38	The Victory
31	The Middle Passage	39	The Stratagem

The title for chapter 22, "The Grass Withereth—The Flower Fadeth," the same in both texts, came from Isaiah 40:7. The numbering of the chapters that follow 19 does not agree, however, because the *Era* carried two chapters designated as 19, one on October 16 and the other on November 6. Consequently, the *Era* concluded with 44, whereas the final chapter in the book is numbered 45. To avoid confusion, all chapter numbers cited here will be to the book version.

Harriet began to add head quotations in chapter 12. The passage for this chapter, which appears in both texts, is misquoted from Jeremiah 31:15; she was probably depending upon her memory. Chapters 13 and 15 through 25 have no quotations in either text. The four lines below the title of chapter 14 in both texts were taken, according to Kenneth Lynn, from Chateaubriand's *In Atala*.[1] Chapter 26 in both texts opens with two lines from Thomas Moore's "Weep Not for Those," one of his *Sacred Songs.* The quotation for chapter 26 in the *Era*, which is minus a title, becomes the title for the corresponding chapter (27) in the novel; it is John Quincy Adams's last words. The next chapter quotation appears at 31 in both texts. The *Era* text slightly misquotes and misattributes. In the novel, the quotation is accurate and the lines correctly noted as coming from "Hab." for Habakkuk, not from "Heb.," Hebrews. The quotation for chapter 32, unattributed in either text, is from Psalms 74:20. The passages which introduce the

[1]Lynn, 148.

next two chapters are from the same place: "Eccl. 4:1." The source is noted in the first chapter but omitted from the second in the *Era*. The novel records the source in both places.

Harriet relied on memory for the five lines at the head of chapter 35, taking them from Byron's *Childe Harold's Pilgrimage* but misquoting a word or two. The full reference, given in neither text, is to canto IV, stanzas xxi–xxii. For chapter 37 in both texts Harriet used a passage from a speech by the celebrated Irish orator, John Philpot Curran (1750–1817): "No matter with what solemnities he may have been devoted upon the altar of slavery, the moment he touches the sacred soil of Britain, the altar and the God sink together in the dust, and he stands redeemed, regenerated, and disenthralled, by the irresistible genius of universal emancipation." No source appears in the *Era* text and only "Curran" is added in the novel. The lines are taken from a "speech on Behalf of Archibald Rowan, Esq. for a Libel in the Court of King's Bench, Ireland, on the 29th of January 1794."[2] For chapter 38 Harriet quoted I Corinthians 15:57 in both texts; for the next chapter she used Proverbs 4:19 both times. She affixed her last head quotation at chapter 40, consisting of eight lines, slightly misquoted, from a hymn by William Cullen Bryant entitled "Blessed Are They That Mourn," first published in Henry Sewall's *Collection of Psalms and Hymns for Social and Private Worship.*[3]

[2] This speech would have been available to Harriet in John Philpot Curran, "Speeches," and in other sources.

[3] H. B. Stowe to Horace Mann, March 20, 1852, in the Massachusetts Historical Society; Harriet Beecher Stowe, "1879 Introduction," xx, xxii. Forrest Wilson, 282, adds the Duke of "Argyle" [*sic*], the Earl of Shaftesbury, and Charles Kingsley to the list in the Mann letter. The Kingsley copy is in the Berg Collection at the NYPL with a presentation letter dated March 20, 1852. The author has been unable to locate the other copies or letters. Charles James Ruthven Howard, 12th Earl of Carlisle, informs me that the copy allegedly sent to his ancestor, the 7th Earl, is not to be found. Ian Douglas Campbell, 11th Duke of Argyll, says that, although he has many copies of Mrs. Stowe's books (his great-grandmother, the Duchess of Sutherland, and Mrs. Stowe were close friends), he does not have a copy of *Uncle Tom's Cabin.* In the absence of a response to the author's query to Anthony Ashley Cooper, 10th Earl of Shaftesbury, it may be assumed that his copy, too, is missing. Mr. Robert Mackworth-

It is not surprising that Harriet used the Bible extensively as a source of the quotations, nor is it remarkable that she remembered *Childe Harold's Pilgrimage* in view of her girlhood adoration of Byron. Her use of Chateaubriand, Curran, and Bryant, however, opens new doors to her reading habits and again illustrates the legendary retentiveness of her mind.

Manuscript leaves F through I (Appendix I, pp. 225–27, 230–31) were dealt with earlier to show that the author's hand was at work revising the text that Jewett set for the novel; they were used to demonstrate that Harriet made changes. Here the discussion will center on the illustrations they furnish of the types of changes she made. The texts for all four leaves are compared with the *Era* text (pp. 222–32). These leaves all cover passages in the chapters in the novel entitled "Cassy" and "The Quadroon's Story," chapters in which Tom defies Legree and Cassy reveals the plight of a black woman in slavery. Just before leaf F begins, Legree has been told that Cassy and Tom have helped to fill Lucy's basket with cotton, and has stated that he will do the weighing of the cotton and thus punish such evil conduct. The laboriously slow process of weighing the picked cotton is much better described in the *Era* than in the manuscript and thus the novel. The pickers, worn out at the end of a long day spent stooped over in the fields, are summoned to judgment before their master. The anonymity of the group is denied them in the *Era;* they are called forth "one by one" to have their baskets weighed and the weights entered on a slate. The phrases "one by one" and "As each was weighed" not only point up the process of judgment in a more detailed manner, but also slow the speed of the action and build suspense, for the reader knows that at least one of the pickers will be accused of being short of her weight. In the *Era* version, Harriet wrote a complex sentence giving the reader a sense of relief when Tom

---

Young, librarian of the Royal Collection, Windsor Castle, reports that there is no presentation copy there from Mrs. Stowe. None of the missing copies is in the British Museum.

passed inspection, but indicating that someone else would not. In the later, manuscript version, Tom merely "looked with an anxious glance" for the fate of the woman; in the earlier text, he "hesitated and lingered" (lines 6, 7), exposing himself to Legree's wrath for idling in case he were to be caught. There seems to be a greater concern on Tom's part in the first version, an attitude of self-sacrifice for others more in keeping with his characterization elsewhere than is conveyed by the almost furtive glance of the revised text.

Legree, it is clear, is not governed by any code of ethical behavior. In the *Era* text he said that Lucy would "catch it this time," revealing that he had been lying in wait for her. The preordained punishment is all but eliminated in the revised text, in which Legree threatens the poor woman with a punishment at an indefinite "pretty soon." In the next paragraph there is a change in the text which also affects the characterization of Legree. Originally, Harriet caused Legree to lose control of himself "for a moment" (line 23), implying that there was some restraint in the man; in the later, manuscript version, however, his rage completely possesses him. The *Era* described Legree's face as becoming "perfectly demoniac" (lines 23–24) when Cassy whispered something to him in French; the manuscript expands the wording: his "face became perfectly demoniacal in its expression," a change of little worth.

At lines 29–30 (p. 228) Legree tells Tom that "to-night yer begin to get yer hand in"; the novel is revised to "to night ye may jist as well begin to get your hand in," adding a more casual and thereby more terrible tone to the action. Flogging school, where dehumanization and bestiality are taught, "[might] jist as well begin" immediately. In keeping with the light tone, the "woman" (line 31) of the *Era* becomes a "gal" in the revision, another improvement. The tense of Tom's refusal to flog, "couldn't" (line 34) is corrected to a more emphatic present "cant." In the same line, an ambiguous "any way," which might mean either "by no method" or "no matter what happened to me," is changed in the manuscript to the dialectal "no way possible," removing the ambiguity. Legree's speech is coarsened here as it was in the revisions in the earlier manuscripts: "You've" becomes "ye'v," "enough" becomes "enough ont," "You'll" becomes "Ye'l," "learn" becomes "larn," "you" becomes "ye," "woman" becomes "gal" a second time; but the "tellin" (line 59) of the *Era* is revised to "telling" in the manuscript.

The addition of "that lay near" (line 37) to describe the location of the cowhide whip is an effective change pointing up the immediacy of punishment. In the revised text, Tom wipes away the blood from his face with one hand rather than two, somehow a more natural gesture, and the blood "trickled" down his face, a more precise verb than the original "was dripping" (line 42). When the manuscript's italics at line 45 (*"never shall do it"* becomes *"never* shall do it") were removed, the remaining italic *never* with an exclamation point added, was reinforced. The addition of "involuntarily" to *Era* line 50 points up the reflexes that Legree has conditioned into his slaves. They know that the first sign of rebellion or insubordination will be met with instant punishment. The slaves are surprised, delighted, filled with "a thrill of amazement" at Tom's reply, but knowing also what will follow, they "involuntarily looked at each other."

Leaf I picks up the story in the seventh paragraph of chapter 34, "The Quadroon's Story." Tom, badly beaten, lies in pain when Cassy arrives with water, as if in answer to his prayer. There are only a few emendations in the manuscript, but they are interesting. The manuscript retains the erroneous quotation mark found at the end of the sentence in the *Era* text (line 3). It is dropped from the novel. The *Era*'s "lower one than you ever can be" (line 5) is changed to the less convoluted "can ever be." The "water" of the *Era* text (line 8) is made "cold," and the manuscript drops the *Era*'s "over." In the same line Tom is asked to roll, "onto" the "pallaise"; rolling "over," a complete revolution, would involve his lacerated back. The *Era*'s "sensation of relief" (lines 10–11) becomes "sensible relief" in the manuscript and the novel, an improvement. In lines 12 and 13, "among the victims of outrage and brutality" in the *Era* becomes "with the victims of brutality," a change of mixed effect. "outrage and brutality" is redundant and should have been condensed, but Cassy does practice "among" the people, that is, perform medical services; she does not practice "with" them. The change from Tom's being "greatly relieved" by Cassy's ministrations in the *Era* (line 15) to "somewhat relieved" in the manuscript increases the severity of Tom's injuries. The formality of "the woman" for the *Era*'s "she" (line 16) reinforces the mystery surrounding Tom's benefactor. Tom does not know her social level; he has been told not to call her "Missis," and as yet he does not know her name. She is still, to him, here and in line 19, "the woman."

Most of the changes made in the revisionary leaves F through I are improvements; certainly Harriet thought they all were. She made other, more extensive changes, however.

When the reader who had followed the serial in the *Era* first opened his copy of volume one of the novel, he was not much surprised to discover that Mrs. Stowe had written a preface to her work. Because she had not known where she was going or how long it would take her to get there when she began the serial, she obviously could not have done a preface in June 1851 even had she wanted to. But now the book was complete, and she could attempt to sum it all up. The movement for social reform, she said, was finally reaching Africa. The "great principles of Christian brotherhood, . . . the hand of benevolence" were "searching into abuses, righting wrongs, alleviating distresses, and bringing to the knowledge and sympathies of the world the lowly, the oppressed, and the forgotten." Her object in writing the story of Uncle Tom had been "to awaken sympathy and feeling for the African race, as they exist among us." She had tried to write without bias, to present a fair picture accurately drawn. The day would come, she hoped, when the sketches would "be valuable only as memorials of what has long ceased to be." The future of the African race lay, she thought, in Africa, where an enlightened, Christianized, Western-oriented civilization would some day view its time in America as a period similar to that of the bondage of the Jews in Egypt (*UTC,* I, v–vi). These sentiments are not surprising; Harriet had not been, was not then, and would never become an immediate abolitionist, contemporary and later critical opinion notwithstanding.

The Preface is somewhat shorter than Jewett had anticipated. He began numbering his pages of text at thirteen, expecting Harriet to write at least six pages of preface; she wrote four. There is, therefore, a gap in the numbering between the end of the Table of Contents and the beginning of the text, and the gathering lacks a leaf. But Harriet did more, much more, than add a preface to the text that had appeared in the newspaper. She deleted a brief passage from Sam's sermon after Eliza's escape. In the *Era* Sam drew upon his religious training to compare himself to characters in illustrations such as those familiar to readers of Foxe's *Book of Martyrs:* "I wouldn't mind if dey burnt me live like dat ar old coon dar missus was a showin us in der catechise. I'd walk right up to de stake" (July 17, 1851). On page 117 of the novel he says he feels so strongly about his principles that he "wouldn't mind if dey burnt me 'live—I'd walk right up to de stake."

Harriet's first major addition to the novel text occurs at page 148. In the *Era* version, August 7, 1851 Tom was called from his cabin, meekly mounted Haley's wagon, was shackled, and expressed regret that young George Shelby was not there to say goodbye. Then, "Haley whipped up the horse, and with a steady, mournful look, fixed to the last on the old place, Tom was whirled away." The paragraph ended here. The next paragraph began, "They rattled on along the dusty road."

In reading this section over while she was revising, Harriet apparently noted that she had forgotten to account for the whereabouts of Mr. Shelby and set about to remedy the error. The novel text reads as follows:

> Haley whipped up the horses, and, with a steady, mournful look, fixed to the last on the old place, Tom was whirled away.
>
> Mr. Shelby at this time was not at home. He had sold Tom under the spur of a driving necessity, to get out of the power of a man whom he dreaded,—and his first feeling, after the consummation of the bargain, had been that of relief. But his wife's expostulations awoke his half-slumbering regrets; and Tom's manly disinterestedness increased the unpleasantness of his feelings. It was in vain that he said to himself that he had a *right* to do it,—that everybody did it,—and that some did it without even the excuse of necessity;--he could not satisfy his own feelings; and that he might not witness the unpleasant scenes of the consummation, he had gone on a short business tour up the country, hoping that all would be over before he returned.
>
> Tom and Haley rattled along the dusty road . . . .

Earlier, the original bargaining scene between Haley and Shelby had been expanded for the *Era*. In her additions, Harriet developed the character of Mr. Shelby more fully, an indication of her increasing awareness of what it might mean to a sensitive, basically humanitarian man to be forced to sell another human being. Shelby's reaction to the transaction with Haley is at first one of relief, but his conscience and his family will not let him rest. Harriet might have had him try to face the facts of the case, harden himself, and stand by his wife and family in the yard as Tom was taken away, but she made him no model slave owner, only an average one, and he flees. Significantly, he rejects the platitudinous rationalizations often mouthed by others, just as earlier, in the *Era* version, he rejected all the easy answers offered by Haley when they haggled over who was to be sold. Thus in two successive expansions of her original concept of a character, Harriet developed a flatly stated dichotomy within her creation and brought out the conflict through action on the character's part, thereby both deepening and enlarging Arthur Shelby.

Harriet puttered along, changing a word here, correcting an obvious printer's error there. When she reviewed chapter 12, she decided to omit the jab at Emerson and Carlyle as noted above and at another point excised a passage from the *Era* version, thereby shortening a time lapse. Originally the boat bearing Haley and Tom southward had progressed for some time before the woman with the child was taken on board and the child was sold from her. The *Era* text reads: "Women sewed, and children played. Suns rose and set, and men did business for some days, till the boat had passed far on her way" (August 28, 1851). Apparently not wishing to give her reader a respite from the nasty realities of slave life and the uncertainty of the morrow, Harriet eclipsed a bit of time. The emended version reads: "Women sewed, and children played, and the boat passed on her way" (*UTC,* I, 183). When she came to the footnote attacking Joel Parker, however, she passed it by, and it was printed on page 191 of the first volume of the novel.

Almost at the end of what was to be the copy for the first volume, Harriet decided that the business about Old Prue and her tickets, in the October 9 *Era,* probably was not clear. She had written that, after Miss Ophelia selected the rusks she wanted from the old woman, she

> paid for a couple of dozen, and the woman, undoing a soiled handkerchief, gave her a couple of tickets.
> "That shows I've sold you so many," said she.
> "I don't understand," said Miss Ophelia.
> "They counts the money and the tickets when I gets home, to see if I've got the change; and if I don't, they half kills me then."

In the novel version, matters are complicated:

> Miss Ophelia took out a couple dozen.
> "Thar's some tickets in that ar old cracked jug on the top shelf," said Dinah. "You, Jake, climb up and get it down."
> "Tickets,—what are they for?" said Miss Ophelia.
> "We buys tickets of her Mas'r, and she gives us bread for 'em."

"And they counts my money and tickets, when I gets home,
to see if I's got the change; and if I han't, they half kills me."

As she revised, Harriet was apparently dissatisfied with the
matter of the tickets. She obviously wanted to present Prue as a
woman untrustworthy in the eyes of her owners, one who
would, given the chance, run off and, as Miss Ophelia says a few
paragraphs later, "make [herself] a brute with" strong drink.
Prue must be made a drunk in order to explain why she steals
money. Harriet therefore had to work out a system of payment
which involved money for Prue to steal, but also involved
noncash payment of a type devised by her owners to prevent
Prue from getting her drinking money. The revised method, as
presented in the novel, is better than the *Era* version in that, in
the *Era,* Prue could collect money, "forget" to give tickets as
receipts, come out right with her owners, and steal cash. In the
novel, Prue is paid, at least part of the time, in tickets or script
rather than hard cash. But this system also has a weakness in that
Prue apparently still gets cash payment from some of her cus-
tomers. She will come home with tickets but can pocket the
change. Harriet's revisions clarify the process, but they stop too
soon.

Up to this point several excellent excerpts have illustrated
Harriet's attempts to use Negro dialect; the preceding conversation between Old Prue and Miss Ophelia, for example, reveals
a growing attention to this dialect and the author's desire to
improve the text. Details having to do with specific changes in
wording or pronunciation are discussed in Appendix II (pp.
233–44). This appendix shows that, regardless of Harriet's
possibly inexpert ear, regardless of inconsistencies that remain
in the speech of an individual character, sometimes even within
the same paragraph, the revisions made between the *Era* text
and the book version were extensive, were generally improvements, were occasionally of artistic importance, and decreased
in number as Harriet progressed with her story and became surer

176

of what she thought was a realistic representation of Negro speech.

The next extensive change occurs in the second volume in chapter 37 at page 238. In the March 4 *Era* she had gotten the Harrises safely to Canada. Now, going over the scene again, she decided that their arrival in a free country should be dealt with a little differently. Originally, the passage read:

> But the boat swept on—hours fleeted—night came down —and morning, bouyant and glorious, looked forth from her gates of gold, as George stood on deck, with his wife by his side. Then it rose before them, the blessed English shore—shores forever charmed with a holy power, by one touch, to dissolve every incantation of slavery, no matter in what langauge pronounced or by what unhallowed national compact sealed! Often in dream of heart-sick desire had they seen those shores, and woke to find them still afar; and now they gazed on them with scarce believing eyes, half fearing that they would fade from their sight.
>
> But this time it is no dream. The lordly boat swept up to the small town of A———, on the Canadian shore. George's breath grew thick and short—a mist gathered before his eyes—he silently pressed the little, trembling hand that lay on his arm—the bell rung—the boat stopped—scarcely knowing what he did, he looked out his baggage, and gathered his company.
>
> They are landed; the deed is done; and the boat swept away, with tears and embracings, the new-made freeman and his wife knelt down, and, with their wondering child in their arms, returned their solemn thanks to God.

The novel version differs in many respects:

> But the boat swept on. Hours fleeted, and, at last, clear and full rose the blessed English shores; charmed by a mighty spell,—with one touch to dissolve every incantation of slavery, no matter in what language pronounced, or by what national power confirmed.

George and his wife stood arm and arm, as the boat neared the small town of Amherstberg, in Canada. His breath grew thick and short; a mist gathered before his eyes; he silently pressed the little hand that lay trembling on his arm. The bell rang; the boat stopped. Scarcely seeing what he did, he looked out his baggage, and gathered his little party. The little company were landed on the shore. They stood still till the boat had cleared; and then, with tears and embracings, the husband and wife, with their wondering child in their arms, knelt down and lifted up their hearts to God!

The influence of the oration of John Philpot Curran, used as a headnote to the chapter, is obvious in both passages. The *Era* treatment appears to give a heroic quality to the description of the coming morning—"bouyant and glorious" morning looking "forth from her gates of gold" is reminiscent of the familiar "rosy-fingered dawn" of Homeric translations. There is also the rather effective contrast of the Harrises' past dream world with their present reality. In these respects, the *Era* text may be superior to that of the novel, but, on the other hand, the conclusion of the novel passage is better than its parallel in the *Era*.

Except for the repetition of "little party"—"little company," the conclusion of the revised paragraph is more direct and contains some very effective rhetorical devices. The addition of the fact that George and his family "stood still till the boat had cleared" points up the shock of their arrival, their inability to comprehend truly what had happened, and presents a more vivid picture than the simple "the deed is done" of the *Era* text. The change from "new-made freeman" to "husband" was also a wise choice, for it emphasizes that the relationship that has been existing in fact but denied by law is now sanctioned by both God and man. In other words, the term "husband" indicates an immediate corollary of being free. Again on the visual plane, the novel text's offering of thanks for their deliverance presents a

THE FUGITIVES ARE SAFE IN A FREE LAND. Page 238.

Cruikshank in the first British edition of *Uncle Tom's Cabin* visualized
this scene showing the arrival of George and his family in Canada.
Courtesy of Stowe-Day Memorial Library and Historical Foundation.

nice up-down juxtaposition: they "knelt down and lifted up their hearts to God!"

Although the death of Uncle Tom may have been the first section of the story written, Harriet continued to revise it, for a number of substantive changes appear in the novel text. She considerably emended one passage which appeared originally in the March 18, 1852, issue of the *Era*. After the description of Tom's death and George Shelby's sorrow, she had written:

> George spread his cloak in the wagon, had the body carefully disposed of in it, moving the seat, so as to give it room.
>
> "Such a fuss for a dead nigger!" said Legree.
>
> The word was a spark to a powder magazine. Prudence was never a virtue of the Kentucky boy. George turned, and with one indignant blow knocked Legree flat upon his face; and as he stood over him, blazing with wrath and defiance, he would have formed no bad personification of his great namesake, triumphing over the dragon.
>
> It was an imprudent thing, George; but it is evident you do not care for that. You are far beyond prudence just now.
>
> Some men, however, are decidely bettered by being knocked down.

For the novel (II, 282–83), a rather lengthy added passage significantly changes both George's character and his motivation:

> George spread his cloak in the wagon, and had the body carefully disposed of in it,—moving the seat, so as to give it room. Then he turned, fixed his eyes on Legree, and said, with forced composure.
>
> "I have not, as yet, said to you what I think of this most atrocious affair;—this is not the time and place. But, sir, this innocent blood shall have justice. I will proclaim this murder. I will go to the very first magistrate, and expose you."
>
> "Do!" said Legree, snapping his fingers, scornfully. "I'd like to see you doing it. Where you going to get witnesses?—how you going to prove it?—Come, now!"
>
> George saw, at once, the force of this defiance. There was not

a white person on the place; and, in all southern courts, the testimony of colored blood is nothing. He felt, at that moment, as if he could have rent the heavens with his heart's indignant cry for justice; but in vain.

"After all, what a fuss, for a dead nigger!" said Legree. The word was as a spark to a powder magazine. Prudence was never a cardinal virtue of the Kentucky boy. George turned, and with one indignant blow, knocked Legree flat upon his face; and, as he stood over him, blazing with wrath and defiance, he would have formed no bad personification of his great namesake triumphing over the dragon.

Some men, however, are decidedly bettered by being knocked down.

In the earlier version, Legree said little to justify George's anger. He had killed Tom, but he seemed almost remorseful when he refused payment for Tom's body—"I don't sell dead niggers"—and gave his permission to George to bury Tom where he liked. "Nigger" apparently did not bother George here; it is curious that the word set him off a few lines later. He had been under great strain, but his reaction came as a bit of a surprise because he did not know what had been going on on Legree's plantation. Apparently Harriet reacted somewhat the same way to the earlier version, for she felt constrained to point out twice that George was not a prudent man. George's lack of "prudence," then, makes him, in a way, just as intemperate as Legree, an emotional person who will strike out quickly and without "prudence" at what displeases him. Imprudence in George is not damnable, however, because the reader sympathizes with his motives, though the *Era* version showed him up, in effect, as too much like Legree.

When she revised, Harriet slowed George's progress toward the boiling point. She added a number of details that entirely change his character.First, George will try to avenge Tom's death through law; he will have Legree tried for murder. To do otherwise is to become a vigilante, to take the law into one's own hands and, in doing so, strike at the foundations of rational society. George is now pictured as superior to Legree, who operates outside the law, at least the law as it is recognized in a nonslavery society. But this is a slavery-based society, one which gives Legree the power to kill at will and, in turn, gives George no recourse against a man who kills a slave. It becomes apparent that the only way George can gain satisfaction in such circumstances is to fight on Legree's level, man to man, equal to equal, and to ignore the "law" upon which Legree's society is based.

Adding to George's frustration at being unable to handle the matter in a rational, "legal" manner is Legree's reply to his threat of arrest, a threat which in Ohio or Maine or any Northern state would have struck fear into a slave owner's heart. Legree knows where he is; George has forgotten. Through his taunting "I'd like to see you doing it," Legree becomes George's superior for the moment; George has made a fool of himself, and he knows it. Then Legree caps his taunt with the "dead nigger" line, and George explodes. Harriet no longer had to apologize for George's lack of prudence, for his actions have been justified.

As she neared the end of the forty-third chapter, she realized that she had tied together all but one of the loose ends in the matter of who went where with whom in the George-Eliza-Emmeline-Madame De Thoux party. Pressed for time, she added to the copy going to Jewett's stereotypers the following passage at II, 304:

> P.S.—It will be a satisfaction to some mother . . . to state that some inquiries, which were set on foot by Madame de Thoux, have resulted recently in the discovery of Cassy's son. Being a young man of energy, he had escaped, some years before his mother, and been received and educated by friends of the oppressed in the north. He will soon follow his family to Africa.

Perhaps there was no time to work this information into the context of the chapter, perhaps she was tired of revising and simply wanted to get the whole business over with, but whatever the reason, this sloppy and unnecessary additional information appears only in the novel.

The last major difference between the *Era* text and that of the novel occurs at the very end of the story. The novel concludes: "Not surer is the eternal law by which the millstone sinks into the ocean, than that stronger law, by which injustice and cruelty shall bring on nations the wrath of Almighty God!" The following passage, which appeared in the *Era* had, appropriately, been deleted:

> The 'Author of Uncle Tom's Cabin' must now take leave of a wide circle of friends, whose faces she has never seen, but whose sympathies, coming to her from afar, have stimulated and cheered her in her work.
>
> The thought of the pleasant family circles that she has been meeting in spirit weekly has been a constant refreshment to her, and she cannot leave them without a farewell.
>
> In particular, the dear little children who have followed her story have her warmest love. Dear children, you will one day be men and women; and she hopes that you will learn from this story always to remember and pity the poor and oppressed, and, when you grow up, show you pity by doing all you can for them. Never, if you can help it, let a colored child be shut out of school, or treated with neglect and contempt, because of his color. Remember the sweet example of little Eva, and try to feel the same regard for all that she did; and then when you grow up, we hope that the foolish and unchristian prejudice against people, merely on account of their complexion, will be done away with.
>
> Farewell, dear children, till we meet again.

Harriet may have felt that she had written a story for children; it is more likely, however, that she knew many children were in her audience and felt that the hope for change in the future lay with them rather than with their parents.

Besides the several preceding extensive revisions, the *Era* and the novel texts differ on a multitude of single points. The substitution of a single word or phrase rather than a paragraph is the more common type of emendation throughout the novel. Two typical paragraphs are presented here as the final illustration of Harriet's revisionary hand at work. They are taken from chapter 40, "The Martyr" (II, 269, in the novel and March 11, 1852, in the *Era*). The *Era* text appears in the left-hand column, the novel text in the right.

The men were two of them overseers of plantations in the vicinity, and others were some of Legree's associates at the tavern bar of a neighboring city, who has come for the interest of the sport. A more hard-favored set, perhaps, could not be imagined. Legree was serving brandy profusely round among them, as also among the negroes who	The men are, two of them, overseers of plantations in the vicinity; and others were some of Legree's associates at the tavern-bar of a neighboring city, who had come for the interest of the sport. A more hard-favored set, perhaps could not be imagined. Legree was serving brandy, profusely, round among them as also among the negroes, who had been detailed from the various plantations for this service; for it was an object to make every service of this kind, among the negroes, as much of a holiday as possible.
Cassy placed her ear to the knot hole, where she could overhear the conversations. A grave sneer overcast the dark, severe gravity of her face, as she listened and heard them divide out	Cassy placed her ear at the knot-hole; and, as the morning air blew directly towards the house, she could overhear a good deal of the conversation. A grave sneer overcast the dark, severe gravity of her face, as she listened, and heard them divide out

the ground, discuss the	the ground, discuss the
rival merits of the dogs,	rival merits of the dogs,
and give the orders about	give orders about
firing, and the treatment	firing, and the treatment
in case of capture.	of each in case of capture.

There is no reason for the tense change in the first line; it should have been left "were" as in the *Era* text. The addition of the "holiday" passage ties in nicely with the scene in the New Orleans slave warehouse in which Harriet had noted that the slaves were to be kept singing and happy at all times. The added passage about the wind supplies a factual detail which explains how Cassy could hear so well through her knot-hole. The additional "of each" in the last line seems to foreshadow Legree's intent to replace Cassy with Emmeline when the two were caught. In short, except for the change of tense, all of these emendations improve the text.

A previous chapter has examined the probable chronology of publication with special emphasis on the probable date of completion of the manuscript that Jewett used as a copy for his stereotypers. If it was as soon as late February or early March, 1852, some problems arise, for four examples of significant changes occur in issues of the *Era* published after March 1. The book was published March 20, but the serial ran in the *Era* until April 1, and two of those four examples appear in it after the March 20 publication date of the book.

What Harriet must have done was to make two copies of the last chapters, one for Bailey and one for Jewett. Conjecturally, one of the twins, Hattie and Eliza, who were fifteen, made them for her; Harriet then sent Bailey's copy off, as Washington was farther than Boston. Before she let Jewett's copy go, she checked it over to see if she or the girls had made any mistakes; as she read, she made changes, and the emendations appeared in the copy sent to Jewett. This hypothesis may explain the variants in the texts preceding publication of the book, but it does not account for those after it.

It would seem logical for Bailey to have procured a copy of Jewett's book and set his type from it. For the *Era* issue of March 18, Jewett surely had galley or page proof for the *Era* to use if Bailey had wanted it, or for Harriet if she had wanted to send it to Bailey. Yet Bailey seems not to have worked from sheets supplied by Jewett. He did not change his chapter numbering to correspond with Jewett's, nor did he use Jewett's paragraphing. He did not capitalize and he did not italicize according to Jewett. Finally, when the issue of March 18 is compared with the book version of chapters 40, 41, and 42, a multitude of variants appear. The following list gives the significant variants found when a sample page (II, 275) is compared with the parallel passage in the *Era* for March 18:

Book	*Era*
that	that awful
soul?	soul—
burning!	burning?
quiet	[omit]
imbruted	Poor, embruted
instruments	instrument
instant	instant that
that	that
we's	we've
hopes	hope
for it	for't
bed, of some refuse cotton, for him to lie down on	bed for him to lie on
tired, and wanted it for himself. He brought	tired, and brought
Tom's	his
"O	[omit]
Quimbo, "we's awful	Sambo, when he revived a little, "we's real
faintly	[omit]
a standin	standin
so	[omit]

One	one
life, him	life and his
everlasting	ever-lasting
and power to save	and his power to forgive
	and save
savage	brutal
this	of this
believe!—I	believe I
Lord Jesus have mercy on us!"	[omit]
critters	critturs
it'll	I could

If Bailey, for some reason, could not have obtained a copy of Jewett's sheets for his March 18 issue, he certainly had access to them for his issue of March 25, and perhaps he used them, for there are no substantive variants in this issue that cannot be accounted for on the basis of typographical errors or house rules. Bailey unbent only twice, printing "O" where Jewett had "O" and where he had been using "Oh" for the past nine months.

But if he used the novel for his copy text for this issue, he did not use it for the final issue, which has the following interesting variants. Bailey does not print Harriet's "P.S." concerning Cassy's brother, has "sadly" where the novel reads "proudly," "1851" for the novel's "1850," "not, as they do" for "not have connived at the extension of slavery, in our national body; the sons of the free states would not, as they do," "B———, from Carolina" for the novel's "B———," "Full black; from Georgia" for the novel's "Full black," and "black of Virginia" for "Black." Finally, and oddest of all, an oversight where a change should have appeared is especially significant: the first line of page 311 in the novel reads "The story of 'old Prue,' in the second volume," and exactly the same line appears in the *Era,* where the reference to "second volume" makes no sense at all.

Again, the only answer seems to be two copies of the manuscript: one sent to Bailey and one to Jewett. There is further support for this theory. In a letter from Harriet to Horace Mann written from Boston on March 20, 1852, she says, "To day I have taken my pen from the last chapter of 'Uncle Tom's Cabin' & I think you will understand me when I say that I feel as if I had written some of it almost with my hearts blood—" The novel appeared the day the letter was written; hence, Harriet surely must have been saying that her revised or emended copy for the *Era* had been completed that day. As this letter is extant and in Harriet's hand, it deserves more credence than the letters to Prince Albert and Macaulay which she reprints in the "1879 Introduction," which are not extant and were dated March 20, 1852, "Brunswick, Me." The letter to Mann, in which she says that she intends to write "McAuley . . . the Earl of Carlysle . . . Charles Dickens & lastly . . . Prince Albert," and asks advice as to how to proceed cannot be taken as proof that she wrote that day. On the basis of the theory that there were two manuscript copies, the "last chapter" referred to in the letter to Mann must have been the final pages of Bailey's *Era* copy. This deduction explains why Bailey did not set type from the novel text consistently: he depended on manuscript revisions from the author.

According to Forrest Wilson, when Calvin Stowe was looking through a copy of the first edition, he came across the Joel Parker footnote, thought "it might make trouble," and urged his wife to have it removed. Dutifully, she "wrote Jewett instructing him to chip Dr. Parker's name from the stereotype-plate of page 191."[4] However, the letter arrived at the print shop just as the first trickles of the eventual flood of orders were beginning. Three thousand of the five thousand copies had been sold the first day, the remainder the following two days. Jewett immediately started a second printing; he either forgot about or ignored the request.

Joel Parker objected to the footnote. Writing to Calvin on May 8, he said that he "was filled alike with sorrow and surprise to find [his] Christian character and professional reputation

[4] Forrest Wilson, 285.

assailed so injuriously from a source which [Calvin's] counsels might fairly be supposed to govern."[5] An enclosed note to Harriet stated that she had "made this assault" without conferring with him or seeking "information from some reliable source" and so injured his "professional reputation and usefulness" that he felt "compelled to demand a full and public retraction of the calumny referred to."[6]

Calvin replied on the eleventh from Brunswick that Harriet had used Parker's name without Calvin's knowledge or consent, that they both had agreed it was wrong and had taken steps to have it erased, that Harriet was now in Brooklyn and would be pleased to see him to set matters straight, and finally that he was "glad to find that [Parker considered] the statement a 'calumny' and a 'serious matter.'"[7]

Harriet was in no hurry to answer Parker. She knew what she had read. If he wanted to set things right, let him publish his own retraction. But he was not in a waiting mood. On May 19, he wrote again, this time directly to Harriet, and refused to retract anything. Her reply, unfortunately, was entrusted to a friend of brother Henry's, who gave it to one of his employees, who gave it to the company mail clerk, who finally mailed it; the hand-to-hand process delayed the letter a week. Before he received it, Parker had written a third letter and placed the matter in the hands of the famous lawyer Benjamin F. Butler. He would sue.[8]

In a note to Parker published in the New York *Tribune* on June 24, Harriet said that her quotation of Parker's speech was entirely innocent of malice, that she had simply quoted what she had seen in both British and American newspapers, and that since "during all this time [he] had never publicly contradicted the truth of this representation, . . . [she] understood [his] silence to be an admission of its correctness." She was "heartily glad to find that a sentiment so shocking to every Christian

[5]*Ibid.*   [6]*Ibid.*, 286.   [7]*Ibid.*   [8]*Ibid.*, 287.

mind" was not his, and she would "order the immediate altera-
tion of the paragraph in question."[9]

The comedy of errors was not to be over for some time, but
the textual implications are clear at this point.[10] Although
Harriet said on June 24 that she would have page 191 corrected,
it had been corrected for some time. The copies labeled "fiftieth
thousand" appeared in late May; by mid-June the book was
selling at the rate of 10,000 copies a week.[11] The footnote
appeared for the last time in some copies slugged "60th
thousand," which must have been published in late May or
early June. When Harriet wrote the letter, Parker, if he had
been checking each succeeding printing of the book, would have
been pleased to find that, even before Harriet's note appeared in
the newspapers, the previously offensive passage now read, "a
trade which is the vital support of an institution which some
American divines tell us has no evils but such as are inseparable
from any other relations in social and domestic life"—no quotation marks, no italics, and no footnote.

Near the end of July 1852 Harriet received her first royalty
check on the sales of the first three months. "It amounted to
$10,300."[12]

In the April 1 issue of the *Era* Bailey noted that the "edition
of five thousand [issued] on the 20th of March . . . [had]
already been exhausted, and another edition of five thousand
[had] appeared." William Harned, publishing agent in New
York who had offered the book for sale in the columns of the *Era*
beginning April 11, announced in an advertisement in the June
17 issue that 50,000 copies had been sold in eight weeks.
Essentially the same information appeared in the June 15 issue
of *Norton's Literary Gazette,* and there the editors dramatized the
point by explaining that the 50,000 copies translated into

[9]*Ibid.,* 288.

[10]*Ibid.,* 281–89, 307–22. See also a letter from Harriet to Charles Sumner,
Brunswick, Sept. 27, 1852, in the Barrett Collection, Univ. of Virginia.

[11]Forrest Wilson, 295.

[12]*Ibid.,* 300.

135,000 SETS, 270,000 VOLUMES SOLD.

UNCLE TOM'S CABIN

FOR SALE HERE.

AN EDITION FOR THE MILLION, COMPLETE IN 1 Vol., PRICE 37 1-2 CENTS.
" " IN GERMAN, IN 1 Vol., PRICE 50 CENTS.
" " IN 2 Vols., CLOTH, 6 PLATES, PRICE $1.50.
SUPERB ILLUSTRATED EDITION, IN 1 Vol., WITH 153 ENGRAVINGS,
PRICES FROM $2.50 TO $5.00.

The Greatest Book of the Age.

Uncle Tom's Cabin, published in many editions and translations, set
sales records that stood for decades. The beginning of the flood is
suggested in this early handbill. *Courtesy of the Harry Birdoff Collection.*

"3,000 reams of medium paper, weighing 30 lbs. to the ream—90,000 lbs. of paper; and that three or four Adams's power presses [had] been kept running at the most rapid rate, day and night, and that from 125 to 200 book-binders [had] been constantly at work in binding. The weight of the books, when bound, would amount to 110,000 lbs. or fifty-five tons." On August 15, Jewett announced that sales had passed 100,000;[13] by the end of September, the figure surpassed 150,000;[14] on the first anniversary of the day of sales Jewett claimed that over 305,000 copies had been sold "with demand as heavy as ever."[15] On January 27, 1853, Jewett's advertisement in the *Era* claimed over 1,000,000 copies sold in England and America.[16]

Uncle Tom's Cabin happened to Harriet only once. She was never again to write a book which would sell on such a scale, partially because she was never again to write as well. When she attempted to prove the truth of what she had said in the *Cabin* by providing a factual *Key* in 1853, the book sold only on the reputation of its author; likewise, the collected sketches entitled *Uncle Sam's Emancipation*, published in 1853, the recollections of her foreign tour (*Sunny Memories of Foreign Lands*) in 1854, and the expanded *May Flower* of 1855 were bought by people who expected another *Uncle Tom's Cabin*. They were disappointed. Harriet's other slavery novel, *Dred* (1856), lacked the indignation of the *Cabin* and was set in an area she had never seen, populated by people she did not know. The remnants of a large press run were sold at a loss.

[13] *Ibid.*, 302.
[14] *Ibid.*, 324.
[15] *Ibid.*, 341.
[16] All the British editions were pirated, of course, there being no international copyright at the time. For a discussion of the various issues of the first edition based on a study of 288 copies, see the author's article "The First Editions of *Uncle Tom's Cabin:* A Bibliographical Study," *Papers of the Bibliographical Society of America* 65 (1971), 365–82.

Between 1858 and 1884 she wrote twenty-four novels and collections of stories, one volume of verse, three collections of biographical sketches, four volumes of semi-belletristic material, a defense of Lady Byron, and hundreds of sketches for newspapers and magazines. Only in those works in which she drew upon her New England heritage—*The Minister's Wooing* (1859), *The Pearl of Orr's Island* (1862), *Oldtown Folks* (1869), *Oldtown Fireside Stories* (1872), and *Poganuc People* (1878)—did she approach the power of *Uncle Tom's Cabin.* In these, she wrote from the heart and knew whereof she spoke.

The decline from the heights of 1852 mystified her as much as had the rapid rise. "God wrote it," she said of *Uncle Tom's Cabin,* and she believed it. But she also believed that having been divinely inspired once, she had been forever blessed; and when the inspiration was no longer there, she became confused. Perhaps she thought that the times had passed her by, and she attempted to join them by writing what was popular, what was selling. Thus she ground out three "domestic" novels in the seventies. They sold respectably, but not like her *Cabin.* The feeling was there—Audacia Dangereyes is probably modeled on Victoria Woodhull, the free-love advocate and women's-rightist who had broken the scandal concerning brother Henry Ward Beecher's alleged adultery—but the book is tedious. *We and Our Neighbors,* the sequel to *My Wife and I,* is filled with examples of innocence and Christianity triumphing over sacrilege and loose living. *Pink and White Tyranny* attacks divorce. Here, the preacher, always an integral part of her character but sublimated in the *Cabin*, had gotten the better of the novelist in her.

A scene which took place in Tremont Temple in Boston on January 1, 1863, illustrates well the heights of success to which *Uncle Tom's Cabin* carried her, from which she fell, and to which she later tried to return. A great crowd had waited most of the night to hear whether or not Lincoln would keep his promise and free the slaves. Finally a formally attired gentleman mounted the platform and announced that "the President [had] signed" the Emancipation Proclamation. In moments, everyone was cheering and waving. Then someone pointed to the gallery and shouted, "Mrs. Stowe! Mrs. Stowe!" The chant grew louder and louder; eager hands opened a path for Harriet. She moved slowly to the railing, a shabby little figure, her bonnet knocked askew by the jostling crowd, and she bowed and waved, tears coursing down her cheeks. The woman who had put down slavery—"the little woman who started this great war," Lincoln had called her—could bow and daub at her eyes with her handkerchief. The whole audience was on its feet. Eventually the cheering subsided, and the audience went home. But to her death on July 1, 1896, in her Hartford home, Harriet could never quite bring herself to accept the fact that she would never again create a work with the moral power or emotional appeal of *Uncle Tom's Cabin*.

Appendices

Appendix I:

COLLATIONS

The materials of this appendix collate corresponding passages in two or more of the stages of composition through which *Uncle Tom's Cabin* went from holograph sheets to the texts for the *National Era* serialized story and the first edition of the book.

Important to this study of revisions and changes are the nine extant manuscript "leaves"—A through I—all in Harriet Beecher Stowe's handwriting and each with a history of its own.

Leaf A, labeled at the top "Part of First Draught of the 1st Chapter of Uncle Tom's Cabin," ruled, white, about 6⅞" wide by 8⅜" long, written on both sides, formerly owned by Jacob Podell, New York, used and published in part by Chester Jorgenson, is now in the Literature Collection, Manuscripts Division, New York Public Library.

Leaf B, on paper like that of Leaf A, written on both sides, is in the Barrett Collection, Alderman Library, University of Virginia, and is labeled "Part of the 1st Chapter of Uncle Tom's Cabin 1st Draught."

Leaf C, labeled *"Uncle Tom,"* is, however, only in facsimile, one side. Charles Stowe, 160; Charles and Lyman Stowe, 160; Forrest Wilson, 270; Johanna Johnston, *Runaway to Heaven,* plate no. 6.

Leaf D also survives only in a facsimile copy, one side, labeled

"Fac-simile of Manuscript Page of 'Uncle Tom's Cabin' "; New York *Press,* Aug. 28, 1889 (clipping graciously sent to the author by the late Philip Brewster, Litchfield, Conn.).

Leaf E, unruled, bluish-gray, same dimensions as Leaf A, written on both sides, is on permanent loan from the Connecticut State Library to the Stowe-Day Foundation Library, Hartford, Conn.

Leaf F, unruled, blue, about 7¾" square, cut from a larger leaf, written only on one side, has a very uneven top edge and a few partial letters of a mutilated line at the top. It is in the Schlesinger Library, Radcliffe; a facsimile appears in Lyman Stowe's biography, facing p. 187, and, in part, in Richard Burton, "The Author of Uncle Tom's Cabin," *Century Magazine* 20 (1896), 700.

Leaves G and H, unruled, bluish-gray, about 7¾" wide and 10" long, numbered "2" and "3" respectively in the upper right-hand corners, both written on one side only, are in the Stowe-Day Foundation Library, Hartford, Conn.

Leaf I, off-white, of the same approximate size as Leaves G and H, is also in the Stowe-Day Foundation Library, Hartford, Conn. The recto is numbered "7"; on the verso is the beginning of a letter: "J P Jewett / Dear Sir / It seems to me that it would" in Harriet's hand.

Leaves A and B contain the conversation between Mr. Shelby and Haley, the slave trader, about the sale of little Harry found in the novel, I, 17–19. Leaves C and D pick up the story on pages 38–39, where Uncle Tom's cabin is described. Leaf E covers the part on pages 64–65 in which Tom decides to let himself be sold to save the others. Leaves F, G, and H form a broken sequence on pages 194–96 of volume two, which cover Tom's refusal to whip another slave. The final leaf, I, begins chapter 34, page 198, where Cassy steals out at night to tend to Tom's wounds.

The remainder of this appendix comprises a succession of collated passages—limited largely by the small coverage of the nine manuscript leaves. All differences are recorded except that no attempt has been made to indicate the exact length and the spacing of Harriet's great number of dashes of varying lengths, usually preceded and followed by wide, unequal spaces. For those dash marks which the *Era* retained, the printer used closed 1-em dashes. It should be pointed out, too, that Harriet's general use of a truncated figure "2" for the ampersand—which the *Era* converted to the word "and"—is represented in this book by the symbol "&." These are stylistic matters which appear clearly in the illustration on page 157. In the light of the discussions and conclusions in chapters 6 and 7, the reader will find the explanations in the headnotes sufficient.

Editorial Symbols

In accordance with the practice of the Center for Editions of American Authors, the following editorial symbols are used to designate emendations to the manuscript leaves:

⟨ ⟩ Canceled matter

↑ ↓ Interlinear insertions, above or below the line
(Mrs. Stowe's occasional ∧ has the same meaning.)

[ ] Editorial suggestions

1. Collation of *National Era* Text and Leaves A and B

i *Passage from* National Era, *June 5, 1851, with lines numbered for convenient reference*

1   At this moment the door was pushed gently open,
2   and a young quadroon woman, apparently about twenty-five,
3   entered the room.
4   There needed only a glance from the child to her,
5   to identify her as its mother. There was the same rich,
6   full, dark eye, with its long lashes, the same ripples

7 of silky black hair; the brown of her complexion gave
8 way on the cheek to a perceptible flush, which deepened
9 as she saw the gaze of the strange man fixed upon her
10 in bold and undisguised admiration. Her dress was of
11 the neatest possible fit, and set off to advantage her
12 finely moulded shape—a delicately formed hand and
13 a trim foot and ankle were items of appearance that did
14 not escape the quick eye of the trader, well used to
15 run up at a glance the points of a fine female article.
16   "Well, Eliza," said her master, as she stopped and
17 looked hesitatingly at him.
18   "I was looking for Harry, please, sir;" and the boy
19 bounded toward her, showing his spoils, which he had
20 gathered in the skirt of his robe.
21   "Well, take him away, then," said Mr. Shelby; and
22 hastily she withdrew, carrying the child on her arm.
23   "By Jupiter," said the trader, turning to him in
24 admiration, "there's an article, now! You might make
25 your fortune on that ar gal in Orleans any day. I've
26 seen over a thousand in my day paid down for gals not
27 a bit handsomer."
28   "I don't want to make my fortune on her," said Mr.
29 Shelby, dryly; and, seeking to turn the conversation,
30 he uncorked a bottle of fresh wine, and asked his
31 companion's opinion of it.
32   "Capital, sir—first chop!" said the trader;
33 then turning and slapping his hand familiarly on
34 Shelby's shoulder, he added—
35   "Come, how will you trade about the gal—what
36 shall I say for her—what'll you take?"
37   "Mr. Haley, she is not to be sold," said Shelby.
38 My wife would not part with her for her weight in gold."
39   "Aye aye! women always say such things, cause
40 they 'hant no sort of calculation. Just show 'em how
41 many watches, and feathers, and trinkets, one's weight

42 in gold would buy, and that alters the case, *I* reckon."

43 "I tell you, Haley, this must not be spoken of;

44 I say no, and I mean no," said Shelby, decidedly.

45 "Well, you'll let me have the boy, though," said

46 the trader; "you must own I've come down pretty

47 handsomely for him."

48 "What on earth can you want with the child?"

49 said Shelby.

50 "Why, I've got a friend that's going into this yer

51 branch of the business—wants to buy up handsome

52 boys to raise for the market—fancy articles

53 entirely—sell for waiters, and so on, to rich 'uns

54 that can pay for handsome 'uns. It sets off one of yr

55 great palaces—a real handsome boy to open door,

56 wait, and tend—they fetch a good sum—and this

57 little devil is such a comical, musical concern—he's

58 just the article."

59 "I would rather not sell him," said Mr. Shelby,

60 thoughtfully; "the fact is, sir, I'm a humane man, and

61 I hate to take the boy from his mother, sir."

62 "Oh, you do—La! yes—somethin of that ar

63 natur. I understand perfectly. It is mighty onpleasant

64 getting on with women, sometimes. I all 'ays hates these

65 yer scrachin, screamin times. They are *mighty* onpleasant;

66 but as I manages business, I generally avoids 'em, sir.

67 Now, what if you get the girl off for a day, or a week,

68 or so; then the thing's done quickly, all over before

69 she comes home. Your wife might get her some ear-rings,

70 or a new gown, or some such truck, to make up with

her."

71 "I'm afraid not."

72 "Lor bless ye, yes. These critters aint like white

73 folks, you know; they gets over things, only manage

74 right. Now, they say," said Haley, assuming a candid

75 and confidential air, "that this kind o' trade is

76 hardening to the feelings, but I never found it so.
77 Fact is, I never could do things up in the way that
78 some fellers manage the business. I've seen 'em as
79 would pull a woman's child out of her arms, and set
80 him up to sell, and she screechin' like mad all the
81 time—very bad policy—damages the articles—
82 makes 'em quite unfit for service sometimes. I knew
83 a real handsome girl, once, in Orleans, as was entirely
84 ruined by this sort o' handling. The fellow that was
85 trading for her didn't want her baby, and she was one
86 of your real high sort, when her blood was up. I tell
87 you, she squeezed up her child in her arms, and talked
88 and went on real awful; it kinder makes my blood run
89 cold to think on't—and when they carried off the
90 child, and locked her up, she jest went ravin' mad,
91 and died in a week. Clear waste, then, sir, of a
92 thousand dollars, just for want of management—
93 there's where 'tis. It's always best to do the humane
94 thing, sir; that's been *my* experience." And the
95 trader leaned back in his chair, and folded his arms,
96 with an air of virtuous decision, apparently consider-
97 ing himself a second Wilberforce.
98   The subject appeared to interest the gentlemen
99 deeply; for, while Mr. Shelby was thoughtfully peeling
100 an orange, he broke out afresh, with becoming
101 diffidence, but as if actually driven by the force of
102 truth to say a few words more.
103   "It don't look well, now, for a feller to be a
104 praisin' himself, but I say it, jest because it's the
105 truth. I believe I'm reckoned to bring in about the
106 finest droves of niggers that is brought in—at
107 least I've been told so. If I have once, I reckon I
108 have a hundred times, all in good case, fat and likely,
109 and I lose as few as any man in the business, and I

110 lays it all to management, sir; and humanity, sir,
111 I may say, is the great pillar of my management."
112   Mr. Shelby did not know what to say, and so he
113 said "Indeed!"
114   "Now, I've been laughed at for my notions, sir,
115 and I've been talked to. They aint pop'lar, and
116 they aint common; but I stuck to 'em, sir; I've
117 stuck to 'em, and realized well on 'em; yes, sir,
118 they have paid their passage, I may say," and the
119 trader laughed at his joke.
120   There was something so piquent and original in
121 these elucidations of humanity, that Mr. Shelby could
122 not help laughing in company. Perhaps you laugh too,
123 dear reader, but you know humanity comes out in a
124 variety of strange forms now-a-days, and there is no
125 end to the odd things that humane people will say and
126 do.
127   Mr. Shelby's laugh encouraged the trader to proceed.
128   "It's strange, now, but I never could beat this
129 into people's heads. Now, there was Tom Loker, my
130 old partner, down in Natchez; he was a clever fellow,
131 Tom was, only the very devil with niggers—on
132 principle 'twas, you see, for a better hearted feller
133 never broke bread; 'twas his *system,* sir; I used to
134 talk to Tom. Why, Tom, I used to say, when your gals
135 takes on and cry, what's the use o' crackin' on 'em
136 over the head, and knockin' on 'em round? It's
137 ridiculous, says I, and don't do no sort of good.
138 Why, I don't see no harm in their cryin', says I;
139 its natur, says, I, and if natur can't blow off one
140 way, it will another. Besides, Tom, says I, it jest
141 spiles your gals; they gets sickly and down in the
142 mouth—and sometimes they gets ugly—particular
143 yallow gals do—and it's the devil and all getting

144 on 'em broke in—now, ses I, why can't you kinder
145 coaz 'em up, and speak 'em fair? Depend on it, Tom,
146 a little humanity thrown in along, goes a heap farther
147 than all your jawin' and crackin'; and it pays better,
148 ses I, depend on't. But Tom couldn't get the hang
149 on't, and he spiled so many for me, that I had to
150 break off with him, tho' he was a good-hearted fellow,
151 and as fair a business hand as is goin'.' "

152   "And do you find your ways of managing do the
153 business better than Tom's?" said Mr. Shelby.

154   "Why, yes, sir, I may say so. You see, when I
155 any ways can, I takes a leetle care about the
156 onpleasant parts, like selling young uns and that—
157 get the gals out of the way—out of sight out of
158 mind, you know—and when it's clean done, and
159 can't be helped, they naturally gets used to it.
160 'Tan't, you know, as if it was white folks, that's
161 brought up in the way of 'spectin' to keep their
162 children and wives, and all that. Niggers, you know,
163 that's fetched up properly, ha'n't no kind of
164 'spectations of no kind; so all these things comes
165 easier."

ii *Leaf A*

—At this moment the door was pushed gently open and a young mulatto woman apparently about twenty five entered the room. There needed only a glance from the child to her to identify her as its mother. There was the Same rich full dark eye with long ⟨silky⟩ lashes the same ripples of silky black hair & the brown of the complexion gave way on the cheek to a perceptible flush which deepened as she caught the eye of the stranger fixed upon her in bold & undisguised admiration. Her dress was of the closest possible fit & set off to advantage her finely moulded form—a delicately formed hand & a trim foot & ancles were ⟨points⟩ ↑items↓ of appearance that did not escape the ↑quick↓

eye of the trader, well used to run up at a glance the points of a fine female article—

Well Eliza said her master as she stopped & looked hesitatingly at him—

I was looking for Henry—please Sir—& the boy bounded toward her showing his various spoils which he had gathered in the skirt of his dress

Well take him away said Mr Shelby & hastily she withdrew ⟨d⟩ carrying the child on her arm—

⟨As the⟩ By Jupiter   said the trader turning to him in admiration—you might make your fortune on that girl in New Orleans any day—Ive seen a thousand—two thousand paid down for girls not half so handsome—

I dont want to make my fortune on her said Shelby drily—& seeking to turn the conversation he uncorked a bottle of fresh wine & asked his opinion of it—

Excellent—first rate—said the trader & then turning said clapping his hand familiarly on Selbys shoulder

Come how will you trade about the girl—what shall I say for her

Mr Haley   she is *not to be sold*—my wife would not part with her for her weight in gold

Ay ay—women always say that—⟨but show⟩ cause they've no kind o calculation, but show em how many silk gowns & gold watches & breast pins & feathers they can get for the money—& that alters the case—I tell you Mr ⟨Stimpson⟩ ↑Haley↓ this must not be spoken of— I *say* no & I *mean* no—said Mr Shelby

Well you'l let me have the boy tho' said the trader—you must own I've made a handsome offer for him— —the fact is I have a friend in N Orleans that s going into this line of business & wants to buy up handsome little boys to raise for the market

iii *Leaf B*

they are to be a fancy article entirely to sell for waiters ⟨w⟩ to rich folks what can pay for a very handsome article—It sets off one of these stylish establishments you know—a handsome boy to open the door & wait & tend & all that—& they fetch a good round sum I can tell you

I would rather not sell him said Mr S↑h↓elby thoughtfully—the fact is   I'm a humane man & I hate to take the boy from his mother Sir—

—Oh you do—law sakes!—well it *is* unpleasant the fuss these women make about their children—I always hate these sc⟨h⟩reeching screamin times they have & as I does business I commonly avoids em sir—Cant you get the woman off for a day or two, for an errand or visit or some such & then the thing can be done quietly—your wife might buy her a new gownd—& some ear rings ⟨&⟩ or some such trap to make it up with her—

Im afraid not—

Lor yes—bless you these creeturs ant like folks you know—they gets over things—that is to say if you know how to manage them—Now they say my kind of trade is hardenin to the feelins—but I never found it so—I never ⟨d⟩ could do things up in the high handed sort of way that some fellows manage the business—Ive seen em as would pull away a womans ⟨baby⟩ ↑baby↓ ⟨out⟩ of her arms & set him up to sell—& she screeching like mad—so that it would take two or three to ⟨b⟩ hold her—bad policy that—damages the article—makes em quite unfit for service sometimes—I knew a real handsome girl once as was entirely ruined by this kind of proceeding—the fellow that was a tradin for her of course didnt want her baby & she was one of your real high sor[t] when her blood was up—& she squeezed her child in her arms & talked real awful—it kinder makes my blood run cold to think ont—& when they pulled away the baby & locked her up s⟨o⟩he j⟨u⟩ist went ravin mad—& died in a week—a clear waste sir of ⟨—⟩ two thousand dollars— —just for want of a little management

—⟨Well Mr Stimpson said Mr Shelby rising Il think over matters & ask my wife said⟩

And did you find that you way of managing did the business any better said Mr Shelby—

—Certainly—to be sure— —get em out of the way—out of sight out of mind—& when the things clean done & cant be helped & they know it they naturally gets used to it—folks can get used to any thing when they must

iv NATIONAL ERA *passage (with lines as numbered above, on pp. 199–204), followed by bracketed variants in manuscript leaves A and B (above, pp. 204–207)*

1 At [(no paragraph)—At]; was pushed [waspushed]; open, [open]

2 quadroon [mulatto]; woman, [woman]; twenty-five, [twenty five]

4 her, [her]

5 same [Same]; rich, [rich]

6 full, [full]; eye, [eye]; its [omit]; lashes, [lashes]

7 hair; the [hair & the]; her [the]

8 flush, [flush]

9 saw [caught]; gaze [eye]; strange man [stranger]

10 and [&]

11 neatest [closest]; fit, and [fit &]

12 shape—a [form—a]; and [&]

13 and ankles [& ancles]

15 article. [article—]

16 "Well, Eliza," [Well Eliza]; master, [master]; and [&]

17 him. [him—]

18 "I [I]; Harry, please, sir;" and [Henry—please Sir—&]

19 her, [her]; his spoils, [his various spoils]

20 robe. [dress]

21 "Well, [Well]; away, then," [away]; Mr. Shelby; and [Mr Shelby &]

22 withdrew, [withdrew]; arm. [arm—]

23   "By Jupiter," [By Jupiter——   ]; trader, [trader]
24   admiration, [admiration—]; "there's an article, now! [omit]
25   ar [omit]; gal [girl]; Orleans [New Orleans]; day. [day—]; I've [Ive]
26   over [omit]; thousand in my day [thousand—two thousand]; gals [girls]
27   a bit handsomer." [half so handsome—]
28   "I [I]; don't [dont]; her," [her]; Mr. [omit]
29   Shelby, dryly; and, seeking [Shelby drily—& seeking]; conversation, [conversation]
30   wine, and [wine &]
31   companion's [omit]; it. [it—]
32   "Capital, sir—first chop!" [Excellent—first rate—]; trader; [trader &]
33   and slapping [said clapping]
34   Shelby's [Selbys]; shoulder, he added— [shoulder]
35   "Come, [Come]; gal—what [girl—what]
36   her— [her]; what'll you take?" [omit]
37   "Mr. [Mr]; Haley, [Haley   ]; not to be sold," [*not to be sold*—]; said Shelby. [omit]
38   My [my]; gold." [gold]
39   "Aye aye! [Ay ay—]; such things, cause [that—cause]
40   they 'hant no sort of calculation. Just [they've no kind o calculation, but]; 'em [em]
41–2   watches, and feathers, and trinkets, one's weight in gold would buy, and [silk gowns & gold watches & breast pins & feathers they can get for the money—&]
42   case, [case]; *I* reckon." [omit]
43   (paragraph) "I [(no paragraph)—I]; you, Haley, this [you Mr Haley this]; of; [of—]
44   say [*say*]; no, and [no &]; mean [*mean*]; no," said [no—said]; Shelby, [Mr Shelby]; decidedly. [omit]
45   "Well, [Well]; you'll [you'l]; boy, though," said [boy tho' said]

46 trader; [trader——]; "you [you]

46–7 come down pretty handsomely [made a handsome offer]

47 him." [him—— ——]

48–9 "What . . . Shelby. [omit]

50 (paragraph) "Why I've got [(no paragraph) the fact is I have]; friend that's [friend in N Orleans that s]; yer [omit]

51 branch [line]; the business—wants [business & wants]

52 boys [little boys]; market—fancy [market they are to be a fancy]; articles [article]

53 —sell [to sell]; waiters, and so on, [waiters to]; 'uns [folks]

54 that [what]; handsome 'uns. [a very handsome article—]

54–5 yr great palaces— [these stylish establishments you know—]

55 real [omit]; open door, [open the door]

56 wait, and tend— [& wait & tend & all that—]; they [& they]; good sum— [good round sum I can tell you]

56–8 and this . . . article." [omit]

59 "I [I]; him," [him]; Shelby, [Shelby]

60 thoughtfully; "the [thoughtfully—the]; is, sir, I'm [is   I'm]; man, and [man &]

61 mother, sir." [mother Sir—]

62 "Oh, [—Oh]; La! yes— [law sakes!—]

62–3 somethin . . . perfectly. [omit]

63 It [well it]; is [is]; mighty [omit); onpleasant [unpleasant]

64 getting on with women, sometimes. [the fuss these women make about their children—]; all'ays [always]; hates [hate]

65 yer [omit]; scrachin, [screeching]; times. They [times they have &]; They . . . onpleasant; [omit]

66 but [&]; manages [does]; business, [business]; generally [commonly]; 'em, sir. [em sir—]

67 Now, what if [Cant]; girl [woman]

67–8   day, or a week, or so; [day or two, for an errand or visit or some such &]
68   thing's done [thing can be done]; quickly; [quietly—]
68–9   all . . . home. [omit]
69   Your [your]; get [buy]
69–70   some ear-rings, or a new gown, [a new gownd—& some ear rings]
70   truck, [trap]; make up [make it up]; her." [her—]
71   "I'm [Im]; not." [not—]
72   "Lor bless ye, yes. [Lor yes—bless you]; These [these]; critters [creeturs]; aint [ant]; white [omit]
73   folks, you [folks you]; know; [know—]; things, [things—]
73–4   only manage right. [that is to say if you know how to manage them—]
74   Now, they say," [Now they say]
74–5   said . . . that [omit]
75   this [my]; o' [of]
76   hardening [hardenin]; feelings, [feelins—]; so [so—]
77   Fact is, [omit]; way [high handed sort of way]
78   fellers [fellows]; business. [business—]; I've [Ive]; 'em [em]
79   pull a [pull away a]; woman's [womans]; child [baby]; out [omit]; arms, and [arms &]
80   sell, and [sell—&]; screechin' [screeching]; mad [mad—]
80–1   all the time—very bad [so that it would take two or three to hold her—bad]
81   policy— [policy that—]; articles— [article—]
82   'em [em]; sometimes. [sometimes—]
83   girl, once, [girl once]; in Orleans, [omit]
84   sort o' handling. [kind of proceeding—]
85   trading [a tradin]; didn't [of course didn't]; baby, and [baby &]
86   sort [sor]; up. [up—]

86–7   I tell you, [omit]

87   she [& she]; up [omit]; arms, and [arms &]

88   and went on [& talked]; awful; [awful—]

89   on't—and [ont &]; carried off [pulled away]

90   child, and [baby &]; up, [up]; jest [jist]; ravin' [ravin]; mad, [mad—]

91   and [&]; week. [week—]; Clear [a clear]; waste, then, sir, [waste sir]; a [two]

92   dollars, just [dollars— —just]; of management— [of a little management]

93–151   there's . . . goin'." [omit]

152   "And [And]; do [did]; your [that your]; ways [way]; do [did];

153   better [any better]; than Tom's?" [omit]; Mr. [Mr]; Shelby. [Shelby—]

154–56   You . . . that— [omit]

157   the gals [em]; way—out [way—out]

158   mind, [mind—]; you know— [omit]; and when [& when]; it's [the things]; done, and [done &]

159   can't [cant]; helped, [helped & they know it]; it. [it—]

160–65   'Tan't . . . easier." [folks can get used to any thing when they must]

2. COLLATION OF *National Era* TEXT AND TEXT OF THE FIRST
EDITION OF *Uncle Tom's Cabin*

Passage from NATIONAL ERA, *June 5, 1851 (with lines as numbered above on pp. 199–204) followed by bracketed variants in* UNCLE
TOM'S CABIN *(1852), I, 17–22*

1   moment [moment,]

6   lashes, [lashes;]

7   hair; the [hair. The]

12   shape—[shape;—]

16   Eliza," [Eliza?"]

25   Orleans [Orleans,]
26   thousand in [thousand,]; day [day,]
35   gal—[gal?—]
38   My ["My]
39   "Aye, aye ["ay, ay]
40   'hant [ha'nt]
41   and feathers [feathers]
52   market—fancy [market. Fancy]
54   yr[yer]
55   palaces [places]
56   tend—they [tend. They]; sum—[sum;]
57   concern—[concern,]
62   do—[do?—]
63   understand [understand,]
64   all'ays [al'ays]
65   scrachin [screachin']; screamin [screamin']; *mighty*
[mighty]
66   but [but,]
68   quickly, [quietly,—]
72   yes. [yes!]; aint [an't]
76   feelings, [feelings;]
77   in [omit]; that [omit]
81   time— [time;—]; articles [article]
83   girl, [gal]
85   baby, [baby;]
87   talked [talked,]
88   awful; it [awful. It]
89   on't—[on't;]
91   then, [omit]
92   management— [management,—]
94   *my* [my]
95   arms [arm]
98   gentlemen [gentleman]
99   for, [for]
100 he [Haley]

103   be a [be]
104   it, [it]
106   in—[in,—]
107   so. If [so; if]
108   times, [times,—]; case, [case,—]
109   business, and [business. And]
111   my [my]
115   aint [an't]
116   aint [an't]
123   reader, [reader;]
131   niggers— [niggers,—]
134   Why ['Why]; Tom [Tom']; when [when]
137   ridiculous, [ridiculous,']; and ['and]; of [o']
138   cryin', [cryin',']
139   its ['it's]; natur, [natur,']; I, and [I; 'and]
140   Tom, [Tom,']; it ['it]
141   gets [get]; sickly [sickly,]
142   mouth—[mouth;]; ugly—[ugly,—]
143   do—[do,—]; getting [gettin']
144   in—now, ses I, why [in. Now,' says I, why]
146   humanity [humanity,]; farther [further]
147–48   better, ses [better,' says]
148   depend on't. ['depend on't.']
149   on't [on't;]
150   tho' [though]
156   that—[that,—]
157   sight [sight,]
158   know—[know,—]

3. COLLATION OF *National Era* TEXT AND LEAF C

i *Passage from* NATIONAL ERA, *June 19, 1851, with lines numbered*
for convenient reference

1   The cabin of Uncle Tom was a small log building,
2   close adjoining to "the house," as the negro par

3 excellence designates his master's dwelling. In
4 front it had a neat garden patch, where every summer
5 strawberries, raspberries, and a variety of fruits and
6 vegetables, flourished under careful tending. The
7 whole front of it was covered by a large scarlet
8 bignonia and a native multiflora rose, which,
9 entwisting and interlacing, left scarce a vestige of
10 the rough logs to be seen. Here also in summer
11 various brilliant annuals, such as marigolds, petunias,
12 four o'clocks, found an indulgent corner in which to
13 unfold their splendors, and were the delight and pride
14 of Aunt Chloe's heart.
15 Let us enter the dwelling. The evening meal at
16 the house is over, and Aunt Chloe, who presided over
17 its preparation as head cook, has left to inferior
18 officers in the kitchen the business of clearing away
19 and washing dishes, and come out into her own snug
20 territories, to "get her ole man's supper;" therefore,
21 doubt not that it is her you see by the fire, pre-
22 siding with anxious interest

ii *Leaf C*

Uncle Tom

The cabin of Uncle Tom was a small log building close adjoining to "the house"—as the negro always par excellence designates the masters dwelling—In front it had a neat garden patch
where strawberries rhaspberries & a variety of fruits ↑& vegetab-
les↓ flourished under careful tending—⟨& roun⟩ The whole
front of the dwelling was covered with a large ↑scarlet↓ bignonia
& a native multiflora rose which entwisting & interlacing left
scarce a vestige of the building to be seen & ⟨in the spring was
redundant with its clusters of roses & in summer no less brilliant
with the scarlet tubes of the honeysuc⟩ Various ⟨qua⟩ brilliant
annuals such as marigolds four o clocks & petunias found here

and there a thrifty corner to ⟨vegetate⟩ unfold their glories & were the delight & pride of aunt Chloe's heart

Let us enter the dwelling—The evening meal at "the house" is over & Aunt Chloe who presided over its preparation as head cook has left to inferior officers in the kitchen the business of clearing away & washing dishes & come out into her own snug territory to "get her old man's supper" & therefore doubt not that it is her you see by the fire place presiding with anxious interest

iii NATIONAL ERA *passage (with lines as numbered above, on pp. 213–14), followed by bracketed variants in manuscript leaf C (above, pp. 214–15)*

1   (paragraph) The [(no paragraph) The]; building, [building]

2   house," as [house"—as]; negro [negro always]

3   his [the]; master's [masters]; dwelling. [dwelling—]

4   patch, [patch]; every summer [omit]

5   strawberries, [strawberries]; raspberries, and [rhaspberries &]

5–6   and vegetables, [& vegetables]; tending. [tending—]

7   it [the dwelling]; by [with]

8   and [&]; rose, [rose]; which, [which]

9   and interlacing, [& interlacing]

10   rough logs [building]; seen. Here [seen &]; Here also in summer [omit]

11   various [Various]; annuals, [annuals]; marigolds, [marigolds]

11–12   petunias, four o'clocks, [four o clocks & petunias]

12   found an indulgent [found here and there a thrifty]; in which [omit]

13   splendors, and [glories &]; and [&]

14   Aunt [aunt]; heart. [heart]

15   dwelling. [dwelling—]

16 the house ["the house"]; over, and [over &]; Chloe,
[Chloe]
17 cook, [cook]
19 and [&]; dishes, and [dishes &]; and [&]
20 territories, [territory]; ole [old]; supper;" [supper"];
therefore, [& therefore]
21 fire, [fire place]

4. COLLATION OF *National Era* TEXT AND LEAF D

i *Passage from* NATIONAL ERA, *June 19, 1851, with lines numbered for convenient reference*

1   of his position as instructor.
2   "Not that way, Uncle Tom—not that way," said he,
3   briskly, as Uncle Tom laboriously; brought up the
4   tail of his g the wrong side out "that makes a q, you see."
5   "La, sakes! now, does it?" said Uncle Tom, looking
6   with a respectful, admiring air, as his young teacher
7   flourishingly scrawled g's and q's innumerable for his
8   edification, and then, taking the pencil in his big,
9   heavy fingers, he patiently recommenced.
10   "How easy white folks all'is does things!" said
11 Aunt Chloe, pausing while she was greasing a griddle
12 with a scrap of bacon on her fork, and regarding young
13 master George with pride. "The way he can write, now!
14 and read, too, and then to come out here evenings
15 and read his lessons to us, it's 'mighty interestin!'"
16   "But, Aunt Chloe, I'm getting mighty hungry,"said
17 George; "aint that cake in the skillet almost done?"
18   "Mose done, mass'r George," said Aunt Chloe,
19 lifting the lid and peeping in—"browning beautiful
20 —a real lovely brown. Ah, let me alone for dat.
21 Missis let Sally try to make some cake

ii *Leaf D*

of his position as instructor
—"Not that way," Uncle Tom—not that way said he briskly
as Uncle Tom laboriously brought up the tail of his g the wrong
side out—you mus'nt make it that way—that makes a "q" you
see
—La sakes—now does it said Uncle Tom—looking with a
respectful & admiring air as his young teacher flourishingly
scrawled g s and q s innumerable on his slate & then taking the
pencil ⟨again⟩ ↑once more↓ in his big heavy fingers he began
patiently again
—How easy white folks ⟨allers⟩ ↑all is↓ does things said
Aunt Chloe—pausing while she was greasing a griddle with a
scrap of bacon fat ↑on her fork↓ & regarding young master
George with pride—the way he can write now!—and read
too!—& then to come out here evenings & read his lessons to
us—its mighty interestin!—
Aunt Chloe Im getting mighty hungry—ant that cake in the
skillet almost done— ↑said Mass'r George↓
Mose done Massr George—said aunt Chloe lifting the lid &
peeping in—browing beautiful a real lovely brown— —ah let
me alone for that—Missis let Sally try to make ⟨some⟩ cake

iii NATIONAL ERA *text (with lines as numbered on p. 216), followed by bracketed variants in manuscript leaf D*

1   instructor. [instructor]
2   "Not [—"Not]; way, Uncle [way," Uncle]; way," said
[way said]; he, [he]
3   briskly, [briskly]; laboriously; [laboriously]
4   out "that [out—you mus'nt make it that way—that]; q,
["q"]; see." [see]
5   "La, sakes! now, does it?" [—La sakes—now does it];
Tom, looking [Tom—looking]
6   respectful, [respectful &]; air, [air]

7 g's and q's [g s & q s];
8 for his edification, [on his slate]; and then, [& then];
pencil in [pencil once more in]; big, [big]
  9 fingers, [fingers]; patiently recommenced. [began patiently again]
  10 "How [—How]; all'is [all is]; things!" [things]
  11 Chloe, [Chloe—]
  12 bacon [bacon fat]; fork, and [fork &]
  13 pride. "The [pride—the]; write, now [write now]
  14 and read, too, and [& read too!—&]
  15 us, it's 'mighty interestin!'" [us—its mighty interestin!—]
  16 But, [omit]; Chloe, I'm [Chloe Im]; hungry," [hun-
gry—]
  16–7 said George; [omit]
  17 "aint [ant]; done?" [done—said Mass'r George]
  18 "Mose done, mass'r George," [—Mose done Massr
George—]; Aunt Chloe, [aunt Chloe]
  19 "browning beautiful—a [browing beautiful a]
  20 brown. [brown—]; Ah, [—ah]; dat [that—]
  21 some [omit]

5. COLLATION OF *National Era* TEXT AND LEAF E

i *Passage from* NATIONAL ERA, *June 26, 1851, with lines
numbered for convenient reference*

  1 with hard work and starving? I'd a heap rather die than
  2 go there, any day! There's time for ye—be off with
  3 Lizzy—you've got a pass to come and go any time.
  4 Come, bustle up, and I'll get your things together."
  5   Tom slowly raised his head, and looked sorrowfully
but
  6 quietly around, and said—
  7   "No, no—I aint going—let Eliza go—it's
  8 her right! I wouldn't be the one to say no—taint

9 in *natur* for her to stay—but you heard what she
10 said! If I must be sold, or all the people on the
11 place and everything go to rack, why,
12 let me be sold. I spose I can bar it as well as any
13 on em," he added, while something like a sob and a
14 sigh shook his broad, rough chest convulsively.
15 "Mass'r always has found me on the spot—he always
16 will. I never have broke trust nor used my pass no
17 ways contrary to my word, and I never will. It's
18 better for me alone to go, than to break up the place
19 and sell all. Mass'r aint to blame, Chloe, and he'll
20 take care of you and the poor"—
21 Here he turned to the rough trundle bed full of
22 little woolly heads, and broke fairly down. He leaned
23 over the back of the chair, and covered his face with
24 his large hands. Sobs, heavy, hoarse, and loud, shook
25 the chair, and great tears fell through his fingers on
26 the floor—just such tears, sir, as you dropped into
27 the coffin where lay your first born son—such tears,
28 woman, as you shed when you heard the cries of your
29 dying babe; for, sir, he was a man—and you are but
30 another man, and woman, though dressed in silk and
jewels.
31 You are but a woman, and in life's great straits and
32 mighty griefs ye feel but one sorrow.
33 ———
34   "And now," said Eliza, as she stood in the door,
35 "I saw my husband only this afternoon, and I little
36 knew then what was to come. They have pushed him to
37 the very last standing-place, and he told me to-day
38 that he was going to run away. Do try if you can to get
39 word to him. Tell him how I went, and why I went;
40 and tell him I'm going to try and find Canada. You
41 must give my love to him, and tell him if I never
42 see him again."

ii *Leaf E*

with hard work & starving!—Id a heap rather die than go there any day!—theres time for ye—be off with Lizy—youve got a pass to come & go any time—come bustle up & I'l get your things together."

Old Tom slowly raised his head & looked sorrowfully but quietly around & said

No no—Im not going—Let Lizy go—its her right. I wouldnt be the one to say no—tant in natur for *her* to stay—but you heard what she said. If I must be sold or all go to rack why let me be sold—I spose I can bar it as well as any body—said he while something between a sob & a sigh shook his broad rough chest convulsively—

—⟨Master⟩ ↑Mass'r↓ always has found me on the spot—he always will. I never have broke trust nor used my pass any ways contrary to my promise—& I wont— — —Its better for me alone to go than to break up all the place & sell em all!—

—"Master ant to blame—he'l take care of you & the poor" Here he turned to a rough trundle bed full of little wolly heads— —& broke fairly down—he leaned over the back of the chair & covered his face with his ⟨heavy⟩ ↑large↓ hands—Sobs heavy hoarse & loud shook the chair—& great tears fell thro his fingers onto the floor—just such tears sir as you dropped into the coffin where lay your first born son—⟨your⟩ such tears woman as you shed when you saw the struggles & heard the cries of your dying baby— —for Sir he was a man & you are but another man—& ⟨you oh⟩ woman tho dressed in silk & jewels are but a woman & in lifes great straits & mighty griefs ye feel all but one anguish—for the heart can feel no more than *"all"*

—And now said Eliza as she stood in the door I want you to get word over to George somehow—Tell him how I went & why say I'm going to try to find Canada & he can come after me—Give my love to him & if I never see him again—

iii NATIONAL ERA *passage (with lines as numbered above, on pp.*
218–19), followed by bracketed variants in manuscript leaf E (above,
p. 220)

1 and starving? [& starving!—]; I'd [Id]

2 there, [there]; day! There's [day!—theres]

3 Lizzy [Lizy]; you've [youve]; and [&]; time. [time—]

4 Come, [come]; up, and [up &]; I'll [I'l]

5 Tom [Old Tom]; head, and [head]

6 around, and [around &]; said—[said]

7 "No, [no]; I aint [Im not]; let Eliza [Let Lizy]; it's [its]

8 right! [right.]; wouldn't [wouldnt]; taint [tant]

9 *natur* [natur]; her [*her*]

10 said! [said.]; sold, [sold]

10–1 the people on the place and everything [omit]

11 rack, [rack]; why, [why]

12 sold. [sold—]

12–3 any on em," [any body—]

13 he added, [said he]; like [between]; and [&]

14 broad, [broad]; convulsively. [convulsively—]

15 (no paragraph) "Mass'r [(new paragraph) Mass'r]

16 no [any]

17 word, [promise—]; and I never will [—& I
wont— — —] It's [Its]

18 go, [go]; up [up all]

19 and [&] all. [em all!— —] Mass'r aint ["Master ant];
blame, Chloe, and he'll [blame—he'l]

20 you and the poor"—[you & the poor"—]

21 (paragraph) Here [(no paragraph) Here]; the [a]

22 wooly heads, [wolly heads— —]; and [&]; down. He
[down. He [down—he]

23 chair, and [chair &]

24 hands. [hands—]; Sobs, heavy, hoarse, and loud, [Sobs
heavy hoarse & loud]

25 chair, and [chair— &]; through [thro]; on [onto]

26   tears, sir, [tears sir]

27–8   tears, woman, [tears woman]; you heard [you saw the struggles & heard]

29   babe; [baby——]; for, sir, [for Sir]; man— and [man &]

30   man, and [man—&]; woman, though [woman tho]; and jewels. [& jewels]

31   You are [are]; woman, and [woman &]; life's [lifes]; and [&]

32   but one sorrow. [all but one anguish—for the heart can feel no more than *"all"*]

33   ———[wide space]

34   "And now," [—And now]; Eliza, [Eliza]; door, [door]

35–8   "I saw . . . to[I want you to]

39   to him [over to George somehow —]; went, and [went &]; I went; [omit]

40   and tell him [say];

40–1   and [&] Canada. You must give [Canada & he can come after me—Give]

41   him, and tell him [him &]

42   again." [again—]

6. COLLATION OF *National Era* TEXT AND LEAVES F, G, AND H

i *Passage from* NATIONAL ERA, *February 12, 1852, with lines numbered for convenient reference*

1   Slowly the weary, dispirited creatures wound

2   their way into the room, and one by one, with crouching

3   reluctance, presented their baskets to be weighed. As

4   each was weighed, Legree noted on a slate, on the

5   side of which was pasted a list of names, the amount.

6   Tom's basket was weighed and approved; but he hesitated

7   and lingered to see the success of the poor woman he

8   had befriended. Tottering with weakness, she came

9   forward and delivered her basket. It was of full

10 weight, as Legree well perceived; but affecting anger,
11 he said:
12 "What, you lazy beast, short again! Stand aside;
13 you'll catch it this time."
14 The woman gave a groan of utter despair, and sat
15 down on a board.
16 The person who had been called Misse Cassy now
17 came forward, and with a haughty, negligent air,
18 delivered her basket. As she delivered it, Legree
19 looked in her eyes with a sneering yet inquiring
20 glance. She fixed her black eyes steadily on him,
21 her lips moved slightly, and she said something in
22 French—What it was, no one knew; but Legree's face
23 became for a moment perfectly
24 demoniac as she spoke, and he half raised his hand, as if to
25 strike—a gesture which she regarded with fierce disdain,
26 as she turned and walked away.
27 "And now," said Legree, "come here, you Tom; ye see
I
28 telled ye I didn't buy you jest for the common work; I
29 mean to promote ye, and make a driver of ye; and to-
night
30 yer begin to get yer hand in. So now yer jest take this yer
31 woman and flog her. You've seen enough to know
how"—
32 "I beg mass'rs pardon," said Tom; "hope mass'r won't
33 set me at that; it's what I aint used to, never did do, and
34 know I couldn't do any way."
35 "You'll learn a pretty smart chance of things ye never
36 did know, before I've done with ye," said Legree, taking
up a
37 cowhide that lay near, and striking Tom a heavy blow
across
38 the cheek, and following up the infliction by a shower of
blows.

39 "There!" he said, as he stopped to rest. "Now will yer tell

40 me yer can't do it?"

41 "Yes, mass'r," said Tom, putting up his hands to wipe

42 the blood that was dripping down his face; "I'm willin to work

43 night and day, and work while thar's life and breath in me;

44 but this yer thing I can't feel it's right to do; and, mass'r,

45 I *never shall do it—never.*"

46 Tom had a remarkably soft, smooth voice, and a habitually

47 respectful manner, that had given Legree an idea that he would

48 be cowardly, and easily subdued. When he spoke these last

49 words, a thrill of amazement went through every one; the poor

50 woman clasped her hands, and said, "Oh, Lord!" and every one

51 looked at each other and drew in their breath, as if to prepare

52 for the storm that was about to burst.

53 Legree looked stupefied and confounded, but at last burst

54 forth:

55 "What! Ye blasted black beast! Tell *me* you don't think it's

56 *right* to do what I tell yer! What have any of you cussed cattle

57 to do with *thinking* what's right? I'll put a stop to 't.

58 Why, what do ye think ye are? May be ye think yer a gentleman,

59 master Tom—to be a tellin your master what's right and what

60 aint. So you pretend it's *wrong* to flog that woman?"
61   "I think so, mass'r," said Tom; "the poor critter's sick
62 and feeble; 't would be downright cruel, and it's what I'll
63 never do, nor begin to. Mass'r, if you mean to kill me,
kill
64 me; as to raisin my hand agin one here, I never

ii *Leaf F*

* Ad ⟨?⟩ Slowly the weary dispirited creatures wound their way into the room & with crouching reluctance presented their baskets to be weighed

Legree noted on a slate on the side of which was pasted a list of names, the ⟨result⟩ ↑amount↓

Toms basket was weighed & approved & he looked with an anxious glance for the success of the woman he had befriended

Tottering with weakness she came forward & delivered her basket. —it was of full weight as Legree well perceived but affecting anger he said

What you lazy beast! short again! stand aside youl catch it pretty soon

The woman gave a groan of utter despair & sat down on a board

The person who had been called Miss Cassy now came forward & with a haughty negligent air delivered her basket. As she delivered it Legree looked in her eyes with a sneering yet inquiring glance

She fixed her black eyes steadily on him, her lips moved slightly & she said something in French—what ⟨wa⟩ it was, no one knew but Legree's face became perfectly

Leaf G

demonaical in its expression as she spoke—he half raised his hand as if to strike—a gesture which she regarded with fierce disdain as she turned & walked away

And now said Legree come here you Tom—ye see I telled ye I

didnt buy ye jist for the common work—I mean to promote ye
& make a driver of ye & to night ye may jist as well begin to get
yer hand in now ye jist take this yer gal & flog her ye'v seen
enough ont to know how

I beg mass'rs pardon said Tom—hopes massr wont set me at
that—its what I ant used to ⟨no ways⟩ never did—& cant do,
no way possible

Ye'l larn a pretty smart chance of things ye never ⟨knew⟩ did
know, before I've done with ye said Legree, taking up a cow hide
& striking Tom a heavy blow across the cheek & following up
the infliction by a shower of blows

"There!" he said as he stopped to rest now will ye tell me ye
cant do it?

"Yes mass'r,"—said Tom putting up his hand ⟨s⟩ to wipe
the blood that trickled down his face

Im willin to work—night & day & work while theres life &
breath in me—but this yer

Leaf H

thing I cant feel it right ⟨d⟩ to do—& ⋀↑Massr↓ I *never* shall
do it—*never*!

Tom had a remarkably smooth soft voice & ↑a↓ habitually
respectful manner that had given Legree an idea that he would
be cowardly & easily subdued—when he spoke these last words
a thrill of amazement went thro every one—⟨the poor w there
was a general drawing in of breath—&⟩ the poor woman
clasped her hands & said "Oh Lord!" & every one involuntarily
looked at each other and drew in their breath as if to prepare for
the storm that was about to burst

Legree looked stupified & confounded but at last burst forth

What! ye blasted black beast! tell *me* ye dont think it *right* to
do what I tell ye—what have any of you cussed cattle to do with
thinking whats right!—Il put a stop to it Why what do ye
think ye are? may be ye think ye'r a gentleman master Tom

to be a telling your master whats right, & what ant   So you
pretend its wrong to flog the gal
    "I think so Massr," said Tom the poor critturs sick &
feeble—'twould be down right cruel & its what I never will do
nor begin to—Mass'r if you mean to ⟨I think⟩ kill me, kill
me—but as to my raising my hand agin any one here I never

   iii NATIONAL ERA *passage (with lines as numbered above,
on pp. 222–25), followed by bracketed variants in manuscript leaves
          F, G, and H (above, pp. 225–27)*

 1   weary, [weary]
 2   room, and [room &]; one by one, [omit]
 3   reluctance, [reluctance]; weighed. [weighed]
 3–4   As each was weighed, (no paragraph) Legree [(paragraph) Legree]
 4   slate, [slate]
 5   amount, [amount]
 6   Tom's [(new paragraph) Toms]; and approved; but [&
approved &]; hesitated [looked]
 7   and lingered to see [with an anxious glance for]; poor
[omit]
 8   befriended. [befriended]; Tottering [(new paragraph)
Tottering] weakness, [weakness]
 9   basket. It [basket.—it]
10   weight, [weight]; perceived; [perceived]; anger, [anger]
11   said: [said]
12   "What, [What]; beast, [beast!]; Stand [stand]; aside;
[aside]
13   you'll [youl]; this time." [pretty soon]
14   despair, and [despair &]
15   board. [board]
16   Misse [Miss]
17   forward, and [forward &]; haughty, [haughty]; air, [air]
18   it, [it]
20   glance. (no paragraph) She [glance (paragraph) She]

21 slightly, and [slightly &]

22 What [what]; was, [was]; knew; [knew]

23 for a moment [omit]

24 demoniac [demonaical in its expression]; spoke, and [spoke—]; hand, [hand]

25 disdain, [disdain]

26 and [&]; away. [away]

27 "And now," [And now]; Legree, [Legree]; "come [come]; here, [here]; Tom; [Tom —]

28 didn't [didnt]; you [ye]; jest [jist]; work; [work—]

29 ye, and [ye &]; ye; and [ye &]; to-night [to night]

30 yer begin [ye may jist as well begin]; in. [in]; So [omit]; yer jest [ye jist]

31 woman and [gal &]; her. [her]; You've [ye'v]; enough [enough ont]; how"— [how]

32 "I [I]; pardon," [pardon]; Tom; [Tom—]; hope [hopes]; mass'r [massr]; won't [wont]

33 that; [that—]; it's [its]; aint [ant]; to, [to]; did do, and [did—&]

34 know I couldn't [cant]; do [do,]; any way." [no way possible]

35 "You'll [Ye'l]; learn [larn]

36 ye," [ye]

37 cowhide [cow hide]; that lay near, [omit]; and [&]

38 cheek, and [cheek &]; blows. [blows]

39 said, [said]; rest. [rest]; "Now [now]; yer [ye]

40 yer [ye]; can't [cant]; it?" [it?]

41 "Yes, ["Yes]; mass'r," [mass'r," —] Tom, [Tom]; hands [hand]

42 was dripping [trickled]; face; [face]; (no paragraph) "I'm [(paragraph) Im]

43 and day, [& day]; and [&]; thar's [theres]; and [&]; me, [me—]

44 can't [cant]; it's [it]; do; [do—]; and mass'r, [& Massr]

45 *shall do it* [shall do it]; *never."* [*never!*]

46   soft, smooth [smooth soft]; voice, and [voice &]

47   manner, [manner]

48   cowardly, and [cowardly &]; subdued. [subdued—];
When [when]

49   words, [words]; through [thro]; one; [one—]

50   hands, and [hands &]; said, [said]; one [one involun-
tarily]

51   breath, [breath]

52   burst. [burst]

53   stupefied and [stupified &]; confounded, [confounded]

54   forth: [forth]

55   "What! [What!]; Ye [ye]; Tell [tell]; you [ye]; don't
[dont]; it's [it]

56   yer! [ye—]; What [what]

57   *thinking* [thinking]; what's [whats]; right? [right!—];
I'll [Il]; "'t. [it]

58   Why, [Why]; May [may]; yer [ye'r]; gentleman,
[gentleman]

59   Tom—[Tom]; tellin [telling]; what's [whats]; right and
[right, &]

60   aint. [ant]; it's [its]; *wrong* [wrong]; that woman?" [the
gal]

61   so, [so]; mass'r" [Massr,"]; Tom; [Tom]; "the [the];
critter's [critturs]

62   and feeble; [& feeble—]; 't would ['twould]; downright
[down right]; cruel, and [cruel &]; it's [its]; I'll [I]

63   never [never will]; do, [do]; to. [to—]; Mass'r, [Mass'r]

64   me; [me—but]; to [to my]; raisin [raising]; one [any
one]; here, [here]

7. COLLATION OF *National Era* TEXT AND LEAF I

i *Passage from* NATIONAL ERA, *February 12, 1852, with lines
numbered for convenient reference*

1   it would be. It isn't the first time I've been out in the

2   night, carrying water to such as you."

3   "Thank you, missis," said Tom, when he had done
drinking."

4   "Don't call me missis. I'm a miserable slave like yourself;

5   a lower one than you ever can be," said she, bitterly. "But

6   now," said she, going to the door and dragging in a small

7   pallaise, over which she had spread linen cloths, wet with

8   water, "try, my poor fellow, to roll yourself over on to
this."

9   Stiff with wounds and bruises, Tom was a long time in

10   accomplishing this movement, but, when done, he felt a
sensation

11   of relief from the cooling application to his wounds.

12   The woman, whom long practice among the victims of
outrage

13   and brutality, had made familiar with many healing arts,
went

14   on to make many applications to Tom's wounds, by
means of which

15   he was soon greatly relieved.

16   "Now," said she, when she had raised his head on some

17   damaged cotton she took for a pillow, "that's the best I can

18   do for you."

19   Tom thanked her; and the woman, sitting down on the
floor,

20   drew up her knees, and, embracing them with her arms,
looked

21   fixedly before her, with a bitter and painful expression of

22   countenance. Her bonnet fell back, and long, wavy
streams

ii *Leaf I*

it would be. It isnt the first time Ive been out in the night,
carrying water to such as you"

"Thank you ⟨N⟩ missis, said Tom when he had done drinking"

"Dont call me missis"— I'm a miserable slave like yourself—a lower one than you can ever be," said she bitterly,—but now said she, going to the door, & dragging in a small pallaise over which she ↑had↓ spread linen cloths wet with ↑cold↓ water "try my poor fellow to roll yourself onto this."—

Stiff with wounds & bruises, Tom was a long time in accomplishing this movement, but when done he felt a sensible relief from the cooling application to his wounds.

The woman, whom long practice with the victims of brutality, had made familiar with many healing arts, went on to make many application to Tom's wounds by means of which he was soon somewhat relieved.

"Now," said the woman when she had raised his head on a roll of damaged cotton which served for a pillow—"there's the best I can do for you."

Tom thanked her, & the woman sitting down on the floor, drew up her knees & embracing them with her arms, looked fixedly ⟨at him⟩ before her, with a bitter & painful expression of countenance

Her bonnet fell back, & long wavy streams

[on verso] J P Jewett

Dear Sir

It seems to me that it would

iii NATIONAL ERA *passage (with lines as numbered above, on pp. 229–30), followed by bracketed variants in manuscript leaf I*

1   isn't [isnt]; I've [Ive]
2   you." [you"]
3   you, [you]; missis," [missis,]; Tom, [Tom]; drinking." [drinking"]
4   Don't [Dont]; missis. [missis"—]; yourself; [yourself—]

5   ever can [can ever]; she, [she]; bitterly. [bitterly,]; "But [—but]

6   now," [now]; door and [door, &]

7   pallaise, [pallaise]; cloths, [cloths]

8   water, [cold water]; try, [try]; fellow, [fellow]; over [omit]; on to [onto]; this." [this."—]

9   and [&]

10   but, [but]; done, [done]; sensation [sensible]

11   of [omit]

12   among [with]; outrage [omit]

13   and [omit]

14   wounds, [wounds]

15   greatly [somewhat]

16   she, [the woman]; some [a roll of]

17   she took [which served]; pillow, [pillow—]; that's [there's]

19   her; and [her, &]; woman, [woman]

20   knees, [knees]; and, [&]

22   countenance. Her [countenance. (new paragraph) Her]; and long, [& long]

Appendix II:

NEGRO DIALECT

This discussion of Negro dialect in *Uncle Tom's Cabin* is not a defense of either the fidelity or the consistency of Harriet Beecher Stowe's use of Negro speech in her novel. It is an attempt to show the types and extent of the revisions in Negro dialect between the *National Era* text and the first edition of the story in book form.

Collations of several corresponding passages in these two texts illustrate Harriet's continual efforts toward greater accuracy and a realistic representation of Negro speech.

Among single dialect words, at least 123 of the spellings in the early text differ from the spellings in the later. As a specific change was sometimes made more than once, there are, in all, over 217 dialect–related spelling variants in the two texts. A sampling of the 217 variants is given in the following table. The *Era* spelling is reproduced in the first column, the novel spelling in the second, and the frequency of occurrence of the particular difference in the third.

allays	al'ays	2
allus	al'ays	2
ally's	al'ays	1
allers	al'ays	1
all'is	al'us	1

all'ys	all'us	I
careful	carful	I
careless	car'less	I
clar	clare	I
der	de	16
the	de	4
de	der	I
de	the	I
jes	jest	4
jest	just	3
jest	jist	I
jist	just	I
just	jist	I
where	whar	I
whar	where	I
yer	ye	20
ye	you	5
you'r	you're	5
you	ye	4
you	yer	3
you	yo	2
ye	yer	2
yer	yere	I
yer	ye're	I
yer	your	I
yer	ye'r	I
yr	yer	I
you'r	your	I
you'll	ye'll	I
you've	ye've	I
yourself	yerself	I
ye's	yeve	I

Even allowing for typesetters' errors and misreadings, it appears that there is a definite pattern of "yer" to "ye," as the change is made twenty times and the reverse occurs only twice. "Der" becomes "de" sixteen times, "the" becomes "de" four times, but "de" becomes "dar" only once and "the" only once. It seems that "ye" and "de" were the desired forms. There is, obviously, less consistency in the attempts to convey the pronunciation of "just," which is spelled four different ways on ten different occasions, and of "always," which appears with nine different spellings in the two texts. It may be that, in the case of "just," the printer misread Harriet's "e" for an "i" or vice versa.

Although little pattern can be found in the sampling just given, the spelling of a few words in the story is changed with great regularity. With the exception of the speech of one character (Adolph), all the *Era* variants "Master," "Masser," "massre," and "mass'r" are regularized in the 1852 edition to "Mas'r." "Aint" is regularly spelled "an't," except where changed to "isn't" (four times) or "am not" (twice). "Oh" in the *Era* is spelled "O" throughout the first edition. These changes are almost entirely, however, the result of the variation between the house rules of Jewett and Bailey, as both texts are consistent within themselves and at variance with Harriet's inconsistent practice.

Of the thirty-seven characters in the novel who might be expected to speak at some time with some sort of dialect in one of the two texts, seven are white men: Haley, Legree, Marks, Symmes, Tom Loker, Van Trompe, and George Shelby. George's grammar sometimes slips in the *Era,* but is impeccable in the novel. The speech of the remaining six is comparatively free from variants. Harriet was more confident when reproducing speech of white men. Of the thirty remaining, all Negroes, some characters appear too briefly (e.g., Dodo, Mandy, Jake, Prue, Susan) to provide a valid basis for study, and others (e.g., George and Eliza Harris, Madame de Thoux) are perfectly consistent in both texts, using non-dialectal English through-out. Tom speaks such a hodgepodge of Negro field dialect, house-servant dialect, quasi-Biblical language intermixed with phrases memorized from sermons, and standard English that he resembles Cooper's Leatherstocking, who, as Twain pointed out, spoke as Cooper wanted him to speak in response to a specific occasion. Therefore only nine Negro characters who appear with some frequency and whose speech admits of variation in the two texts will be discussed. Of the nine selected, six fall into a lower social class and three into an upper class of either valet or mistress.

The variants in the speech of these two groups exhibit two trends in the development of the novel: first, as Harriet wrote the story for the *Era,* weekly chapter by weekly chapter, she improved considerably in the reproduction of Negro speech; secondly, when she returned to revise each chapter for the novel publication, she made spelling changes and corrections with both dialectal and artistic intent. Therefore, although there are variants between the *Era* text and that of the novel throughout the whole of the story, the larger number occur in dialectal words early in the texts.

In an attempt to illustrate both trends, the discussion will take up the characters according to whether they appear early or later. The order of their appearance in the novel will be found to approximate, in descending order, the number of variants in the speech of each character. Harriet seems to have become more confident the more she wrote. Strict chronological order of appearance will not be observed; rather, the division of the story into the early part and the later part will provide the structure for the discussion.

In the story, Chloe is the first of the lower-class Negroes to be introduced. It is not surprising that Harriet, attempting the reproduction of dialect for the first time, should make what she later considered errors and thus, returning to the passage as she reworked the text for the 1852 book, revise here more than in the speech or any other character.

As the changes in Chloe's speech are numerous, they are presented as parallel passages to aid in the comparison. The *Era* text is on the left, that of the 1852 edition on the right, the parenthesized numbers referring to the pages in the novel.

June 19, 1851	Volume I
all'is	al'us (41)
feelins	feelin's (41)
spilt	spilled (42)
der first	de first (42)
your ole aunty'd	your old aunty'd (42)
de best	the best (42)
flucky	flecky (43)
yer know	ye know (43)
spose	suppose (43)
yer telled Tom	ye telled Tom (44)
yer did	ye did (44)
yer crawed	ye crawed (44)
yer wouldn't	ye wouldn't (44)
yer oughter	ye oughter (44)
jist	just (44)
you. You know	ye, ye know (44)
yer oughtenter	ye oughtenter (44)
der heavist	de heavist (45)
yer may say	ye may say (45)
sparklin	sparkling (45)
the dew's	de dew's (45)
der Lord	de Lord (45)
der pie crust	de pie crust (45)
just	jist (45)
those	dem (45)
the parlor	de parlor (45)

de parlor	der parlor (45)
der head	de head (45)
where tis	whar 'tis (45)
der kitchen	de kitchen (45)
der dining-room	de dinin'-room (46)
der Gineral	de General (46)
der Gineral	de Gineral (46)
der Gineral	de Gineral (46)
ole	old (46)
der Gineral	de Gineral (46)
or as orter be	or oter be (46)
der pints is	de pints is (46)
aggravatin	aggravating (47)
you'r	you're (48)

June 26, 1851

Lizzy	Lizy (62, 63, 64)

July 17, 1851

ter bed	to bed (117)

August 7, 1851

ought ter	oughter (142)
hisself	himself (142)
jes likely	jest like (144)
careful	carful (144)
make yer	make ye (144)
oughter	ought ter (145)
jes	jest (145)
ye spect	she spect (147)

November 13, 1851   Volume II

mornin	morning (59)

April 1, 1852

That's all	dat's all (308)

This list of variants at first seems to reveal a slant toward the informal. The personal pronoun "you" (spelled either "yer" or "you") is, in all cases, regularized to "ye." In all instances but one, "der" and "the" are changed to "de." On the other hand, a tendency to give up dialect forms for standard English appears: the "-ing" ending replaces the "-in" regularly; "spilt" becomes "spilled"; "spose" becomes "suppose"; "ole" becomes "old"; "ter" becomes "to"; and "hisself" becomes "himself."

If the evidence is for both standardizing and unstandardizing of words in the lines assigned to a single character, the list also reveals that, even with specific words or vowel sounds, Harriet was unable to make up her mind as to how her characters would pronounce them. Chloe says both "jest" and "jist."

The next of the selected group of Negroes to appear in the novel, Shelby's Sam and his companion, Andy, provide much of the humor in the first volume, but it is Sam who frustrates Haley's attempts to recapture Eliza, who tells Mrs. Shelby of Eliza's passage over the Ohio and who spellbinds the other slaves with a recounting of the adventure. Although the number of the variants in Sam's and Andy's speech is great, it is smaller than the number for Chloe.

July 3, 1851	Volume I
d'idee	de idee (70)
ter know	to know (70)
knowd	knowed (70)
dis nigger	this nigger (70)
you see	yer see (74)
catch him, catch him	cotch him! cotch him (76)
start this way	start dis way, no how (77)
commend	'commend (78)
dout	doubt (78)
bound	boun (78)

July 10, 1851	
every nigger on us keeps a pup of some natur ur uther	every nigger of us keeps a pup of some natur or uther (89)
the straight	de straight (90)

yer thinks	ye thinks (91)
der straight	de straight (91)
der matter	de matter (91)
der natives	de natives (93)
feels	feel (96)
bless ye	bless you (110)

July 17, 1851

the lord	de lord (110)
o' fire	of fire (110)
o'wallop	g'wallop (112)
fur	for (116)
burnt me live like dat ar old coon dar missus was a showin us in der catechise	burnt me 'live (117)

Here again is the change of "the" and "der" to "de" found in Chloe's speech. Uses which convey ignorance, but not sound differences, seem to be regularized: "knowd," "ur," and "dout," are changed to "knowed," "or," and "doubt." The "ter-to" change found in Chloe's speech is repeated here. The most significant difference between the changes made here and in Chloe's speech occurs in the deletion of a passage of dialect of considerable length which contains spellings found nowhere else in either version: "ar" for "there," and "dar" for "the" (*Era,* July 17, 1851).

By September 18, 1851, the date of Jewett's publication announcement, Harriet had written sixteen chapters and had ensconced Tom on the St. Clare plantation. Through practice, her rendering of Negro dialect should have been better by this time than it had been the preceding June when she began the work, and therefore fewer variants should appear in the chapters that followed. Adolph, Emmeline, and Cassy are semieducated, intelligent house servants who appear toward the middle of the novel or later. Of the three, Adolph has the smallest number of variants in his speech.

Mrs. Stowe made only one change in Adolph's speech, but she made it consistently and wisely. In the *Era,* he says "Massa" when he addresses St. Clare; in the 1852 text, the title becomes "Master," a change which purges Adolph of whatever servileness remains in his Negro pronunciation of the word. He speaks to St. Clare in standard, if not florid, English as a man talking to a friend. His choice of words and their pronunciation sets him apart from all other slaves on the plantation and raises him to the level he thinks he so richly deserves.

Emmeline slips into dialect only twice, each time under emotional pressure. In both texts, as Emmeline rides to the plantation in Legree's wagon, he leans over, tweaks her ear, and asks if she has ever worn earrings. "No, Mas'r" she replies, "trembling and looking down" (*Era,* Jan. 29, 1852; II, 178). Later, when she arrives at the house and discusses escape with Cassy, she says, "I an't afraid of snakes" (*Era,* Feb. 26, 1852; II, 222), again in a moment of unusual stress. Considering the many inconsistencies in the handling of dialect throughout the novel, it might be a bit presumptuous here to remark upon Harriet's great sensitivity to the right phrase. Considering the revised character of the text as a whole, however, the fact that these two inconsistencies appear in both texts would seem to indicate that they are intentional.

Of those of her class, Cassy exhibits the largest number of lapses and textual variants. When she carries water to Tom after he has been beaten, she addresses him as "you" in the *Era* (Feb. 12, 1852), but "ye" in the 1852 text (II, 198). In trying to persuade Emmeline to take strong drink, she says in the *Era* (Feb. 26, 1852) that after a few drinks, things don't "look near so dreadful"; in the later text they don't "look so dreadful" (II, 223). A few lines later, an obvious slip on Harriet's part was picked up and corrected as she went over the text for the 1852 version. In the *Era* (Feb. 26, 1852), Cassy, speaking to Legree, asks, "Aint it just as I told you?"; rereading the passage and perhaps noting that two lines above were the words "said Cassy, in French," the author prudently changed the "Aint" to "Isn't (II, 230). Later, however, when Cassy asks Legree why he fears her haunted garret and he tells her that it is none of her business, she replies, in both texts "O, it an't?" (*Era,* March 11, 1852; II, 260).

Cassy may have addressed Tom as "ye" and not "you" to show him she thought of him as an equal. She may have used the "an't" to Legree to mock his lack of the culture she has acquired, although she was black and he white. The change from "near so dreadful" to "so dreadful" may indicate an attempt to diminish the colloquial tone. Whatever the answer to these questions, the most significant fact is that toward the latter part of the work the number of corrections involving dialect seems both to diminish and to be based on explainable artistic grounds.

In the second volume, Harriet created a second pair of characters of about the same class and intelligence as Shelby's Sam and Andy, namely, Sambo and Quimbo. If the reader finds that he has difficulty in distinguishing one from the other without their speech tags, he will be comforted to discover that some lines given to Quimbo in the 1852 text (II, 271, 275) were originally assigned to Legree's Sambo in the *Era* (March 11, 18, 1852). (Another Sambo belonged to Skeggs, the New Orleans slave auctioneer.) Because of the reassignment of lines, the following list of variants is a composite taken from the speeches of both Legree's Sambo and his Quimbo. Again the *Era* text precedes that of the 1852 edition, volume II, with paging in parentheses.

January 29, 1852	Volume II
donno	dunno (183)
February 5, 1852	
Ho, you	Ho, yo (184)
Thar, you	Thar, yo (184)
catch	cotch (192)
der debil	de debil (194)
March 11, 1852	
mass'r	Mas'r's (272)

we've	we's (275)
hope	hopes (275)
for't	for it (275)
rall wicked	awful wicked (275)
standin	a standin' (275)

The change from "der" to "de" has occurred before. The emendation of "we've" to "we's" and "hope" to "hopes" is more significant. Both words appear in the same sentence; the subject of the sentence is plural. In going over the text, Harriet, aware of the characteristic lack of subject-verb agreement in low-class white and Negro speech, changed the verbs to make the sentence consistent with the characters. The change from "mass'r" to the possessive "Mas'r's" is necessitated by the sense of the sentence. "Rall" to "awful" may have been the result of a fear on the author's part that the former would not be understood by all of her readers. The "you" to "yo" change occurs only twice in the novel, both times on the same page in an episode in which the occurrences of "yo" far outnumber those of "you." It would appear that in single passages Harriet is striving for a kind of consistency. Finally, although the individual changes have significance, there are eleven instances of variants in the speech of Sambo/Quimbo, whereas in the lines assigned to Sam and Andy, more than twice that number occur.

A speech of Chloe, Tom's wife, contains some fifty-four variants. Since Chloe appears in both volumes, the distribution of these variants takes on greater meaning than their nature or number. In the passage in volume I there are fifty-two changes; in that in volume II there are only two. The first passage in which Chloe speaks (I, 41–49) has forty-one changes; the first passage in the second volume (pp. 56–59), one change; and the second passage in the same volume (pp. 304–8), also one change.

If Sam and Andy are early models for the later Sambo and Quimbo, certainly Chloe has her counterpart in Dinah, the St. Clares' cook. Dinah speaks on about ten pages (I, 299–303,

306–10), a sample large enough to permit a comparison of her speech with Chloe's. The two characters rank at about the same social level; Dinah's character and general attitudes are much like those of Chloe, although we do not see Chloe's kitchen. In brief, except for the fact that she is not Tom's wife, Dinah is almost a Louisiana Chloe.

An examination of the ten pages on which Dinah speaks reveals that Harriet made only one change in the text of the *Era* when she was readying it for book publication. In the early text Dinah told Sam not to "git the baby dat ar sugarbowl" (*Era,* Oct. 9, 1851); in the later text, she tells him to "gib" it to the baby (I, 301). Thus the single change that Harriet felt she had to make in Dinah's speech has nothing to do with dialect: it is purely word choice.

What, then, can be said about Harriet and Negro speech? Some of the dialect changes have artistic importance, but the majority do not. That Harriet was concerned with representing Negroes as they actually spoke, or rather as she thought they did, is certainly evidenced by the number of changes she made in the two versions. That she made these changes with any great consistency is out of the question. But that, at least to her own ear, she was transcribing with greater and greater fidelity the pronunciation and grammar of the people she longed to see free is proven by the decreasing frequency with which she emended the text.

BIBLIOGRAPHY

MANUSCRIPTS

The largest depositories of manuscript material relating to Harriet Beecher Stowe are at the Arthur and Elizabeth Schlesinger Library on the History of Women in America, Radcliffe College; the Henry Huntington Library; the Clifton Waller Barrett Collection, Alderman Library, University of Virginia; the Stowe-Day Foundation Library, Hartford, Connecticut; and the Library of Congress. Other important collections and depositories from which holograph data for this study were drawn include the following: the Henry W. and Albert A. Berg Collection, New York Public Library; the American Antiquarian Society; the Cincinnati Historical Society; the Connecticut Historical Society; the Boston Public Library; the Beinecke Library, Yale University; the Sterling Library, Yale University; the Historical Society of Pennsylvania; the Houghton Library, Harvard University; the Estelle Doheny Collection of the Edward Laurence Doheny Memorial Library, St. John's Seminary, Camarillo, California; the Massachusetts Historical Society; the Vassar College Library; the Ohio Historical Society; and the Oberlin College Library.

PERIODICALS

Biblical Repository and Theological Review, 1831–1850
Bibliotheca Sacra, 1843–1855
Christian Examiner, 1824–1844

Christian Spectator, 1819–1838
Emancipator, 1833–1850
New York *Evangelist*, 1830–1855
Hesperian, 1838–1840
New York *Independent*, 1848–1855
Cincinnati *Journal and Western Luminary*, 1836–1855
Ladies Repository, 1839–1855
Liberator, 1831–1855
National Era, 1847–1855
Hartford *Observer*, 1825–1840
Cincinnati *Weekly Herald and Philanthropist*, 1836–1847
Spirit of the Pilgrims, 1828–1833
Western Messenger, 1835–1841
Western Monthly Magazine, 1832–1837

WORKS BY HARRIET BEECHER STOWE
Books

The Key to Uncle Tom's Cabin. Boston, 1853.
The Mayflower; or, Sketches of Scenes and Characters among the Descendants of the Pilgrims. New York, 1843.
The Mayflower; or, Scenes and Sketches among the Descendants of the Pilgrim Fathers. London, 1853.
The May Flower, and Miscellaneous Writings. Boston, 1855.
Men of Our Times. Hartford, 1868
Prize Tale: A New England Sketch. Lowell, Mass., 1834.
Uncle Sam's Emancipation; Earthly Care, a Heavenly Discipline; and Other Sketches. Philadelphia, 1853.
Uncle Sam's Emancipation; Earthly Care, a Heavenly Discipline; and Other Tales and Sketches. London, 1853.
Uncle Tom's Cabin; or Life among the Lowly. 2 vols. Boston, 1852.

Shorter Works

"Art and Nature." *Godey's Lady's Book*, 19 (1839), 241–44.
"Atonement—A Historical Reverie." *Evangelist*, Dec. 28, 1848.
"Aunt Mary." *Western Monthly Magazine* 2 (1834), 362–67.
"Bring Up Your Child in the Way He Should Go." Cincinnati *Journal*, June 2, 1836.
"Canal Boat." *Godey's Lady's Book* 23 (1841), 167–69.

"Catharine E. Beecher." *Our Famous Women*. Ed. Harriet Beecher Stowe et al. Hartford, 1884, pp. 75–93.

"Christmas; or, The Good Fairy." *National Era*, Dec. 26, 1850.

"Clara Delafield." *The Violet: A Christmas and New Years Present*. Philadelphia, 1840, pp. 17–56.

"The Coral Ring." *The Christian Souvenir: An Offering for Christmas and the New Year*. Ed. Isaac Shepard. Boston, 1843, pp. 265–81; rpt. in *Godey's Lady's Book* 36 (1848), 340–43.

"Cousin William." *The Gift: A Christmas and New Years Present for 1839*. Ed. Miss Eliza Leslie. Phildelphia, 1839, pp. 207–19.

"The Dancing School." *Evangelist*, April 6, 13, 1843.

"Deacon Enos." *The Gift, A Christmas and New Years Present for 1840*. Ed. Miss Eliza Leslie. Philadelphia, 1840, pp. 144–87.

"De Rance and Fenelon." *Evangelist*, July 7, 1842.

"The Drunkard Reclaimed." *Evangelist*, Nov. 30, Dec. 7, 1839.

"Eliza; From My Aunt Mary's Bureau." *Godey's Lady's Book* 20 (1840), 24-26.

"Feeling." *The Religious Souvenir for MDCCCXXXIX*. Ed. Mrs. L. H. Sigourney. New York, 1838, pp. 252–60; rpt. in *The Christian Keepsake: A Christmas and New Years Gift*. Ed. Mrs. L. H. Sigourney. New York, n.d., pp. 252–60; *Godey's Lady's Book* (1848), 102–4.

"Frankness, by a Lady." *Western Monthly Magazine* 2 (1834), 266–73.

"The Freeman's Dream, a Parable." *National Era*, Aug. 1, 1850.

"Heinrich Stilling." *Evangelist*, Feb. 6, 1851.

"Immediate Emancipation." *Evangelist*, Jan. 2, 1845; rpt. in Cincinnati *Weekly Herald and Philanthropist*, Feb. 5, 1845.

"Independence." *National Era*, Jan. 30, 1851.

"The Interior or Hidden Life." *Evangelist*, April 17, June 19, 1845.

"Introduction." *Uncle Tom's Cabin; or, Life among the Lowly*. Boston, 1879, pp. ix–xlii.

"Introduction." *The Works of Charlotte Elizabeth*. 2nd ed., New York, 1845, pp. v–vii.

"Isabelle and Her Sister Kate, and Their Cousin." *Western Monthly Magazine* 2 (1834), 72–75; rpt. in Lexington (Ky.) *Observer and Reporter*, Aug. 3, 1839, Cincinnati *Chronicle*, Sept. 28, 1839.

"Jesus." *Evangelist*, Feb. 19, 1846.

"Let Every Man Mind His Own Business." *The Christian Keepsake and*

Missionary Annual. Ed. Rev. John A. Cooke. Philadelphia, 1839, pp. 239–64; rpt. in Charleston (S.C.) *Chicora*, July 23, 1842; *The Christian Keepsake and Missionary Annual*. Ed. Rev. John A. Cooke. Philadelphia, 1848, pp. 98–128.

"Literary Epidemics—No. 1." *Evangelist*, July 28, 1842.

"Literary Epidemics—No. 2." *Evangelist*, July 13, 1843.

"Lord if Thou Hadst Been There." *Evangelist*, Sept. 11, 1845.

"Mark Meridan." *Godey's Lady's Book* 22 (1841), 242–44; rpt. in Cincinnati *Weekly Herald and Philanthropist*, Sept. 29, 1841; Eliza Leslie's *Mr. and Mrs. Woodbridge with Other Tales*. Providence, R.I., 1841, pp. 129–40.

"Modern Uses of Language." *Western Monthly Magazine* 1 (1833), 121–25.

"A New England Sketch by Miss Harriet E. Beecher." *Western Monthly Magazine* 2 (1834), 169–92; rpt. in *The Family Visitor*. Ed. John Hayward. Boston, 1840, pp. 29–47; *The Boston Book*. Ed. George W. Light. Boston, 1841, pp. 100–39.

"Now We See through a Glass Darkly." *Evangelist*, June 8, 1843.

"Old Testament Pictures—No. 1." *Evangelist*, Nov. 14, 1844.

"Olympiana." *Godey's Lady's Book* 18 (1839), 241–43.

"The Only Daughter." *Godey's Lady's Book*, 18 (1839), 115–29.

"On the Ministrations of Departed Spirits in the World." *Evangelist*, Jan. 25, 1849.

"A Parable." *Evangelist*, Feb. 24, 1842.

"The Sabbath." *The Christian Keepsake and Missionary Annual for 1840*. Ed. Rev. John A. Cooke. Philadelphia, 1840, pp. 130–57.

"Salmon P. Chase." *Men Of Our Times*. Ed. Harriet Beecher Stowe. Hartford, 1868, pp. 241–68.

"A Scholar's Adventures in the Country." *National Era*, Nov. 7, 1850.

"The Seamstress." *The Religious Souvenir for Christmas and New Years Presents*. Ed. Mrs. L. H. Sigourney. New York, 1840, pp. 99–114; rpt. in *Godey's Lady's Book* (1840), 363–66; *The Gem Annual*. Ed. E. H. Butler. Philadelphia, 1855, pp. 39–53.

"Sketches from the Notebook of an Old Gentleman. Number 1, The Old Musty House." *Godey's Lady's Book* 21 (1840), 61–63.

"So Many Calls." *Ladies Repository* 3 (1343), 278–79.

"The Tea Rose." *Godey's Lady's Book* 24 (1842), 145–47; rpt. in Cincinnati *Weekly Herald and Philanthropist*, April 27, 1842; *The Bouquet for 1847*. Ed. Alfred A. Phillips. New York, 1847, pp. 43–50; *Flora's Gem; or The Bouquet for All Seasons*. New York, n.d., 43–50; Woodstock, Vt., *Spirit of the Age*, Aug. 28, 1851; *The Female Prose Writers of America, with Portraits, Biographical Notices and Specimens of Their Writings*. Ed. John S. Hart. Philadelphia, 1852, pp. 246–53; *Women's Record; or, Sketches of All Distinguished Women from 'The Beginning' Till A.D. 1850 Arranged in Four Eras with Selections from Female Writers of Every Age*. Ed. Sarah Josepha Hale. New York, 1853, pp. 837–38.

"Trials of a Housekeeper." *Godey's Lady's Book* 18 (1839), 4–6.

"The Twelve Months: A New Year's Dream." *The Christian Keepsake and Missionary Annual*. Ed. Rev. John A. Cooke. Philadelphia, 1849, pp. 115–22.

"The Two Altars; or, Two Pictures in One." *Evangelist*, June 12, 19, 1851; rpt. in *The Republican: A Journal of Politics, Literature and General Intelligence* 3 (July 17, 1851), 113; *Liberty Tract, Number 1*. Boston, 1852; *Autographs for Freedom*. Ed. Julia Griffiths. Boston, 1853, pp. 127–47; *American Association Tracts, Number 13*. New York, 1855.

"Uncle Abel and Little Edward." *The Gift: A Christmas and New Years Present for 1839*. Ed. Miss Eliza Leslie. Philadelphia, 1839, pp. 59–65.

"Uncle Enoch." *Evangelist*, May 30, 1835.

"The Unfaithful Steward." *Evangelist*, April 7, 1842.

"What Will the American People Do?" *Evangelist*, Jan. 29, Feb. 5, 1846.

"The Yankee Girl." *The Token and Atlantic Souvenir: An Offering for Christmas and the New Year*. Boston, 1842, pp. 63–81.

Other Sources Cited

Adams, John R. *Harriet Beecher Stowe*. New York, 1963.

———. "The Literary Achievement of Harriet Beecher Stowe: A Survey of Her Writings, Collected and Uncollected." Ph.D. diss. Univ. of Southern California, 1940.

Allen, James Lane. "Mrs. Stowe's 'Uncle Tom' at Home in Kentucky." *Century Monthly Magazine* 34 (1887), 852–67.

Allison, Young E. ["Picador"], "The Cradle of Uncle Tom's Cabin." Louisville *Courier Journal*, May 16, 1881.

Bacon, Leonard Woolsey. *Anti-Slavery before Garrison.* New Haven, 1903.

Ballou, Ellen. *The Building of the House: Houghton Mifflin's Formative Years.* Boston, 1970.

Barnes, Gilbert Hobbs. *The Antislavery Impulse 1830–1844.* 1933; rpt. New York, 1964.

Beecher, C[atharine E]. *An Essay on Slavery and Abolitionism with Reference to the Duty of American Females.* Philadelphia, 1837.

———. "Song for the Youth's Temperance Society of Cincinnati." *Western Monthly Magazine* 3 (1835), 182–83.

———, and H[arriet E]. Beecher. *Primary Geography for Children on an Improved Plan, with Twelve Maps, and Numerous Engravings by C. and H. Beecher, Principals of the Western Female Institute.* Cincinnati, 1833.

Beecher, Charles. *The Duty of Disobedience to Wicked Laws: A Sermon on the Fugitive Slave Law.* Newark, N.Y., 1851.

Beecher, Edward. *Narrative of the Riots at Alton.* Alton, Ill., 1838.

Beecher, Lyman. *Autobiography of Lyman Beecher.* Ed. Barbara M. Cross. 2 vols. Cambridge, Mass., 1961.

———. *Remedy for Duelling: A Sermon Delivered Before the Presbytery of Long-island at the Opening of Their Session at Aquebogue, April 16, 1806.* Sag Harbor, N.Y., 1807.

———. *Six Sermons on the Nature, Occasion, Signs, Evils, and Remedy of Intemperance.* New York, 1827.

Beecher, William C., and Samuel Scoville. *A Biography of Henry Ward Beecher.* New York, 1888.

Bibb, Henry. *Narrative of the Life and Adventures of Henry Bibb, an American Slave, Written by Himself.* New York, 1849.

Birney, James Gillespie. *Letters of James Gillespie Birney: 1831–1857.* Ed. Dwight L. Dumond. New York, 1938.

———. *Narrative of the Late Riotous Proceedings against the Liberty of the Press in Cincinnati with Remarks and Historical Notes Relating to Emancipation.* Cincinnati, 1836.

Birney, William. *James G. Birney and His Times.* New York, 1890.

————. "Some Account of Mrs. Beecher Stowe and Her Family." *Fraser's Magazine* 46 (1852), 518–25.

Blanchard, J., and N. L. Rice. *A Debate on Slavery: Held in the City of Cincinnati, on the First, Second, Third, and Sixth Days of October, 1845, upon the Question: Is Slaveholding in Itself Sinful, or the Relation between Master and Slave a Sinful Relation?* Cincinnati, 1846.

Boyle, Regis Louise. *Mrs. E. D. E. N. Southworth, Novelist.* Washington, D.C., 1939.

Brandstater, Evan. "Uncle Tom and Archy Moore: The Antislavery Novel as Ideological Symbol." *American Quarterly* 26 (1974), 160–75.

Brazeale, Phanor. "Denies Uncle Tom's Cabin is Tale of Louisiana." New Orleans *States*, Dec. 29, 1929.

————. "Uncle Tom's Cabin and the Spanish Post of the Adaias." *Louisiana Historical Society Quarterly* 7 (1924), 304–7.

Brookway, Wallace, and Bart K. Winer. *A Second Treasury of the World's Great Letters.* New York, 1941.

Brown, Anna Burnside. "Where Uncle Tom's Cabin Stood." *Kentucky Progress Magazine* 3, No. 12 (Sept. 1930), 19–21.

Brown, Herbert Ross. *The Sentimental Novel in America: 1789–1860.* Durham, 1940.

Brown, William W. *Narrative of William W. Brown, an American Slave.* London, 1849.

Brownson, Orestes. "The Laboring Classes." *Boston Quarterly Review* 3 (1840), 358–95, 420–510.

Buckmaster, Henrietta. *Let My People Go: The Story of the Underground Railroad and the Growth of the Abolition Movement.* Boston, 1941; rpt. 1959.

Burton, Richard. "The Author of 'Uncle Tom's Cabin.'" *Century Magazine* 20 (1896), 698–704.

"Chartism." *Western Messenger* 8 (1840), 57–90, 108–15, 162–68.

Child, Alfred T., Jr. "Prudence Crandall and the Canterbury Experiment." *Bulletin of the Friends Historical Association* 22 (1933), 35–55.

Chopin, Kate. *At Fault: A Novel.* St. Louis, 1890.

Cincinnati Colonization Society. *Proceedings of the Cincinnati Colonization Society at the Annual Meeting, January 14, 1833.* Cincinnati, 1833.

Clarke, Lewis, *Narrative of the Sufferings of Lewis Clarke, during a Captivity of More than Twenty-five Years among the Algerines of Kentucky, One of the So Called Christian States of North America.* Boston, 1845.

———, and Milton Clarke. *Narratives of the Sufferings of Lewis and Milton Clarke.* Boston, 1846.

Clayton, Herbert. "The Original Uncle Tom." *Notes & Queries*, 9th ser. 11 (1903), 445.

Coffin, Levi. *Reminiscences of Levi Coffin, Reputed President of the Underground Railroad.* Cincinnati, 1876.

Cole, Charles C., Jr. "Horace Bushnell and the Slavery Question." *New England Quarterly* 23 (1950), 19–30.

Coleman, J. Winston, Jr. "Mrs. Stowe, Kentucky, and Uncle Tom's Cabin." *Lincoln Herald* 48, no. 2 (1946), 2–10.

Corley, D. B. *A Visit to Uncle Tom's Cabin.* Chicago, 1892.

Crandall, John C. "Patriotism and Humanitarian Reform in Children's Literature 1825–1860." *American Quarterly* 21 (1969), 3–22.

Crozier, Alice. *The Novels of Harriet Beecher Stowe.* New York, 1969.

Curran, John Philpot. "Speeches of the Right Hon. John Philpot Curran, Master of the Rolls in Ireland." *Irish Eloquence: The Speeches of the Celebrated Irish Orators Philips, Curran and Grattan.* Philadelphia, 1849.

Davis, Curtis Carroll. *That Ambitious Mr. Legaré.* Columbia, S.C., 1972.

Drayton, Daniel. *Personal Memoirs of Daniel Drayton.* Boston, 1855.

Dunn, Jacob Piatt. *Greater Indianapolis.* 2 vols. Chicago, 1910.

Edgeworth, Maria. *The Works of Maria Edgeworth*, 13 vols. Boston, 1825.

"Education and Slavery." *Western Monthly Magazine* 2 (1834), 266–73.

Elsmere, Jane Shaffer. *Henry Ward Beecher: The Indiana Years 1837–1847.* Indianapolis, 1973.

Entrikin, Isabelle Webb. *Sarah Josepha Hale and Godey's Lady's Book.* Philadelphia, 1946.

Erskine, John. *Leading American Novelists.* New York, 1910.

"Extract from Dr. Beecher's Speech." *Connecticut Observer*, July 28, 1834, p. 118.

"Facsimile of Manuscript Page of 'Uncle Tom's Cabin.'" New York *Press*, Aug. 28, 1889.

Fields, Annie. *Life and Letters of Harriet Beecher Stowe*. Boston, 1897.

Filler, Louis. *The Crusade against Slavery: 1830–1860*. Rpt. New York, 1963.

Finley, Ruth E. *The Lady of Godey's: Sarah Josepha Hale*. Philadelphia, 1931.

Finney, Charles G. *Sermons on Important Subjects*. New York, 1836.

Fisher, Walter, "Introduction," *Father Henson's Story of His Own Life*. New York, 1962, pp. v–xi.

Fladeland, Betty. *James Gillespie Birney: Slaveholder to Abolitionist*. Ithaca, N.Y., 1955.

Fletcher, Robert S. *A History of Oberlin College from Its Foundation through the Civil War*. Oberlin, Ohio, 1943.

Foote, John P. *Memoirs of the Life of Samuel E. Foote*. Cincinnati, 1860.

Foster, Charles H. *The Rungless Ladder: Harriet Beecher Stowe and New England Puritanism*. Durham, 1954.

Furnas, J. C. *Goodbye to Uncle Tom*. New York, 1956.

Gaines, Francis Pendleton. *The Southern Plantation: A Study in the Development and the Accuracy of a Tradition*. New York, 1925.

Garrison, Wendell P. and Francis J. *William Lloyd Garrison 1805– 1879: The Story of His Life*. 4 vols. New York, 1885–1894.

Garrison, William Lloyd. *Thoughts on African Colonization; or, An Impartial Exhibition of the Doctrines, Principles and Purposes of the American Colonization Society. Together with the Resolutions, Addresses and Remonstrances of the Free People of Color*. Boston, 1832.

Gilbertson, Catherine. *Harriet Beecher Stowe*, New York, 1937.

"A Gray Old Man Now." Minneapolis *Evening Journal*, May 30, 1888.

Grimké, Angelina. *Appeal to the Christian Women of the Southern States*. New York, 1836.

————. *Letters to Catherine [sic] E. Beecher in Reply to an Essay on Slavery and Abolitionism Addressed to A. E. Grimké. Revised by the Author*. Boston, 1838.

Gysin, Brion. *To Master—A Long Goodnight: The Story of Uncle Tom, a Historical Narrative*. New York, 1946.

H. "Brownson on the Laboring Classes." *Western Messenger* 3 (1840– 1841), 316–30, 433–49.

Hale, Sarah Josepha. *Northwood: A Tale of New England.* New York, 1827.

———. *Northwood: or, Life North and South, Showing the True Character of Both.* New York, 1852.

———, ed. *Women's Record; or, Sketches of All Distinguished Women from "The Beginning" till A.D. 1850 Arranged in Four Eras with Selections from Female Writers of Every Age.* New York, 1853.

Hartgrove, W. B. "The Story of Josiah Henson." *Journal of Negro History* 3 (1918), 1–21.

Henry, Stuart C. *Unvanquished Puritan: A Portrait of Lyman Beecher.* Grand Rapids, Mich., 1973.

Henson, Josiah. *Autobiography of the Rev. Josiah Henson (Mrs. Harriet Beecher Stowe's 'Uncle Tom') from 1789 to 1879 with a Preface by Mrs. Harriet Beecher Stowe. Introductory Notes by Wendell Phillips and John G. Whittier and an Appendix on the Exodus by Bishop Gilbert Haven.* Boston, 1879.

———. *The Life of Josiah Henson, Formerly a Slave, Now an Inhabitant of Canada, as Narrated by Himself.* Boston, 1849.

———. *Truth Stranger than Fiction: Father Henson's Story of His Own Life (with an Introduction by Harriet Beecher Stowe).* Boston, 1858.

Hibben, Paxton. *Henry Ward Beecher: An American Portrait.* New York, 1927.

[Hildreth, Richard]. *The Slave; or, Memoirs of Archy Moore.* Boston, 1840.

Hill, Herbert. "Uncle Tom, an Enduring American Myth." *Crisis* 72 (1965), 289–95, 325.

History of the Foundation and Endowment and Catalogue of the Trustees, Alumni, and Students, of the Lane Theological Seminary. Cincinnati, 1848.

Johnson, Oliver. *William Lloyd Garrison and His Times; or, Sketches of the Anti-Slavery Movement in America and of the Man Who Was Its Founder and Moral Leader.* Boston, 1894.

Johnston, Johanna. *Runaway to Heaven: The Story of Harriet Beecher Stowe and Her Age.* Garden City, N.Y., 1963.

Jones, Howard Mumford, ed. *Uncle Tom's Cabin.* Columbus, Ohio, 1969.

Jorgenson, Chester E. *Uncle Tom's Cabin as Book and Legend: A Guide to an Exhibition.* Detroit, 1952.

Kennedy, George. "Uncle Tom Legend Points to Log Cabin on Old Georgetown Road," Washington (D.C.) *Star*, Feb. 12, 1957.

Kirkham, E. Bruce. "The First Editions of *Uncle Tom's Cabin:* A Bibliographical Study." *Papers of the Bibliographical Society of America* 65 (1971), 365–82.

———. "Two Abolitionists and a Pearl." *Journal of Negro History* 50 (1965), 123–25.

Lader, Lawrence. *The Bold Brahmins: New England's War against Slavery 1831–1863.* New York, 1961.

"Life of Isaac Shelby." *Western Monthly Magazine* 5 (1836), 462–70, 516–63.

Lincoln, William S. *Alton Trials: Of Winthrop S. Gilman* [and others] . . . *Written Out from Notes Taken at the Time of the Trial.* New York, 1838.

Littlefield, Louise. "Letter." Portland (Me.) *Sunday Telegram*, July 19, 1931.

Litwack, Leon F. *North of Slavery: The Free States 1790–1860.* Chicago, 1961.

Loggins, Vernon. *The Negro Author: His Development in America.* New York, 1931.

Lynn, Kenneth S., ed. *Uncle Tom's Cabin; or, Life among the Lowly.* Cambridge, Mass. 1962.

McCray, Florine Thayer. *The Life-work of the Author of Uncle Tom's Cabin.* New York, 1889.

MacTavish, Newton. "The Original Uncle Tom." *Canadian Magazine* 30 (1907), 25–29.

May, Samuel J. *Some Recollections of Our Anti-Slavery Conflict.* Boston, 1869.

Meredith, Robert. "Introduction." *Narrative of the Riots at Alton by Edward Beecher.* New York, 1965, pp. v–xxix.

———. *The Politics of the Universe: Edward Beecher, Abolition, and Orthodoxy.* Nashville, 1968.

Mitchell, William M. *The Underground Railroad.* London, 1860.

Mott, Frank Luther. *A History of American Magazines 1741–1905.* 4 vols. Cambridge, Mass., 1938–1966.

N. "The Chartists." *Western Messenger* 7 (1839), 365–95.

Nichols, Charles H. *Many Thousands Gone.* Leiden, 1963.

————. "The Origins of *Uncle Tom's Cabin*." *The Phylon Quarterly* 19 (1958), 328–44.

"Not His Real Home." Chicago *Tribune*, Nov. 20, 1892.

Nye, Russel B. "Eliza Crossing the Ice: A Reappraisal of Sources." *Bulletin of the Historical and Philosophical Society of Ohio*, April, 1950, pp. 106–12.

"The Original George Harris." New York *Tribune*, July 22, 1870.

P. "Moral Emancipation of the Negro." *Western Monthly Magazine* 2 (1834), 26–30.

Page, John T. "The Original Uncle Tom." *Notes & Queries*, 11th ser. 6 (1912), 367.

Paynter, John H. "The Fugitives of the *Pearl*." *Journal of Negro History* 1 (1915), 243–64.

Pennington, James W. C. *The Fugitive Blacksmith; or, Events in the History of James W. C. Pennington, Pastor of a Presbyterian Church, New York, formerly a Slave in the State of Maryland, United States*. 3rd ed. London, 1850.

"*Primary Geography for Children*–Review." *Western Monthly Magazine* 1 (1833), 287.

Quinn, Arthur Hobson. *American Fiction: An Historical and Critical Survey*. New York, 1936.

Rankin, Daniel S. *Kate Chopin and Her Creole Stories*. Philadelphia, 1932.

Rankin, John. *A Review of the Statement of the Faculty of Lane Seminary in Relation to the Recent Difficulties in That Institution*. Ripley, Ohio, 1835.

Ratner, Lorman. *Powder Keg: Northern Opposition to the Anti-Slavery Movement 1831–1840*. New York, 1968.

Rhea, Linda. *Hugh Swinton Legaré: a Charleston Intellectual*. Chapel Hill, 1934.

Ross, Alexander Milton. *Recollections and Experiences of an Abolitionist from 1855 to 1865*, 2nd ed. Toronto, 1876.

Rourke, Constance Mayfield. *Trumpets of Jubilee*. New York, 1927; rpt., 1963.

Rusk, Ralph Leslie. *The Literature of the Middle Western Frontier*. New York, 1925.

S., W. B. "The Original Uncle Tom." *Notes & Queries*, 11th ser. 6 (1912), 436.

Saxon, Lyle. *Old Louisiana.* New York, 1929.

Scudder, Harold H. "Mrs. Trollope and Slavery in America." *Notes & Queries* 187 (1944), 46–48.

Seyersted, Per. *Kate Chopin: A Critical Biography.* Baton Rouge, 1969.

Sketches of Old Virginia Family Servants with a Preface by Bishop Meade. Philadelphia, 1847.

Sklar, Kathryn Kish. *Catharine Beecher: A Study in American Domesticity.* New Haven, 1973.

"Slave Raid." Cincinnati *Enquirer*, Sept. 14, 1895.

The Soldier, The Battle, and The Victory, Being a Brief Account of the Work of Rev. John Rankin in the Anti-Slavery Cause. Cincinnati, n.d.

Southworth, Mrs. E. D. E. N. *Retribution; or, The Vale of Shadows.* New York, 1849.

Starling, Marion Wilson. "The Slave Narrative: Its Place in American Literature." Ph.D. diss., New York Univ., 1946.

Staudenraus, P. J. *The African Colonization Movement 1816–1865.* New York, 1961.

Stebbins, Lucy Poate, and Richard Poate. *The Trollopes: The Chronicle of a Writing Family.* New York, 1945.

Stephens, John Vant. *The Story of the Founding of Lane Seminary.* Cincinnati, 1940.

Stern, Philip Van Doren, ed. *The Annotated Uncle Tom's Cabin.* New York, 1964.

"The Story of Eliza." Hartford *Daily Courant*, Nov. 23, 1895; rpt. in Boston *Evening Transcript*, Nov. 30, 1895.

Stowe, Charles Edward. *The Life of Harriet Beecher Stowe.* Boston, 1891.

―――, and Lyman Beecher Stowe. *Harriet Beecher Stowe: The Story of Her Life.* Boston, 1911.

Stowe, Lyman Beecher. *Saints Sinners and Beechers.* Indianapolis, 1934.

Taylor, William R. *Cavalier and Yankee: The Old South and American National Character.* Garden City, N.Y., 1963.

Tebbel, John. *A History of Book Publishing in the United States, Volume I: The Creation of an Industry 1630–1865.* New York, 1972.

Thomas, Benjamin P. *Theodore Weld: Crusader for Freedom.* New Brunswick, N.J., 1950.

Thomas, John L. *The Liberator: A Biography of William Lloyd Garrison.* New York, 1963.

"Thrilling Incident Near Cincinnati." *The Antislavery Bugle*, Nov. 26, 1847.

"Thrilling Incident Near Cincinnati." *The Liberty Almanac for 1848.* New York, 1848, p. 42.

Ticknor, Caroline. *Glimpses of Authors.* Boston, 1922.

Trollope, Mrs. Frances. *The Life and Adventures of Jonathan Jefferson Whitlaw; or, Scenes on the Mississippi.* Paris, 1836.

Twitchell, Joseph H. "Authors at Home, XXIII: Mrs. Harriet Beecher Stowe in Hartford." *The Critic* 9 (Dec. 18, 1886), 301–2.

"Uncle Tom Lived in Daviess County, Kentucky," Owensboro (Ky.) *Messenger-Register,* Oct. 22, 1967, Sect. 3.

"Uncle Tom's Cabin." *The Manhattan: An Illustrated Literary Magazine* 1 (1883), 28–31.

"Uncle Tom's Cabin." New Orleans *Times-Democrat*, Dec. 4, 1892.

"Uncle Tom's Cabin." New York *Tribune*, July 22, 1840.

Van Doren, Carl. *The American Novel 1789–1939.* New York, 1946.

Venable, W. H. *Beginnings of Literary Culture in the Ohio Valley: Historical and Biographical Sketches.* Cincinnati, 1891.

Wagenknecht, Edward. *Harriet Beecher Stowe: The Known and the Unknown.* New York, 1965.

Weld, Theodore Dwight. *American Slavery as It Is: Testimony of a Thousand Witnesses.* New York, 1839.

———. *Letters of Theodore Weld, Angelina Grimké Weld, and Sarah Grimké: 1822–1844.* Ed. Dwight L. Dumond and Gilbert Hobbs Barnes. 2 vols. New York, 1934.

[———]. *A Statement of the Reasons Which Induced the Students of Lane Seminary to Dissolve Their Connection with That Institution.* Cincinnati, 1834.

Westbrook, Perry D. *Acres of Flint: Writers of Rural New England, 1870–1900.* Washington, D.C., 1951.

Wilson, Edmund. *Patriotic Gore: Studies in the Literature of the American Civil War.* New York, 1966.

Wilson, Forrest. *Crusader in Crinoline: The Life of Harriet Beecher Stowe.* Philadelphia, 1941.

INDEX

259